Highveld Ways

Recollections of life in Johannesburg in the 1990s

By

Valerie Poore

ISBN: 9781095566183

A Rivergirl Publications book: first edition

Cover photo: Melanie Bendixen and Tyler Brimson

Disclaimer

The contents of this book are the product of my recollections, and have
both inaccuracies as a result of time passed, and embellishments
needed to turn a series of memories into readable stories. Names have
been changed in the interests of discretion, but some people
represented are referred to by their given names. As a result, if there
are mistakes regarding the 'characters', the content or the time, I
would like to make it clear that these are my errors and mine alone.

In addition, please note I am a British writer and I use British spelling
and grammar. This will sometimes differ from what US readers are
accustomed to, so I hope those of you in America will be indulgent
with me on this. Valerie Poore (2019)

This book is dedicated to Moira Datson, Annette Dunbar
Marian Weissenborn-Mcfarlane and Melanie Bendixen
All real friends when I needed them most
and to my beloved sister, Toots, who has always been there

It is also for Colin Pryce

CONTENTS

INTRODUCTION

Images of our first visits to places that become important to us tend to stay in our memories, don't they? For me, this is especially true of Johannesburg, and my first encounter with the city remains in my mental picture archive to this day. On the whole, I'm not a fan of large urban areas, but Johannesburg was special. For one thing, it was my home for more than a decade, and for another, despite its bad press, I became surprisingly attached to it. In fact, even before I knew how much it would come to mean to me, my first exploration of its busy centre was one I will never forget.

Although we'd spent a night there when we first arrived in South Africa at the start of the 1980s, I only really saw the city centre some time later. It must have been in 1985, a few months after my husband Bill was transferred from Durban, or it may have been a little earlier. Whatever the case, my first venture into Johannesburg, known variously as iGoli, the Reef (an abbreviation of *Witwatersrand)*, Joeys or Joburg – any of which will be acceptable to locals – was an experience for both of us: for me, because I was exploring a whole new environment; for Bill, because I did something he'd never done despite having spent so much time there: I drove into the heart of its downtown area on my own and with just a basic tourist map to guide me.

Given the reputation the city later acquired, that may sound risky, but in those days the commercial capital of South Africa wasn't quite so notorious for danger and crime, although it still wasn't a place many people would have ventured into alone. I didn't know this then; my ignorance saved me. I suffered no feelings of anxiety about waltzing into the centre and wandering around with wide-eyed wonder. To me, everywhere in South Africa was safe, so why should Joburg be any different? I realise now I was naive, but I'd only known kindness and warmth from people in Natal where we'd lived since arriving in the country four years previously.

As a matter of fact, I was still living in Natal but on this occasion, I was up in Joburg for a long weekend to visit Bill. Normally, he would have travelled back down to our home in the Byrne Valley, so it was a sort of holiday for me and one I was determined to make the most of.

The morning of my adventure was a bright sunny one, but whether it was winter or summer, I can't recall. It would be true to point out here that most mornings on the Reef were sunny in any season. I believe climate change may have upset that stability, but it was one of the key attractions of the *Highveld* for me. By the way, *Highveld* is the name given to the high-altitude escarpment on which Johannesburg and Pretoria are built. The odd combination of English (high) and Afrikaans (*veld*) is one of many in South Africa's local glossary of terms and phrases.

In any event, I remember going to Bill's office with him and being handed the car keys of his small white Toyota.

"I've got a couple of hours work to do here. Why don't you take the car and go into Sandton?" he said. "It's just down the road and it's a fabulous mall. You'll love it, I know. There's nothing like it in 'Maritzburg."

"Okay," I agreed, and did as suggested.

The trouble was it didn't take me long to realise this wasn't what I wanted to see.

Sandton City was certainly impressive; the height of luxury shopping. And Bill was right. There was nothing like it in Pietermaritzburg, the closest city to rural Richmond where I was living at the time. Anyway, I appreciated this was a whole new ball game in the retail world. Even in England I'd never been to a shopping mall on this scale.

With its wall-to-wall polished marble, soft lighting, piped music and classy stores, it felt like entering a luxurious and very affluent world. And although you needed a magnifying glass to see the tiny, discreet price tickets, you needed very large eyes to absorb the size of the numbers. It seemed that if you had to ask, you couldn't afford it and peering at the price, well, that was just "too common, doll".

I suppose I spent an hour or so wandering round the well-known stores: Edgars, Truworths, and Woolworths, the last being very different from the 'Woolies' I knew from my youth in England. I'd already noticed the South African Woolworths looked very much like Britain's Marks and Spencer's in another guise and research tells me there were and still are close ties between the two. In any event, the store sold genteel fashion for the not so needy. By the time I'd bored myself looking at clothes I couldn't afford and wouldn't wear even if I could, I'd had enough; more than enough for the farm girl I was.

Where to go next? I pulled my cheap tourist Johannesburg street map out of my bag and studied it. The city was built on a grid system, so from where I was in Sandton it looked pretty easy to drive into the centre. On the map I saw a small square sector saying 'Oriental Plaza'. That sounded interesting. I could imagine an array of exotic stalls with goods from Asia and the East. Since I'd come from Natal with its large Asian population, I'd feel more at home there, I was sure.

In those days, the streets in Johannesburg had names like Smit Street, President Street and Bree Street. These have mostly changed now, and Bree Street is Lilian Ngoyi Street, named after an activist in the struggle to liberate South Africa from apartheid. Other than the names, not much has changed since then and the one-way grid system remains, its only downside being that it can be a minefield of one-way traffic rules.

In Johannesburg, each alternate street goes in one direction and the in-between streets go in the other. The Oriental Plaza was just off Bree Street and I saw I could reach it quite easily by heading from Sandton City across to William Nicol Drive, a major arterial road I could follow until I reached Jan Smuts Avenue, thereafter continuing into the city. As Bree Street was one that went in a westerly direction, to reach the Plaza, I had to make a right turn into the next, Jeppe Street (now called Rahima Moosa Street if you look at a current map).

This might sound confusing, but it looked easy enough as long as I followed the road names and didn't confuse my left with my right – always a risk as I had zero sense of direction, no clue about north and south, and if you turned me round once, I was completely disorientated. For my own security, I focused on road names and numbers. But directional challenge problems aside, at least I wasn't daunted by my lack of familiarity with the city. So off I went.

William Nicol Drive sped me through the suburb of Bryanston and then Jan Smuts Avenue took me through some of Johannesburg's oldest and classiest neighbourhoods. High walls and impressive gates, behind which I could see gracious villas, spoke of wealth and elegance. Names like Hyde Park, Parktown, Rosebank and Saxonwold suggested the same. The roads were lined with beautiful jacaranda trees as graceful as the houses. I passed Zoo Lake Park on one side and the zoo itself on the other. But then the classic, if busy, elegance changed as I reached the inner-city area.

Braamfontein looked grimy, scruffy and maybe a little forgotten, but it was near the railway station, so maybe that was the reason. However, after crossing the bridge over the rail tracks, I made the necessary turns and arrived at the Oriental Plaza without any trouble. Parking the car was also easy. There was a convenient space in a side street next to a workshop where I could see they were making attractive pine furniture. I remember this because I stopped to watch and thought how nice it would be to have some of the lovely kitchen units they were making.

Then I walked down a street lined with slightly shabby lock-up garages on one side and faded apartments on the other, crossed another road and found an entrance to the Plaza. I'd arrived. My first impression was of an explosion of colour. Small shops and stalls overflowed with the most gorgeous fabrics; there were crammed outlets selling saris, Indian and oriental clothing and jewellery. There were also food kiosks from which spicy smells wafted, as well as grocery stalls and bag shops.

It was at the Plaza that I ate my first *samoosa*, which is the local version of the Indian *samosa,* and was a small triangular shaped deep-fried patty filled with spicy vegetables or meat. I wasn't sure if I liked it, but it was typically South African fare and I was proud of myself for being so adventurous.

I wandered round in awe and even bought myself a large green suitcase. It must have been cheap as I can't imagine why I should have wanted it, although it served its purpose very well in later years. As far as I know, it's still in one of the family attics today, far too bulky to be used for anything but a major travel event.

Eventually, I left the overwhelming sights, smells and sounds of the Oriental Plaza and walked back to the car bearing my booty. I then made my way back through the grid-lined streets of Johannesburg before heading back towards Sandton again. These city centre roads were fairly narrow, which was probably why they were all one way, but with the towering height of the office blocks, they looked imposing. The stonework of the buildings had a mostly brown hue and I could imagine that New York was similar. With the press of people, the hawkers on the pavements and the hooting of horns, it felt vibrant and exciting.

Judging from the names spread large across their facades, the skyscrapers were mostly occupied by banks and insurance companies, all soaring above the humming bustle and colour of streets lined with shops, both classy and run down. I decided I liked Johannesburg and even in the future, when its reputation fell, I never changed my mind. Despite its gradual deterioration into an almost no-go zone, I retained a fondness for the eclectic mix of Africa, Europe and the Orient that could be found in its downtown areas; its meld of first and third worlds.

Back in Sandton, I collected Bill from his office.

"What have you been up to then?" he asked, as I shifted back into the passenger seat and he got in behind the wheel.

"I've been to the Oriental Plaza."

"You what?"

"I've been to...."

"Yes, I heard you, but what on earth did you go there for? How did you get there? You didn't drive into town, did you?"

"Well, yes, I did. Why?"

"Because for one thing, even *I've* never had the nerve to drive straight into the city, and for another, it's just not safe ... well, not for tourists anyway!"

"Oh? It seemed fine to me. I rather liked it."

"But how did you find it? I know you and your sense of direction. Or lack of it."

"Um, I just followed that map you gave me. It was quite easy really."

"Really? Even for you?" I decided to ignore the jibe.

"Yes. Everything's in squares, you see, so if you go wrong, you just go round the block again. No problem."

Bill shook his head. He was either impressed or flummoxed. I wasn't sure which at the time, but he certainly hadn't expected to hear where I'd been.

Later, I learnt he was genuinely amazed and just a little proud of my excursion. The thing was, I didn't know any better, so to me it was just normal to want to go exploring. I couldn't very well spend a weekend in the country's foremost commercial centre without having a look at it, could I? I didn't know I was taking chances, so perhaps my innocent demeanour was my saving grace. I enjoyed driving and the city's grid system most definitely helped a *loskop* (airhead) like me.

Another thing I didn't know then was that I would eventually be living and working in Johannesburg and there would come a time when I would walk its streets and travel the entire *Witwatersrand* area wearing a corporate suit with a business briefcase in hand.

And that is where this collection of anecdotes comes in.

After my innocent introduction to the city in the mid 80s, I saw very little of it until 1989 when I moved there with my two daughters to be with Bill. We'd been separated since 1987 but decided to give our relationship another try, and so began a decade of life in South Africa's biggest, baddest city.

It was an exciting period with the country was on the cusp of huge changes. It was also when the whole process of dismantling apartheid started to accelerate. The first ANC government was elected in 1994 with Nelson Mandela as president, a major milestone in South Africa's history. For the people, the 90s were accompanied by violence and hope, by tragedy and joy. Personally, we had both good and bad spells, and we moved five times in those ten years, which was too much. Even so, as time went by I became increasingly fond of 'my Joburg' as I hope these stories of our life in Africa's city of gold will show.

The chapters that follow are arranged according to the suburbs in which we lived, but other than that, there is no specific time continuum. Each of the five sections (one for each suburb) contains the memories and anecdotes that belonged to each home: the incidents that stood out during the years we spent in them; the journeys we took to other parts of the region; and above all, the people who filled our lives at the time.

South Africa's political changes are part of the backcloth to the stories and set the scene for some of our activities. But just as they didn't play a prominent role in our life until late in our stay, they are not prominent in these recollections.

Having said that, these are my memories and the accuracy of the timeline has become blurred over the years, hence the lack of precise chronology. Overall, my aim is to give an impression of what life was like for a young family striving to make a living in Johannesburg during these formative years of the new South Africa.

There were ups as well as downs, but I hope you enjoy them; I did.

SUNNINGHILL

The background

The plane touched down, and the *Witwatersrand* welcomed us with bright sunshine and the scent of that warm spicy earth that was all Africa. We'd arrived. My heart was pounding as I looked out at the red soil, the pale grass and the beaten steel-blue sky. This was it: a new life in South Africa far from the tranquillity of our Natal farm and sleepy Richmond. It was November, 1989, the beginning of the southern hemisphere summer, and this was Johannesburg, the most crime-ridden city in the African sub-continent.

My husband, Bill, had been living and working in Joburg since 1985 following his transfer from Durban. The German car company that employed him promoted him that year, so he had to move up country as well as up the career ladder. As could have been expected, the rural pace of our home in the Natal Midlands didn't correspond with his increasingly corporate lifestyle, and a rift between us developed. This widened further when one of his female colleagues drove her fashionable high-heels into the marital cracks to ensure they couldn't be repaired. We separated shortly afterwards and although I loved South Africa, my daughters and I went back to England in 1987 to be close to my father and siblings.

By 1989, however, Bill and I had found common ground again and decided to give our marriage another chance. The children, Jodie and Mo, pined for the things we'd done as a family: the travelling, camping holidays and social activities I couldn't maintain as a single mother. They were now aged ten and eight respectively, and although we'd enjoyed spending time with my family and all their cousins, they missed the outdoor life in South Africa. I had to admit I did as well, and we all felt it was time to take on a new challenge.

It wasn't going to be easy, though. I'd got used to being alone and making my own decisions. More importantly, I liked being in control of my own finances, something I wouldn't relinquish easily. My job in London was a good one with regular pay-rises and promotions. I worked for a prominent health insurance company in their Corporate

Services department and had my own portfolio of clients to look after, one of which was the Bank of England.

It felt good to be trusted with the customer service for such an important organisation, and I still treasure the personal messages my contacts at the Bank sent me when I left the company. The card signed with all their heartfelt good wishes is tucked in a box of my most precious bits and pieces. They were good days.

For all that, the call of Africa was powerful. I longed for the wide cerulean skies, the rolling hills of the Natal Midlands, the infinite golden stretches of the Free State and the lonely arid scenery of the northern Cape. I missed the space, the empty landscape with its impressive and almost overwhelming nothingness. I also missed the wide smiles of the Zulus and the generous hospitality of all the people. Africa had become part of me and I was homesick.

Of course, most people would point out that 'crime capital' Johannesburg was a far cry from the remote landscapes of my nostalgic yearnings, and they'd be right. On the other hand, the city wasn't only overcrowded and dangerous; it had distinct benefits too. Being a massive conurbation, it was geographically well-positioned, and from its metropolitan heart we could travel to every part of the country.

Another plus was that because I still needed to work, it was the best place to find a job. Despite not being a city girl, I also knew Joburg had quiet leafy suburbs and I was happy with the prospect of living in one of them. It wasn't too difficult to reason that having lived in London for eighteen months, the transition wouldn't be as hard as if I'd just moved up from Natal.

As for my children, all the activities they'd enjoyed in England, albeit briefly, would be more readily available in Johannesburg than somewhere more provincial. For instance, Jodie was learning to play the cello, and I felt sure music teachers would be in greater supply in the big city than in a sleepy Natal village. I, or rather we, convinced ourselves it would be a good move. Even so, I'm sure it's true that all three of us were nervous as we stepped off the plane into the vivid sharpness of the *Highveld* morning, but it was butterflies of excitement more than fear.

All the same, I should have known it wouldn't be a walk in the park. And it wasn't.

The beginning

Bill met us at the airport and guided us swiftly to his smart white VW Camper beside which a smiling and bulky African man was standing.

"Val, Jojo, Mo, this is Nicky, my driver."

Goodness, I thought, a driver? Why would he need someone to drive him around? Now was obviously not the time to ask. I smiled at Nicky and shook his hand. He grinned as if in possession of a naughty secret and then chuckled. He was a cheerful sight, but his presence made me suspicious.

"Pleased to meet you, Nicky."

"I am very pleased to meet you too, madam," he twinkled. Ah, I thought, that 'madam' thing again. I'd got out of the habit of it and hoped it wouldn't create a division.

Meanwhile, my daughters had other priorities.

"Daddy, Daddy, can Mo and I sit right at the back?" squeaked Jodie. She was bouncing with excitement. Camper vans meant holidays to her and sitting at the back was somehow the ultimate travel experience.

"Yes, Jojo, of course you can," Bill agreed, almost too eagerly. I could see he was on edge and a few minutes later I was to find out why he was so glad his daughters would be out of earshot.

"I'm taking you to a hotel for a few days," he said as soon as we were loaded into the van.

"A hotel? Why? I thought we were going to the house in Sunninghill."

"Yes, well, there's a few problems. A certain someone hasn't moved her stuff out and is making things generally awkward," he explained, shuffling with unease. "But don't worry. It's all in hand and we'll have it to ourselves in a couple of days, I promise."

I didn't ask what that meant. I didn't want to know. Anyway, Nicky was with us, and it was too private a matter to discuss openly. Perhaps, I thought uncharitably, that was the reason he was there. It sort of confirmed my suspicions, as Bill knew I wouldn't say anything much in front of someone else.

He turned from the front seat, reaching out to take my hand and squeezing it. I smiled, but it was a damper on our arrival. Was this how things were going to be? I'd been full of anticipation about starting over again, but I might have guessed it wasn't going to be that simple; things with Bill rarely were. Complications seemed to sniff him out like dogs after a nice smelly titbit. They always found him too, I thought with somewhat wry amusement.

However, we survived. The girls and I were good at that even though we didn't have any choice. There was nothing left of our home in England, so we really had to muddle through. I swallowed my irritation and decided to wallow in the luxury of a hotel stay instead; there was always an upside.

When the 'couple of days which became a week' were over, we finally arrived at the house I'd heard so much about. It was in the Sandton suburb of Sunninghill, a new neighbourhood of new housing developments of which Bill's house was in the newest.

At the time, all it consisted of was an area of cleared pine woodland on which some clusters of houses had been built around a grid of a few streets. Sunninghill was reached from Witkoppen Road, an almost rural arterial route that linked some of Johannesburg's most pleasant northern suburbs. Being on the outer perimeter of the area, it was a long way from the frenetic buzz of the big city downtown area.

When I saw it, I was instantly charmed by its quiet village-like feel. The oldest of the developments was two streets of brick-built double storey homes with well-established gardens. These were lush, richly floral and very lovely. Since they'd only been there a few years, this boded well for the future of the newer gardens. Plants appeared to grow and thrive in the sandy soil.

Another couple of streets had gorgeous thatched houses, also double storey, but the house to which Bill led us was in a brand-new cluster complex of bungalows. Cleverly, all the houses in the street were detached from each other but otherwise connected by shared garage walls. More high walls along the front also made them very private.

From outside, however, the estate looked a bit forbidding. The brickwork was grey and the road frontage was only relieved by meranti garage doors and garden gates. Young trees were planted on the grass verge, which was neatly trimmed, but on the other side of the road it was a mess of scrubland and building rubble.

Once inside the garage, a side door led directly into the garden and over a path into the house. The garden looked rather like a grass squash court with its unnaturally high walls, an impression compounded by the lack of flowers or shrubs. Bill hadn't been there long enough to cultivate anything other than a lawn, although there was a single tree growing next to the front gate. I looked at its trunk with curiosity.

"Why has the tree got all those scratches on it?"

"Ah, that's Sasha. She has a serial climbing habit," Bill said, pulling a face.

"A cat? Making that mess of the trunk?"

"Well, no. Look, here she is now."

Across the grass bounded a large cheerful Boxer dog, followed by a small but unidentifiable furry mass on legs.

"Meet Sasha," Bill grinned, pointing to the Boxer.

I was flabbergasted.

"A dog did that? Goodness, I've never heard of a dog scaling trees."

"Well, I should rather say she tries but doesn't really succeed, hence the numerous claw marks."

Sasha bounced around us, snuffling the girls, who were more or less at her level. They screeched and giggled, predictably enough.

"At least she's friendly," I laughed, although I wasn't quite so keen on all the slobber making streaks of slime on our clothes. She seemed to leave trails of it in her wake every time she shook her head, which was often.

"Yes. She's also very old but you'd never think so."

"How old?"

"Sixteen."

"You're kidding, surely! She looks about six, not sixteen!"

I bent over to give Sasha a pat and got smeared with a new patch of slime as a reward, but she was obviously a sweet-natured dog. I decided we could be friends.

"And who's this, Daddy?" Mo asked, crouching down to try and befriend the furry mass.

"It's Claude, Mo. You know, I told you about him. He's a Shih Tzu. Be gentle with him, though. He's only got one eye, so he can't see too well."

Bill had told me about Claude in his letters. He was a small dog with a massive ego. How he'd had a fight with a Sheltie Collie and lost an eye in the skirmish was the subject of one of Bill's more dramatic anecdotes; he hadn't mentioned Sasha, though.

"Erm, who does Sasha belong to?" I ventured.

"Yes, well, she's Anna's actually." Bill's embarrassment was all too clear. "I said we'd look after her until she's settled. Anna, that is."

Anna was the certain someone who'd been resisting relocation; the high-heeled girlfriend who'd taken my place when Bill moved from Natal. I couldn't help feeling that leaving Sasha behind was her way of showing she hadn't gone willingly. Still, I might have done the same in her shoes. The situation was a bit awkward, but the best thing I could do now was to make light of it.

"Well, I realised it wasn't Sasha who needed settling. She looks perfectly at home here. As settled as the slobber on your jeans."

We all laughed; however, I was aware there was some emotional quicksand I'd have to either deal with or avoid in the coming months. Typically for me, I found avoidance was the easiest and least stressful policy, so I set about putting my sensitivities on the back burner.

The house was the next surprise: it was empty. There was no furniture in the living room other than a desk and a stereo set. Even Bill looked nonplussed. A small round African woman dressed in the regulation maids' uniform of matching housecoat, pinny and scarf came through from what looked like the kitchen.

"Betty," Bill turned to her. "Where's all the furniture? What's happened here?"

Betty glared at him.

"Madam Anna, she take everything today. A friend bring big van. He help her. She say everything hers."

"Everything? Even the beds? They're mine!"

"She leave beds."

"Well, that's a relief," Bill said, turning to me and grinning. "At least we'll have something to sleep on, and there are built-in cupboards in the bedrooms for your clothes."

"But Dad, there's no sofa. Or TV!" Jodie whined.

"Not to worry, Jo. We'll get one tomorrow. Then it'll be all our own stuff." He threw a pleading glance at me. I could only shrug. This wasn't exactly the welcome I'd been expecting; none of what had happened since we arrived was, but I decided not to let it get to me. Okay, so we were in an empty house with the aura of Bill's departed girlfriend still present and a maid who obviously wasn't happy with our presence. It wasn't exactly ideal, especially when Betty disappeared back into the kitchen and made no attempt to make our acquaintance. I could only guess where her loyalties lay. Welcome to Sunninghill, I sighed. Things could only improve, couldn't they?

On the upside, we were here now, we'd had a few days luxuriating in the comforts of a Sandton hotel, and we knew we loved South Africa: its people, its scenery and its weather. Betty excluded, warm hospitality was what the country was known for and despite the ongoing political problems, I was happy to be back.

It was also wonderful to be reunited with my cat, Mitten. She was the only one left of the three we'd had in Natal, and was our first pet when we lived on the farm. I found her on Bill's bed when I walked through the house. She rolled onto her back and purred furiously. As I picked her up, I wanted to believe she remembered me, and I was easily convinced when she rubbed her chin against my cheek. It was a mutually affectionate meeting for us both, and from that first day, she resumed her pole position on my lap. The other two cats, Stanley and Spooky, were new arrivals and very much Bill's but that didn't matter. With a house full of animals, I felt sure life would regain its balance.

As for the future, I'd get the girls into school and find myself a job, and somehow or other Bill and I would sort things out. Although in many respects he was pretty volatile, he was an incurable optimist and I was usually a glass half-full sort of person too. This time I knew I'd need to nurture that attitude well.

Apart from all this, I remembered Joburg from 1985 as a bustling lively city and I relished the idea of getting to know it better. It was time to adapt to the situation, let go of the past and move forward.

As Bill promised, we spent the next few days organising furniture for the living and dining areas. We bought a modern but comfortable mushroom coloured lounge suite, a large square pine-framed coffee table with a glass top and some bookshelves. With a couple of opulent pot plants, a second-hand TV and the pictures and stereo equipment Bill already had, we were quickly in our own home.

The dining area took a little longer. When we went to choose a table, I fell for an oak set with matching chairs. It was just so classy I had to have it.

"Now, madam," said the salesman, pen poised to take our order, "would you be happy with this veneered chipboard table, which you can have now, or do you want a solid oak top? If so, that'll take another six weeks as we have to have it custom made."

He smiled, looking from one to the other of us.

How I wished he hadn't told me; I'd never have known about the veneer unless we actually chipped the thing. I also wish he hadn't asked what I wanted; there was only one possible answer.

"It has to be solid wood."

"Are you sure, Val?" Bill cut in, a little anxiously.

"Quite sure. I'm not buying a fake and that's that."

Given my pre-South Africa career in furniture restoration it shouldn't have surprised him. When we met, I was doing restoration as a business and I specialised in stripped pine country cupboards and dressers – all one hundred percent solid wood and wholly authentic. Call me a snob, but in those days just the idea of having something made from veneered chipboard made me shudder.

The downside of my sensibilities was not only the extra time the table would take to make; it was the money too. I could see the Rand signs floating in Bill's worried eyes. The cost would be another R1000 on top of the displayed price of R1500. We both knew this, but since I was intending to use my pension money from London to pay for it, I just smiled sweetly. There wasn't much more he could say.

In spite of my extravagance, we went home pleased with both the choice and the decision. Even so, it became something of a legend among us that I kept the family eating off trays for months because I wouldn't compromise quality for convenience. In South African culture, the concept of mañana (tomorrow will do) was already considered much too urgent, so it was predictable that the table finally arrived somewhat later than the six weeks promised. The consolation was that it fitted our furnishings perfectly. We were all very happy with it and the inconvenience of the extended wait was forgotten. Now we could behave like normal people and eat, drink and relax in a home that was all ours.

My next challenge was to try and make friends with Betty, but she resisted all my efforts at drawing her both out and in. She lived on the premises in her own very nice modern flatlet. It had a bedroom, full bathroom and small kitchenette, all well furnished with smart fitted cupboards and appliances. Our own kitchen was at the back of the house with a door that led out to a small yard. Betty could go outside and into her flat without ever coming through the main house and she did this quite pointedly.

 Where I was concerned, she bristled with animosity. In her favour she was very fond of Bill, but she obviously disapproved of me and had no truck with the girls. Her 'madam' had been Anna and she didn't intend to betray that loyalty for any reason, however good. I later discovered she'd been Anna's maid for years, so it was quite understandable. But I still tried, even though I realised I was waging a campaign that was destined to fail.

It became quite comical at times. I would go into the kitchen while Betty was there and make an attempt to strike up conversation.

"Good morning, Betty. How are you today?"

"Madam."

"Is everything okay? It's a lovely day, isn't it?"

Yes, madam."

Well, that's good. Do you need anything? Food, cleaning materials...?"

"No, madam."

"Okay. Will you let me know if there's anything I can get you?"

"Yes, madam. I ask the master."

How to be dismissed in one easy lesson.

Meanwhile, she would be furiously wiping tops, washing down cupboards and doing everything possible not to look at me. The harder I tried to win a smile from her, the deeper her frown became.

What made things more difficult was that she was an Afrikaans speaker, a language I didn't know other than the odd words and phrases our Dutch landlord and landlady taught us when we lived in Natal.

Apart from what I'd learnt from them, I'd rarely heard any Afrikaans except for some programmes on the radio, because the Natal Midlands was almost entirely an English area. Bill didn't speak it either, although he understood quite a bit as it was Anna's mother tongue. Anyway, he would have heard it more on the Reef than in that 'last outpost of the British Empire', Natal. In Betty's eyes, however, my lack of bi-lingual skills was another point against me.

Eventually it became impossible to communicate with her, so when the day came that Anna asked if she could have Betty back, I agreed with almost indecent alacrity. I was quite happy to do the housework myself and life became much more relaxing when we didn't have a small pink-aproned thunder cloud in the house, ready to rumble at the slightest provocation.

Work, school and home

Before this relief came, I had to acknowledge that having someone else to do the dusting and hoovering liberated me to sort out the other urgent aspects of our new life. The first of these was to get the girls into school.

Bill was working out of an office in Halfway House, a loosely assembled centre of shops and business premises that had evolved from an eponymous village halfway between Pretoria and Johannesburg. There was a growing film industry there and Bill was working with a production company on a script he'd written. It was showing distinct and encouraging signs of making it onto the big screen and Bill was at the offices almost daily, intent on realising his dream of stardom; in other words, getting his name on the credits.

Since there was a primary school in Halfway House, we applied for the girls to go there. It happened to be the only school we knew about, but the fact that it was also a *laerskool*, as it was called in Afrikaans, and therefore bi-lingual seemed like a good idea. The benefits of being fluent in both English and Afrikaans were obvious in a country with two official languages. Jodie had Afrikaans lessons when she was at school in Richmond, but I don't suppose much of it registered then because no one in our circle of acquaintances spoke it. As for Mo, she only started primary school in England, so she'd had no exposure to it at all.

Having the girls at school in Halfway House turned out to be handy for the first employment I managed to find, which was located in roughly the same area. I say roughly because there were always distances to travel wherever we lived and worked. Being such an out of the way and new suburb, Sunninghill wasn't really handy for anywhere, but it was closer to Halfway House and Midrand than it was to Sandton and the centre of Johannesburg.

My job was with a wildlife book distributor, whose premises were on a plot that was as isolated as any outlying game lodge and had a rough track leading to it worthy of a remote mountain pass.

I was employed as a data entry clerk. I can't imagine now what possessed me to think I would enjoy it other than knowing I'd be surrounded by beautiful books about Africa. But I got the job and every day I dropped the girls off at school before tearing ten kilometres across country and then bouncing up the deeply rutted track to my new office. I would be there until four o'clock, punching numbers into a desktop computer until I was free to tear back again and collect the girls from the school's aftercare centre. They hated their school and I hated my job.

Being English speakers was not a happy situation for children in a predominantly Afrikaans environment. Despite its claims of bilingualism, all the teachers at Halfway House Primary spoke Afrikaans and most of the attending children did too. My daughters found themselves being discriminated against in various wretched ways and disciplined harshly for minor misdemeanours that were ignored in the other children. It was miserable for them. This was probably not typical of Afrikaans schools per se; it was just this school at this time. Maybe if they'd gone a few years later or earlier, it might have been completely different.

As for me, my boss was a brilliant and inspiring man, but he didn't suffer fools gladly and when it came to numbers, I was the ultimate fool. At my last job in the UK, I'd started off as a medical claims assessor until my employers realised I was worse than useless at calculating payments. I might have had a degree but it didn't include basic accounting skills, or even simple addition.

Instead of firing me, though, they moved me to their customer service and communications department where I could use what I was better with: words. I flourished there and although I still had to enter data into a computer, it was reports and letters, not numbers and codes. Even better, I had personal contact with the clients.

Given these circumstances, it was unfortunate for me and my boss that I was quite good at interviews (those words, you see), so when I went to Wildworld Books to talk about the job, I bluffed my way into it by citing my computer and claims assessing experience. It was a big mistake. Ross Leon had a short fuse which blew with increasing frequency the more he realised I was a mathematical idiot.

Unknown to me then, I had a form of dyscalculia and to this day, anything to do with numbers sends me into a spin. Hopelessly. I never know what I'm doing. What makes it worse is that if anyone attempts to explain numerical data to me, I lose any capacity to understand anything at all – at any time. Idiocracy takes over and my face has a vacant sign pinned to it.

This was not behaviour of much use in a data entry clerk where speed and accuracy were required – all the time. Poor Mr Leon. He didn't know what to make of me. His frustration was justifiable, but I wasn't good at tension at the best of times and the atmosphere became fraught.

That apart, what had appealed to me about the work in the first place was being around all the books, and these were breathtaking. I loved being sent from the office down to the storeroom. As Ross Leon was a keen conservationist, the grounds of his several-acre plot were largely left to their natural state. There was a rock path down the steep hill to the neatly built outhouse that housed the stock. On either side, indigenous plants grew between the boulders and a few acacia trees provided shade. It was like being on safari just outside the city and the panoramic view across the valley was gorgeous. It was often still and hot and with an almost uninterrupted outlook, I could imagine myself in Zululand again.

Ross Leon had other employees besides me, and one of these was Robert, the storeman, a young and good-looking African with a broad smile and a good sense of humour. We were partners in sin quite often as he was also inclined to arouse our employer's ire. Admittedly, he too managed to be quite dim at times, so I can imagine the pair of us drove Mr Leon to distraction.

All the same, Robert was essentially intelligent and very interested in wildlife and conservation, so together we browsed through the new consignments of books as they came in and passed them to each other with due reverence. Some of the editions were filled with stunning photography; others were illustrated with fine watercolour paintings or pen and ink drawings. It was such a delight to be allowed to handle them, and because I was entitled to a staff discount, I bought a number of them myself as gifts for family or simply to keep for the sheer pleasure of leafing through them.

While talking to Robert one day, I asked him if he was happy in his job. He was responsible for the stock taking and picking, as well as keeping track of mail orders. He was also the company driver and did all the deliveries, so it was quite a varied position.

"I like my work here, Mrs Val, but one day I want to be a guide on safaris."

"Oh really? Actually, yes, Robert, that would be perfect for you. What's stopping you from doing it now?"

"I need more money. I must study to be a guide, but I have a wife and a child. I must support them first."

"Ah, yes. I see your problem. Can you apply to the government for a scholarship, perhaps?"

"No, the government say they have no money for this thing. It makes me angry. I don't know why they cannot print more money. So many people are hungry. If the government print more money, we could all get food and education!"

"But Robert, you can't just print more money," I objected. "Paper notes have no value in themselves. They just represent the thing that has the real value, for instance gold and diamonds."

"I don't believe that, Mrs Val. If I go to the bank with a hundred Rands, they will not give me a piece of gold!" he scoffed. "No. The government have the power and they can print more money to stop the poverty. But they don't want to do that in case they lose their power."

I was disconcerted by his reasoning and conviction. It seemed such a simplistic view, but in hindsight, I realised he might have had a point. The gold standard had long been gone and it was hard to know what the numbers in our bank accounts meant. If there was nothing tangible to support them with, were they just figures? What was a Rand or a Dollar anyway? Robert's argument got me thinking.

That said, this was 1990 South Africa and despite the moves to dismantle apartheid, along with Nelson Mandela's much lauded recent release from prison, Robert's words might still have been regarded as belligerent talk. Under the circumstances, I thought it wiser not to pursue the subject.

I didn't know too much about the laws on inflammatory speech; they may not have been too harsh by then as so much was changing. But it occurred to me such outspoken criticism could get him into trouble. I should say it was the only time I ever heard or saw Robert angry although I can imagine he was frustrated. He had a dream and could see no way of achieving it.

Being among all those magnificent books was about the only benefit of the job for me. As a child, I was an avid reader and used to threaten to leave home and take all the books with me if I was upset about something. It was a family joke; our lounge had wall-to-wall bookshelves containing hundreds of books. With this as my background, it stands to reason that I'd taken the position because the idea of working with a book company really appealed to me.

Within a couple of months, I was regretting my decision. The books aside, my duties both worried me and bored me. My colleague in the office wasn't much fun either. Sandra was the operations manager and she ignored me most of the time, so it was lonely work during which I had little to no contact with other people apart from Robert. Even worse, I spent far too much time on the mind-numbing task of copying numbers into the computer terminal.

After five months I decided I'd had enough and handed in my notice. I no longer remember what excuse I gave for leaving, but Mr Leon was sympathetic and kind, which made me feel guilty. I must have fibbed my way out of the job just as I'd bluffed my way into it. Anyway, whatever it was I said, I didn't feel good about leaving although I couldn't have been more relieved when I did.

After extracting myself from terminal boredom – literally and figuratively – I wasn't sure what to do next. Having paid work was essential, but for the time being it wasn't quite so financially pressing. Bill was on a retainer from the production company, which meant that for once I had the luxury of choice when it came to my own career.

For some time, I'd been interested in the real estate business. I'd worked as the secretary in a property sales firm in Natal and enjoyed it. I'd also typed innumerable property transfer deeds in my next job with a Richmond attorney. But to become an agent myself would involve some studying because the proper qualifications were a legal requirement; I would need to take the Estate Agents' Board exams.

I signed up with an estate agent's firm in Midrand run by a glamorous woman by the name of Catherine Earl. The deal was that I would follow a distance-learning course to gain the qualifications necessary to work as a sales agent, and in the meantime, I'd be general dogsbody in the office for a minimal salary.

Distance learning in the early 90s was conducted by snail mail post as it was before email had arrived in South Africa. Once I'd enrolled on an accredited course, I received modules through the letterbox on a regular basis. I had to study these materials and then write essays on questions posed at the end of the module.

The one snag was the amount of maths involved. We had to be able to calculate mortgage rates for all sorts of properties and work out the amortisation and devaluation amounts for things like car parks, blocks of flats, and what are known in South Africa as Sectional Title properties. These would be complexes where the flats or cluster houses would have shared areas and external walls, but the interiors belonged to the individuals.

It was all quite complicated, and I was immensely grateful I had a special and rather expensive calculator to do the necessary sums for me. I'd have been back to square one otherwise, as I didn't have a clue how to work these things out myself.

It was a very interesting course, especially as I'd already had some hands-on experience with house sales and transfer documents in Natal. I learnt fascinating facts about old rights of way, servitudes, legal ownership, occupation rights and all sorts of other information about South African property law. I've never tried to sell houses anywhere else, so I don't know if all these land laws are the same everywhere, but I was impressed by how carefully the various legal aspects of property ownership, leasing and renting were dealt with in my studies.

Meanwhile, we were generally content in our squash-court house in Sunninghill. There were good walks in the pine woodlands that bordered the suburb and Sasha and Claude took every advantage of having the girls for company. We usually strolled around the few streets that made up our quiet neighbourhood and then over the newly laid roads into the trees beyond.

There was much less need for security then; there were no gated communities or armed guards as there are these days. We didn't have electric fencing either, although everyone had a burglar alarm and steel security gates for when the front door was open. While not as carefree as we'd been in Natal, we felt quite safe to explore the surrounding areas on foot. This was not downtown Johannesburg after all.

Adventures in Namibia

While we were in Sunninghill, we also went on an extensive camping holiday for the first time in a few years. I hadn't been able to afford real holidays in Natal after Bill left, and in England, we'd had just one long weekend break in a caravan in Cornwall. Then during our first Christmas back in South Africa, we took the camper to the east of the country and spent a few days driving round the magnificent Blyde River Canyon. While the scenery was dramatically beautiful, the weather was oppressive and sticky and we were eaten by mosquitoes the size of small drones. With too little time to relax and temperatures too hot to enjoy, it didn't count as a real holiday, either. So when Bill suggested a two-week camping trip to Namibia the following July, we were all excited.

The film he was working on was a wartime story set in the Namibian desert and he wanted to take us to the Namib-Naukluft National Park, where he'd spent some time doing research for the script. He'd been so taken with the country he wanted us to see it too.

"It's just incredible up there," he enthused. "And now it's independent and the border war is over, it's perfectly safe to drive there too."

Namibian independence was just a few months old at this time, but Bill's outlook was so buoyant and positive he swept us along on his wave of good cheer. Of course nothing bad could happen. It wasn't allowed to.

"How will we get there? What's the route? It looks very empty on the map. Are there many camp sites on the way?" I asked, my interest piqued. The terrain west of Joburg looked suspiciously like a desert already with towns few and far between.

"We'll go to Kuruman first so we can see Die Oog."

"What's that? Something to do with an eye, I take it?"

"Yes, it's a natural spring, supposedly one of the biggest in the world. It comes up in a large pool between the rocks. I haven't been there yet but apparently it's lovely. Full of fish and plants. We can't go through the northern Cape without seeing that," Bill said, pointing to it on the road map. "And then we'll go on to Upington and spend a night at Augrabies Falls. I went there last time I drove to Namibia and it's fantastic, a stunning nature reserve. And the falls are just beautiful."

His excitement had us buzzing. One of Bill's greatest qualities was his infectious enthusiasm for adventure. Everything was described in superlatives.

After Augrabies, we would drive north into Namibia beyond Windhoek, the capital, following which we'd head first west then south down the Skeleton Coast, so named because of the number of ships wrecked along its treacherous shores. From Swakopmund, we could go into the desert, before heading back to Windhoek and home.

I say all that quite casually now, but it was a huge distance of around 4000 kilometres and very ambitious for a two-week trip passing through terrain usually covered by Land Rovers and other four-wheel-drive vehicles. We would be driving a VW Golf, in those days just a small hatchback car only a step up from a tin can.

That was also typically Bill. He had no doubts at all about our safety and was completely confident we'd be fine in our totally unsuitable vehicle. As a result, we (the girls and I) were convinced as well. As it turned out, his conviction was not entirely groundless, but it wasn't totally accurate either.

The holiday was a great success and did much to allay my uncertainties about the wisdom of our return, although I have to admit there were one or two minor crises. At Augrabies, which was indeed stunningly beautiful, we were so cold during the night none of us slept a wink. We were sadly unprepared for the bitter overnight temperatures of the southern Kalahari Desert with our thin ground mats and summer sleeping bags. We got up stiff and wretched, the girls crabby from lack of sleep.

"Did you know it would be so cold?" I asked Bill.

"Well, I knew in theory ..."

"But not in practice or experience, I take it."

"No, but it's just numbers when you read about it, isn't it? When they say overnight temperatures around three degrees, it doesn't sound so bad, does it?"

"I never imagined it would go so low in this area."

"Ah, but deserts *are* cold in the winter. I think it was actually freezing last night."

I should have thought of that myself.

In a sterling effort to make up for our discomfort, Bill introduced the girls and me to the 'snack buck' as he called the local antelope herd.

They were elegant, graceful creatures and they gathered round the perimeter fence of the campsite, clearly looking for some supplements to their breakfast.

"Look Jojo and Mo. They're cheeky, aren't they? They want your breakfast as well as theirs," he joked. "You'd better watch out; there's a snack buck about," he chuckled.

The girls were fascinated to see wild antelope so close up and it dispelled their niggling and irritable behaviour like magic. Mine too. Clever Bill.

The other crisis was much later in the Namib Desert, but before that we had the most exhilarating time ever. Namibia was awesome in the real sense of the word; truly magical. The road from Augrabies to Windhoek was just short of a thousand kilometres of nothing with Keetmanshoop, a railhead town, about half way between the two. It was almost surreal in its vast deserted emptiness, and even more so when we saw a cyclist on the road

"Where on earth can he be going?" I asked. "We've come from nothing and there's nothing ahead for kilometres!"

"Beats me," said Bill. "Crazy, isn't it? There must be villages somewhere around, but I've never seen one and I've driven this road a few times now."

"Have you seen many bikes before too?"

"Not many, but it's bizarre when you do. I mean, where is there to go anyway?" A fact made even more mind boggling when a few years later a well-meaning British first lady started a campaign to donate thousands of bikes to the Namibian people. I'm not sure she succeeded, but all of us who knew Namibia were speechless.

When we arrived in Windhoek, we found a clean, pleasant and spacious town surrounded by mountains. It seemed quiet and tranquil, a bit of a backwater, which I suppose it was. However, our next stop at Khorixas was memorable for being a different kind of backwater.

We approached it at night, crawling along roads populated with more buck than we'd ever seen before. They wandered out in front of the car, often freezing in our headlights and we had to be constantly on the alert to avoid them. In one heart stopping moment, we nearly ran into a Kudu bull, a near miss that had me sweating with anxiety. Kudus are huge, heavy beasts with massive horns. All of us would have been a mess if we'd hit it.

Khorixas itself was just a small crossroads town in the Namibian wilderness, so we found the campsite easily and got ourselves set up in total darkness, a feat unwitnessed by any. In the morning, our fellow campers watched in fascination as we loaded all our equipment back into the Golf.

"We wouldn't have believed that if we hadn't just seen it," one of them said to me.

"You mean how we pack everything in?" I asked.

"Yeah ... that's just amazing! And you manage to find room for two kids as well!"

"Well, actually, we strap them on the roof," Bill winked.

We all laughed, but our fellow camper was right; it was quite remarkable. How we did it still surprises me. The car was crammed so full we couldn't see anything in the rearview mirror at all, and there wasn't a chink of light between any of our well compressed belongings.

The Petrified Forest on the road west of Khorixas was next on our itinerary. When we arrived, we found an open site where the fossilized remains of millennia-old trees lay resting on the open ground. Washed down in flood waters at the end of a former ice age, they'd been buried for millions of years under mud and sand, only exposed in recent times through erosion.

Silent and still, the atmosphere of the place breathed peace and a sense of time suspended. I could easily imagine it held the key to a wealth of ancient wisdom. There wasn't another soul there as we stepped among these relics of another age in the desert's history, and later I was glad we'd seen it before it became a tourist attraction.

About thirty kilometres further west, we turned off the main road to wind our way through the desert to Twyfelfontein, where Bushmen rock paintings were visible to those who could find them. The sand roads were narrow with no clear markings, but Bill had been there before and eventually we tracked them down. They were definitely worth the diversion.

Clearly distinguishable on the rock face, the delicate lines of animals and hunters were timeless images, still full of action and life. I found them especially poignant given the decimation of the San people by later more dominant occupants of the land.

All these marvellous experiences took place under the clear blue skies and warm winter sun of the desert. It continued being cold at night but nothing like the icy conditions we had at Augrabies.

The weather changed dramatically when we reached Kaap Kruis on the Skeleton Coast. In swapping the heat of the interior for a cool misty climate reminiscent of Europe, we were physically reminded about the influence the cold waters of the Atlantic exerted over the coastal region.

Kaap Kruis itself was another highlight we were privileged to witness. It was home to one of the few great seal colonies on the African continent. The sheer numbers of these heavy, lumbering creatures lying around and communing in small groups would have been hard to imagine without being there. The smell was appalling, but the impression was unforgettable.

The cool, damp conditions continued all the way down to Swakopmund, a quaintly German town fighting a constant battle against invading desert sands. I remember camping on the beach close to Mile 4 and waking to an almost impenetrable fog that shrouded the town for part of each day.

Our last rest days were spent in the Naukluft desert, the National Park of the Namib. We needed a permit to enter and set up camp, and we had to give specific details about where we were going and when we were leaving. All of this was arranged at a national parks' tourism office in the centre of Swakopmund. When we received our entry papers, they told us we also had to carry all our own water and agree to camp only at the designated sites. Entry was strictly controlled in an effort to conserve the delicate ecology of the desert, so we felt quite honoured to be granted the permits.

Once we drove through the park entrance, we were on our own. During the days we were there, we saw no one and heard no other human activity at all. It was incredible, and for the first time in my life I became aware that silence could be filled with sound and noise, but of a unique kind. I still find it hard to describe how deeply it moved me to be there.

The campsites were marked and easy to find along the route. The ones we used were next to massive rock formations, but that was all the protection or amusement available. Even so, it was heartening to see how little our two children needed to entertain them. With their father mostly, they climbed the rocks, investigated crannies and flew homemade kites. We walked, cooked on our campfire, and relished the lonely peace of this vast landscape.

Far from being deserted, though, the desert was alive with life: insects, birds, rock rabbits (known as *dassies*) and plant life. It was overwhelming and inspiring in its grandeur; uplifting in the feeling of sheer unhampered space. We could stretch our eyes forever and see nothing but an unblemished, natural world with no manmade structures anywhere. I haven't been anywhere like it since and it remains a cherished memory.

But about that other crisis I mentioned, it happened, or rather nearly happened, on our way out of the Naukluft Park when we were driving towards Windhoek again. We were taking the most direct route and hoping to see the Spookhuis (Ghost House) at Khomas Hochland on the way.

It was said to be a lonely and isolated mansion with a mysterious and ghostly history, but the deep sand on the steep climbs to the interior's highlands finally defeated the little Golf. It's true we'd seen a sign warning us the road was only suited to four-wheel-drive vehicles; indeed, it stated 'Four-Wheel-Drive Vehicles Only' but Bill was never one to be daunted, so on we went.

All was well at first, but at the steepest part of the sharpest bend, when the ground fell away with gut-wrenching finality to our right, the wisdom of the warnings hit home. We got well and truly stuck. Despite the combined pushing of the girls and myself, the wheels just dug further and deeper into the ruts of the road.

There was nothing for it; we had to turn round and go to Windhoek the long way round. We three girls stayed out of the car holding hands and breath together as, in reverse, Bill edged his way back round the bend, aiming for a wide spot where he could manoeuvre safely. The hot sun and still air made the situation even more fraught. Every few metres, the wheels would lose purchase and the car just slid back. We gasped. It was worse than a movie; it was real, and with terrifying frequency, it looked as if Bill and the car would go over that unforgiving edge.

But he didn't, and with calm presence of mind as well as skill, he steered it back to the point where he could make the turn. All he said was: "Well, that was fun," and laughed. But I saw the beads of sweat on his brow.

As it was quite late in the day, and we had a long round trip to make, we pounded along the rippled surface of the desert floor at ludicrous speeds. Sand roads become corrugated if they aren't graded regularly, and I suppose in Namibia the desert wasn't visited often enough for the authorities to make it a routine job. It was cripplingly uncomfortable.

The road we were traversing seemed to go on forever and disappeared ahead in the midst of endless yellow hills dotted with sparse scrubby bushes. And then suddenly, with no warning, it made a sharp right-hand turn. In an astonishing reflex action, Bill pulled on the handbrake and we hurtled skidding and screeching round the corner. When I opened my eyes, we were facing back the way we'd come.

"Well, that was fun," Bill quipped for the second time that day.

"Only if you're a disaster junkie," I replied, teeth gritted. I hated handbrake turns and remembered my angry reaction some years before when a friend did one 'just for fun' on a mountain road in Natal. That wasn't fun at all.

Anyway, that was the end of our tyres. By the time we'd limped the 1500 kilometres back to Sunninghill, they'd worn through the rubber and the canvas beneath to the steel reinforcement. In fact, the car didn't survive long after our trip either.

Although it had done us proud, 4000 kilometres of bone jarring terrain proved too much for the poor Golf and it started developing problems. Before the spring, Bill traded it in for another car with significantly less wear. It's said that a car is only as old as its mileage, but I think it also depends on what kind of mileage it's done.

Changes both animal and mineral

Once we were back home, the reality of normal life bit again and the girls had to go back to their dreaded school. I felt guilty knowing I'd sorted out my own wretchedness but not theirs. Never one to miss an opportunity, Mo made it quite plain that life would only be worth living if she had her own puppy. Not only that, it had to be a Labrador.

She'd been honing her skills in the powers of persuasion since she was in nappies and far from losing her edge while we were overseas, she'd merely acquired some new tricks, one of which was some fairly effective emotional blackmail.

"Mummy, if I had a puppy, I wouldn't be unhappy at school anymore," she wheedled. "And now we don't have to stay at aftercare, I could look after it." While I wasn't at work in the afternoons, this was true. She had a point, but it didn't stop there.

"Mummy, Sasha and Claude are old. They're going to die soon. I need a puppy so I won't be sad when they've gone."

Little wretch. But it was the tearful pleading that really got to me. I never told her, but that was much more effective than her other tactics.

"Please, Mummy, please Daddy. Please, please can I have a puppy? I so want my own doggy," she sobbed, tears dripping off the end of her nose. The pathos was unbearable.

Against such a war of attrition, we had no defence. I'd defy anyone not to capitulate when faced with utter desolation in one so young. Even armour-plated hearts would have melted when confronted with a small person of so much earnest and tearful intent. So it wasn't all that long before we accepted our fate and went off to see a breeder with a litter of Labrador puppies.

The actual process of choosing and buying the black sausage that eventually evolved into Daisy the Labrador is something I don't remember anymore, but the six-week old bundle of chewing, biting mischief that arrived in our Sunninghill midst made a major impact on our lives. From day one, Daisy knew she was Mo's puppy; much to our relief. It would have been dire if she'd chosen another of us as her human, but since Mo was completely smitten with her four-footed baby, there wasn't much danger of that.

House training was the usual cross between despair and hilarity and kept us all busy. Until we could be reasonably sure she wouldn't leak at the slightest excitement or provocation, she had to sleep in the kitchen; our living room and bedrooms were all carpeted and thus out of bounds. That was the theory, anyway. In practice, the sight of one or other child, or even Bill, pelting through the house with a puppy borne on outstretched arms was the cause of much mirth from the rest of us. If the bearer hadn't caught her in time, the resulting trail of pee that Daisy dribbled on the carpet during the dash for the door had a rather more sobering effect.

Sasha and Claude tolerated the new infant without protest and carried on being the 'little and large' chums they were. It may have been their apparent indifference that irked Daisy, or it might just have been her nature anyway, but as soon as she was sporting a few teeth she started a chewing spree the like of which I have never experienced in any dog.

We'd started planting the garden out with a variety of both indigenous and border plants. We had wonderful 'elephant ears' growing under the windows of the bedrooms and plenty of big ferns, monstera (which we called 'monstrosity' plants) and other tropical greenery. Then we'd put in geraniums, the most tolerant of all flowering plants. We also had marigolds, begonias and impatiens in the beds.

Sadly, these were fair game to a lively puppy. Daisy dug our garden up with the enthusiasm of a competition ploughman. After each session, she would bounce onto the veranda and deposit what she saw as her prizes, these being the mangled remains of my cherished borders.

She then started on our LPs (we didn't have any CDs yet) and cassette tapes. LP covers were a special favourite and I still have a copy of Queen's A Kind of Magic with Daisy tooth marks in the chewed-off corner of the cover. What was worse was the carnage inflicted on Bill's Bose speakers. She nearly didn't survive that crime. I half expected her to be despatched to the SPCA on a charge of aggravated assault.

Fortunately for Daisy, Bill had more patience with dogs than people. If the children had done something as appalling, they'd have been packed off to boarding school before they'd had time to blink. That's not to say Daisy got away free. The sparks emitting from Bill's ears said much about what was coming out of his mouth when he discovered what she'd done, and she was banished to the kitchen for at least an hour.

But it didn't seem to matter what sins she committed; he forgave her in the end. This even extended to the time she caused us crippling embarrassment by having an accident of note in the middle of Sandton City's glitzy shopping mall – on a shining marble walkway next to the top designer stores. The steaming pile of evidence was hastily removed, as were we. Bill laughed his socks off about that.

What all this led up to was the realisation that the house and garden in Sunninghill were becoming a little small for our growing menagerie. Call it coincidence, but Daisy's increase in wickedness occurred at roughly the same time as I passed my estate agency exams and started viewing properties with potential customers.

As things transpired, I only sold two houses in my career as an agent. One was in the north Midrand suburb of Noordwyk and was a house bought by a young African lawyer and his family. The repeal of the Land Act prohibiting black people from owning property in white areas was tabled and approved early in 1990 but only effected in June 1991. But as I recall, relaxations were already occurring in outlying areas.

In Noordwyk, one part of the suburb was already deregulated and small houses on their own stands were available for purchase to non-white owners. I was quite pleased that my first sale was representative of an emerging new South Africa.

The second sale was to myself. While I was showing clients round properties in the Midrand area, I came across another Noordwyk house on the agency books that seemed to have everything we needed. The house in Sunninghill was rising in value, but so was the cost of the mortgage, known in South Africa as the bond. Interest rates were reaching silly levels. Within the last couple of years, they'd escalated from 12.5%, which was bad enough, and were heading for 20%. If we sold the Sunninghill house and made a profit, we could buy a cheaper home in Midrand with a larger garden and save money on the bond. That was the idea, anyway.

It has to be said I wasn't doing all that well as an agent. Catherine Earl complained I was too soft and too candid. I felt obliged to tell prospective purchasers what was wrong with the properties I showed them, if of course I knew. She didn't agree.

"Let them find out for themselves, Val. That's what they have surveyors for. Don't put them off before you've even started," she admonished with a mixture of disbelief and exasperation.

I was also not assertive enough. Estate agents in South Africa were very driven; it was a highly competitive business and if you didn't have that 'killer instinct', then you wouldn't make the sales. I failed in that department miserably, but with my training and past experience, I understood about negotiating prices and calculating costs. I also knew how the conveyancing worked, which meant I was a well-informed buyer if not a gifted seller. The house I'd seen was empty and neglected, but it was attractive in many respects, so I took the family to see it.

Its most appealing feature was its position. Like Sunninghill, it was in a neighbourhood apart that consisted of a single street with the name Francis Drive. Although Noordwyk was a distinct village with its own small shopping centre, Francis Drive was separated from it and accessed by a dirt road. This was, and still is, 14th Road, now tarred and lined with commercial buildings and new housing developments. In 1990, it was a quiet and rural outlier. When we turned off the rutted 14th and drove down Francis Drive to view the property, there was a surreal sense we were on a road to nowhere. In a way we were, but we would only realise that later.

What we saw was a white house set down off the street with steps leading between well-grown tropical plants to the front door. There was a garage to one side, behind which was a maid's room. Inside, the house was on different levels and sported some slightly bizarre features. It was tiled throughout the living area (a bonus given that we had three dogs) but it had a split-level bright purple and pink lounge. This eye-watering confection led to the dining room, where there was a Jacuzzi oddly placed behind a bar counter. Even stranger, it was right next to the kitchen.

"What do you think prompted whoever it was to put that there?" Bill asked. "It looks as if they had luxury ideas bigger than the space to put them in. Either that, or they thought they could combine dining with bathing."

"Well, at least that would be efficient, wouldn't it?"

"Who on earth wants efficiency with their food?"

I did but I didn't say so. Bill was an enthusiastic cook and spent hours preparing curries and Mexican dishes that were so hot I'd long since lost all sense of taste. But then he ate chopped up chillies on his breakfast toast, so there was no accounting – or complaining.

Beyond the kitchen there was a further step down to a passage, off which were two bedrooms and a bathroom. Right at the end, down yet another step, was the main bedroom with an *en suite* bathroom (as they're called in any good property prospectus). The different levels gave the house character and despite the garish paint in the living room and the quirk of the Jacuzzi in the dining room, we all liked it.

Another appeal was the garden. There were sliding doors in the living room and the dining room. Both of these gave onto a paved patio and beyond that came the feature that clinched it completely for the girls. This was a good-sized swimming pool set into the paving and surrounded by what was once a fine lawn bordered with bushes and flowering shrubs. I say once because it was rather overgrown, but it would be lovely when tidied up.

"Oh wow!" breathed Jodie, delight suffusing her face. "A proper pool!"

"I thought you might like that," I smiled. I'd kept the pool part of the description a secret.

"Daisy can learn to swim too, can't she, Mum?" Mo piped up. It wasn't really a question. I knew it would be more of an issue to keep her out of it when she was older. She was a Labrador.

"Yes, Mo, Daisy can learn to swim, although I don't think she'll need much teaching."

At this point, I had a light bulb moment. We'd already reached the stage of psychological ownership by discussing Daisy's introduction to the pool. The house had clearly scored a hit with the whole family in spite of its strange interior features.

"Do I take it that you'd all like to move here then? Away from Sunninghill?"

The answer was a fairly predictable and unanimous 'yes'.

We decided to use my position as the agent to make an offer on the spot. I convinced 'me the buyer' that the seller on whose behalf I was acting would accept our bid. The Sunninghill house would probably sell quickly; it wasn't a certainty, but if it did, we'd have to move fast. Our offer was conditional on being able to move in before the transfer date, if need be. This was possible in South Africa and Sale Agreements made provision for occupational rental. In other words, it was rent that was paid to the seller to cover mortgage costs until the transfer was complete.

What we didn't appreciate was that it was a system rife with risk. It happened that we *did* have to move early and this proved to be the beginning of a long drawn out and rather sorry process.

The bigger picture

U p until our move Johannesburg's northern suburbs had been the
centre of our social and cultural universe. Although we claimed
to live in the city, our Sunninghill home was about twenty-five
kilometres from the centre and even twelve from the important
commercial hub of Sandton. Joburg was not just one unified city. It
consisted of several municipalities that were all large and established
urban conglomerations in their own right.

In the Johannesburg of 1990, the southern and eastern towns like
Germiston, Benoni, Boksburg, Springs and Alberton had their own
character and were older and more conventional in style than the
northern suburbs. They were home to a mix of cultures, but I think it's
true to say Afrikaans was a more dominant language in those areas.

North of the city, the municipalities of Randburg, Sandton and
Kempton Park enclosed older suburbs such as Parktown and
Rosebank and were home to the more affluent sectors of Johannesburg
society but also to more English speakers.

To the west were Soweto, Roodepoort and Krugersdorp, towns that
evolved from the mining industry on the West Rand. The entire
Johannesburg area, including all its municipalities and suburbs had a
population of several million people from a wide variety of cultures.
Roughly half of these lived in the city itself.

In other words, Sunninghill was on the outskirts of a huge
metropolitan sprawl and because we were so much closer to the
northern suburbs and Midrand, we didn't need to go into town very
often. Mostly, we did our shopping locally. Only the older inner-city
neighbourhoods had high streets; in the newer developments,
shopping centres were the norm and newly built malls were popping
up everywhere.

At the weekends, we went to Bryanston, Sandton or Randburg, all
of which had busy shopping and business districts. Heading towards
Pretoria, Halfway House in Midrand was also a good location with a
variety of stores. The big supermarket chains, Pick 'n Pay and
Checkers had branches in almost all the malls, so our normal practice
was to head for one of these, do our bulk buying and then resort with
exhausted relief to a café for much needed coffee and breakfast. The
food was always delicious and the café owners created an inviting

environment. It was always a treat to look forward to after enduring the crush of Saturday morning in the hypermarket, especially at month end.

There was one particular café we liked going to in Bryanston where the staff were cheerful welcoming people who made us feel like personal friends. We went there for the music too and it was where we often heard Sugar Man by the singer, Rodriguez. We all thought he was a world-famous star as his music had been popular in South Africa since the seventies.

It was only when the film *Searching for Sugar Man* came out in 2012 that I learnt his phenomenal success was confined to South Africa and Australia. He was hugely influential in the South African music scene, inspiring anti-apartheid activists like Steve Biko with his protest songs. In a bizarre twist of fate, all of this was completely unknown to the singer himself, which made it such a special story. As we munched on our breakfast toasted sandwiches, we would hum along to his songs as oblivious to the story behind the singer's fame in South Africa as we were to the fact that he was virtually unknown elsewhere.

Anyway, during the early 90s, these northern suburbs were populated mainly by white Europeans although within a few years of the '94 election (when Nelson Mandela became president), the denizens would start to be much more cosmopolitan and mixed. Before this development, the only African residents were domestic workers, and while others served in the shops and businesses, they didn't live in the white residential areas. They came in daily from the townships like Soweto and Alexandra, travelling by public transport. This was mostly provided by privately run minibus taxis (minibuses fitted with bus style seats), much as it still is in many African and eastern European countries.

Altogether, Joburg was a city of extremes: in size, in population mix, in diversity and in wealth; it was tragically tough for many, extremely luxurious for others. But it can't be denied that to be white, working and middle class was a comfortable place to be in South Africa's foremost city at the time. We had an unfair advantage and were aware of it.

On the positive side, one of the aspects of this urban life I came to enjoy was simply driving. The arterial roads were long and not too busy. Witkoppen Road was a pretty, winding, shrub-lined and quite narrow road that wound its undulating way from Sunninghill down to the Sand River, a rather grand name for what was just a lively stream. The road then continued on to Jukskei Park, one of the most northern of the northern suburbs. We usually followed it until we reached Main Road at a landmark called the Clay Oven where we would turn left to Bryanston.

The whole area was still largely undeveloped and the Clay Oven was just an old-fashioned thatched restaurant in a semi-rural setting. It seems it has now expanded into a much grander lifestyle centre.

Behind the tall trees lining Main Road, there were plots with houses we didn't really see. Without much traffic either, it was a straight run through to the more exclusive Bryanston and other elegant locations such as Hyde Park, Rosebank and Parktown.

The roads were wide with smooth surfaces and there were plenty of traffic lights, known locally as robots. However, the stretches between them were long enough to make driving a pleasure. When we reached the junction with William Nicol Drive, there would always be tradesmen at the lights trying to sell us a variety of goods: anything from sun shades to boxes of fruit.

I loved the cheerful banter we had with these chirpy personalities and quite often we slipped them a few Rand coins even when we didn't want to buy anything. Making eye contact was fatal, but I could rarely help smiling. They beamed their way into our purses.

"Hey, mama," one of them would call, weaving his way through the cars as soon as he caught my glance. "You take some oranges for the chill-dren today?"

"Ah no, sorry, Baba, not today, thank you. Maybe next time."

"Ah please, mama. You a kind lady. I can see that. And the chill-dren, they *need* plenty fruit. You can make juice, jam, *even* English marmalade." He would pause, for maximum effect. "See, I give you this *whole* box for five Rand!" The grin would be dazzling as he knew he'd got me. I enjoyed the game as much as he did.

"Okay, okay. Give me a box then, but next time I come, don't even look at me," I would chide, smiling and handing over a five Rand note. I knew my scolding would have no effect whatsoever.

"No mama, yes mama, thank you mama!" And off he'd go, laughing, to grab another box and accost another unwary customer.

On that note, being able to drive was essential. Buses were few and not really set up for the European commuter. Their routes were mainly from the black townships and although I think there were a couple of lines that ran from the northern suburbs, I rarely saw them. It was always possible to take the minibus taxis, of course, and some people I knew did use them now and then, but you needed to be made of stern stuff and have nerves of steel to risk riding in one of these.

It's a phenomenon of countries where minibuses are used for public transport that they all seem to be driven by maniacs whose one wish is to terrify their passengers. In South Africa, they filled them to the point where no one could move a muscle and barely breathe. Sardines in cans came to mind. Then they hurtled through the city (or country), jumping red traffic lights, cutting off other drivers, especially other taxis, and generally slaloming their way round the traffic to get to the next stop first and pick up a new load of sardines. In a word, it was a terrifying experience. For this reason, and the lack of other options, having a car was a must.

Incidentally, my first car in Johannesburg was a white Ford pick-up, known as a *bakkie*, but it wasn't really fit for a school run where other people's children were often on my passenger list. So it wasn't long before I was driving one of the best cars I've ever owned: an Alfasud Sprint Veloce with a 1500 engine.

It was around ten years old, an ugly bronze colour and not a particularly pretty model, but when I got in it, I felt I was a kind of Jody Scheckter, the South African racing driver. It was such fun to drive: very sporty with neat bucket seats and as much acceleration as the old MG sports car I'd had as a twenty-something in the UK.

There was room enough in the back for three small people and one in the front passenger seat too (not yet forbidden then); maybe it still wasn't ideal as a mum's taxi, but driving it made up for all its other shortcomings. I was completely enamoured of my Alfa Sprint and would roar down the N1 highway from Halfway House to Sunninghill for the sheer pleasure of feeling it take off.

Swooping down the hill past the Kyalami racetrack and then negotiating the curves of the road to Midrand was also exhilarating and always put a smile on my face. I mourned it when Bill traded it in for a Fiat Uno. To my frequent dismay he had a habit of selling off my cars and buying others without much of a by your leave. Because of this, I had a series of vehicles during my years in Joburg but the Sprint remains one of my all-time favourites.

A different kind of entertainment that also involved cars was going to the drive-in cinema to watch current movies. We'd started going there from time to time, enjoying an evening out where we could take the kids, the dogs and a picnic with us.

Essentially, the drive-in was just a large car park where every space had a connection to the movie sound system that you could clip onto your car window. They're probably the same everywhere but it was a new experience to us and we really enjoyed it. The one we went to was next to the off-ramp of the N1 highway at Randburg. A huge open space, it was ideally suited to a drive-in as it couldn't disturb anyone in the no-man's land of a motorway exit.

All the cars faced the big screen and we sat in the comfort of our own seats and watched the movie through our windscreens. If it was raining, we put the wipers on; if warm, we put blankets on the ground and sat outside. When the children got tired, we put the back seats down and they snuggled under duvets with the dogs.

We loved going as it was a reminder of days gone by in other countries. It was living nostalgia for me as I'd never been to a drive-in until I went to South Africa. Like so many things that were old-fashioned or simply not part of life in Europe, it was one of the charms of living there.

As for the weather, the *Highveld* had the best climate in the world. Summers were warm to hot, but hardly ever too hot. The usual temperature in December and January was around 26C; on a winter's day in July, it was around 17C. Perfect. And that was the average. It could be both hotter and cooler respectively, but it was generally pretty stable and rarely so hot that all action had to be suspended.

Even the rain tended to be in short, regular, torrential bursts during spring and summer afternoons, after which it turned bright and sunny again. In winter, there was no rain, none at all, which was absolute bliss for me. Just like the desert, the nights were cold, even freezing at times, but it stayed dry for a good four months and once I knew what to expect, I could take measures to cope with the low temperatures (something I learnt quickly in the more extreme Natal Midlands). The only downside was the static electricity. After weeks with no rain, everything we touched would give off a spark and brushing our hair became almost risky.

Of all the seasons, however, autumn (being April and May) was my favourite. Still very warm but with little rain and reasonable overnight temperatures, it had a golden glow to the light that I loved. But whatever the time of year, I'd found my personal climate heaven in Joburg. I was never one of those who longed for heavy rain in spring, and I could more or less guarantee being able to walk around without a jacket on a winter's day. That said, there was one year when we had a few bleak cold days and even a sprinkling of snow, but it was such a rarity it stood out.

I suppose all this goes to show that by the end of 1990, I'd become an enthusiastic Joburger, and as a family, we were getting back on track again. Our Namibian adventure, Daisy the Labrador and the prospect of a real family home in Noordwyk created the bonds that tied us together again.

The next phase of our life on the *Highveld* was one of significant change in both our personal lives and in the country as a whole. Ultimately, the move was a mixed blessing. While it opened us up to many more possibilities, it also proved to be a mistake of mammoth proportions.

NOORDWYK

House and home

The house in Noordwyk belonged to a man we never met nor had direct contact with. It later transpired that no one else had or did. He was elusive and mysterious, a fact which in itself should have sounded alarm bells, but if they rang we must have ignored them. After going through the formalities of making the offer, I left it to the Earl Real Estate office administration machine to take it through the usual channels. Since I'd held that role myself when I worked for the estate agency in Richmond, I knew what the procedure was and it normally took a few months.

From our side, Bill put the Sunninghill home up for sale. As we expected, it sold quickly and the transfer was arranged for the earliest possible date. Sunninghill was an up and coming neighbourhood; a 'good' address perceived as the smart option by the yuppies, which was very much in our favour. Having agreed to pay occupational rental if we had to move before we took possession of our Noordwyk home, we were out of one house and into the other by early autumn 1991. That part was simple.

Once we'd moved, life immediately took on a new perspective, and we suddenly had a feeling of great space. The house had quite a low garden wall, unlike the Sunninghill squash court, and from the back patio we could see across a wide valley to the hill beyond. Crowning our view was a solid and solitary building that housed the Development Bank of South Africa. There was nothing else between us and the horizon and I loved being able to look out on such a wide panorama.

The Development Bank wasn't the most beautiful of structures, but its position was imposing and it looked quite impressive cresting the hill when the sun was going down behind it. In other aspects too, our world changed. With the girls still at school in Halfway House and Bill's office close by, we had much less travelling to do and even less need to drive into Johannesburg, at least not for a while.

I initially spent my energies settling into our new home and getting used to life on the outskirts of another developing area. Where

Sunninghill had been on the periphery of Joburg's posh northern suburbs, Noordwyk was most definitely a move down the social scale, but we didn't care. We had a great house, the unimaginable luxury of a pool, a lovely garden and the best view on the Reef – well, we thought so.

Within weeks of moving in, the purple and pink walls were transformed into a more soothing soft white and we found our furnishings suited the clean-tiled split-level design of the house perfectly. The dogs and cats loved the sunny patio and the girls took to the pool with the enthusiasm of ducks reunited with a long-lost pond; not that my water babies had ever had a pond of their own, but they behaved as if they'd been born in one.

Overall, it felt as if life was falling into its proper place, although that's not to say it wasn't hard work; it was.

Cleaning the pool was a new challenge for us. Even though we'd spent several years in South Africa, we'd never lived in a house with a pool before, and we soon discovered there was a whole manual involved in keeping one. Firstly, ours was completely green when we moved in. Between the time we first saw it and our occupation, it was quite clear no one had bothered to maintain it. I suppose our mystery owner decided he didn't need to keep up any kind of show once he'd accepted our offer and left it to nature to do what it would. Nature being what it is favoured a nice green coating over everything. As we didn't, we felt this had to be removed.

We spent a month's salary on cleaning chemicals and new filters for the pump, which was by now nicely clogged up with leaves. Then we did what most people hired others to do for them; we emptied the pool, climbed in wearing shorts and scruffs and scrubbed its sides and floor free of all the dirt and debris. Filling it again cost another month's salary (water was not free in South Africa) and in addition to these already hefty expenses we bought a Kreepy Krauly.

For those who've never seen one, this is like a roving vacuum cleaner with a long suction hose attached to it. Completely independent once switched on, it potters around the pool sucking up everything that settles in and on the water. It's marvellous, and watching it work can be quite addictive. It has a kind of meditative and therapeutic effect, and I often sat by the pool following its progress; I found it a good quiet time for the soul, if not for the skin. My shins got horribly sunburnt on one of my Kreepy Krauly vigils one morning and I couldn't walk for days. I didn't always learn fast enough.

Anyway, like a kind of robotic helper, the Kreepy Krauly became an essential item of household equipment; or rather we thought it was. Not so, Daisy who decided it was an evil monster that had to be killed – regularly. In six months, she murdered more metres of the Kreepy Krauly's hose than would go around the garden three times over, and the pool shop employees looked at me in disbelief the third time I went to buy some more.

"Again?" one young assistant asked. "Sorry, lady, but isn't that just careless, *ja*? How come you let your mutt *donner* it this time?" *Donner* was slang for 'hit hard'; in other words, 'destroy'.

"Because it's almost impossible to stop her. We can't watch her all the time. We do have to go to work, you know."

"Well, keep her in when you're not there, man," he muttered, turning away to fetch another length of hose for me.

I couldn't tell him I'd been there during her last assault. The problem was she'd wait until none of us was watching before diving in. She'd then make a beeline for the Kreepy Krauly, which was making wafting undulating movements in the water like some kind of seductive monster eel. Irresistible. Hauling it out onto the grass by its hose, she would proceed to shake the living daylights out of the 'snake' until it was properly and thoroughly dead. By this time, it had several puncture holes along its expensive length, rendering it completely unfit for purpose any longer.

I knew this because one of our neighbour's maids saw her do it and told me with tears of laughter rolling down her face. Very funny, yes. We would dutifully go off to the pool shop to buy more, only to have it murdered again a few weeks later. After the dressing down the shop assistant gave me, I started looking for other outlets and discovered the larger supermarkets sold Kreepy Krauly equipment too. It was such a relief to know I could buy the hose anonymously and save myself further shame at my inability to prevent the ongoing destruction.

In Daisy's defence, she was still very young and when she turned two years old, all the chewing miraculously stopped, but while it lasted it was hard to bear, especially the extra costs of keeping the Kreepy Krauly alive. Luckily, we all adored her although I have to admit my own affection was severely tested when she dug up the Plumbago climber I'd been nurturing for months and presented its shredded remains to me along with the contents of the pot. In the lounge. On the carpet.

As for the Jacuzzi, it developed a distinctly white elephant aura. We didn't quite know what to do with it and never used it. The problem was potentially solved for us one Sunday a few months after we'd moved in. The spring rains were falling with more than usual gusto and we were having a torrential downpour. What we'd failed to anticipate when buying a house with parts lower than the road was that it might get flooded. It didn't but we were constantly afraid it would. On this particular day, while we were waiting out the deluge in the lounge, there was an almighty bang, a kind of ripping crack that sounded like a gunshot in the house.

Leaping out of his reclining position on the sofa, Bill was on his feet in one easy movement. I was impressed. He wasn't the agile type normally, but I suppose adrenaline makes athletes of even the most horizontal couch potato.

"What the hell was that?"

We looked at each other.

"No idea, but we'd best find out," I replied.

Together we headed through to the dining room, the apparent source of the bang. On reflection, it probably wasn't the wisest move. Had there been someone with a gun, we'd both have been in the line of fire.

At first sight, there was nothing amiss: no smashed windows, no pistol toting gangsters and nothing out of place. We looked in the kitchen and bathroom too but nothing was broken there either. The girls had both heard the noise and came out of their rooms to see what was wrong, so it was clear it hadn't come from their end of the house. It was a mystery.

"What was that, Mum?" Jodie asked, alarm written on her face. Mo just looked curious.

"We don't know, pet, but there's nothing to worry about. At least we don't think so."

Reassured, both girls disappeared back into their rooms. Unexplained noises weren't their area.

I walked back into the dining room and happened to look over the counter into the Jacuzzi. At first, I didn't register what I was looking at, but then it hit me; it was no longer the Jacuzzi as we knew it.

"Um, Bill. I think you'd better come and have a look at this," I called out to him.

I looked back. Instead of sitting in its hole in the ground with its top rim flush with the floor, the Jacuzzi was sticking up on one side at a peculiar angle. Water seeped out through the plughole and it wasn't coming from a tap or pipe.

"Hmm, so that's what it was."

"Yes, but what was it that did it? D'you suppose the water level beneath the house pushed it out?" I asked.

"Must have. It's been one heck of a storm. Who'd have thought it?" he breathed, a kind of awe on his face.

"I'd better check out the front too. If it's come down that hard, the area at the bottom of the steps is probably flooded."

Fortunately for us, the front door step was quite a bit higher than the paving in front of it and although the water was a good couple of centimetres deep outside the door, it hadn't come in. Despite the heavy downpour, the drains seemed to be coping quite well.

However, as with all storms on the Reef, this one was fairly short-lived and it wasn't long before the rain stopped. The sun came through again and half an hour later, it was as if it had never happened, except for our uplifted Jacuzzi, that is.

By this time, we'd been at the house for about five months and we already had a further addition to our family. Bill's son, Tim, had come to live with us. Tim was seventeen. He'd been having some issues at home in England and his mother and Bill agreed he should spend some time in South Africa with us. As luck would have it, we didn't have a maid in Noordwyk so the room behind the garage made an ideal teenager's lair. He arrived late in July and apart from some natural squaring up to his father he settled in well.

I'd always been fond of Tim and I liked having him around. He was funny, quick-witted and intelligent; in other words, good company.

That afternoon, Tim was unaware of the drama going on in the house but had of course noticed the unusual volume of water being deposited on us all from above. When it stopped, he sloshed his way through the back door into the kitchen, mug in hand, coffee in mind.

"Hi Val," he grinned. "Some storm, wasn't it?"

"It was," I sighed. "Come and look at what it's done."

I beckoned him through to the dining room and pointed to our upended Jacuzzi. He looked at it in admiration.

"Wow! Far out! Did it really do that? How come?"

"Well, we think the water table under the house rose and pushed it out. It made the most unbelievable bang. We thought someone had fired a gun in here it was so loud."

"Really? That's totally rad!" Tim was full of street talk we hadn't heard before. "What are you going to do with it, Dad?" he asked Bill.

"Dunno yet. This might be a good opportunity to get rid of the thing."

"But we can't do that," I chipped in. "The house doesn't even belong to us yet."

The whole transfer process was beginning to be a concern. The attorneys handling the sale were being vague about the seller's situation. He still hadn't signed the documents and everything was on hold until they'd pinned him down.

"True," Bill nodded. "Then maybe we'd better just move it outside."

"I like that idea," grinned Tim. "An outdoor Jacuzzi. Yeah! I can see it now. We'll be sitting out there, wallowing in warm water in the winter, even when it's freezing. Love it!"

"Well, I'm glad you approve, sunshine," said Bill, "because you're going to be helping me dig the hole for it."

Tim grimaced but then laughed.

"I suppose I walked into that one, didn't I?"

"And we haven't even started digging," Bill grinned.

When it came to projects, Bill didn't let any moss grow on his stones. During the weeks following the storm, he and Tim dug up a suitable circle of paving and excavated a hole in the sandy soil below. They then hauled the Jacuzzi out through the sliding doors and deposited it in its new home. Sadly, that was as far as it ever got because before we could manage to have water fed to it, we'd moved again. But I'm leaping ahead of myself here; that was many months later.

The state of the state

In the wider world of South Africa's development, all our personal changes, challenges and activities took place against a background of surging political turbulence in the country. Like almost everyone in our circle of friends and acquaintances, we tried not to let the uncertainty and unrest affect us or prevent us from leading a normal life.

For me, the realisation that we were living in a volatile world began when I was in Richmond in 1986. That was during the State of Emergency which was imposed as a result of increasing pressures for change. However, the closer we came to the end of apartheid, the more polarised the political parties seemed to become and the struggle for power stepped up. It was a fact of 1990s life. We watched the approach of a more inclusive political construct with hope, but the eruptions of violence as well as the heavy-handed reaction of the authorities were disturbing and often shocking.

1991 marked significant progress, but it was made with equal amounts of pain. On the plus side, in January, black children were admitted to white government schools for the first time. February saw the president, F.W. de Klerk, announcing the upcoming scrapping of the Land Act, the Group Areas Act and the Population Register Act, all key legislation in maintaining racial segregation since the beginning of apartheid. All three acts were finally repealed in June. In addition, both the ANC and the Inkatha Freedom Party, the two largest black movements, made commitments to end violence and work towards a peaceful settlement. These were positive developments that gave us all a boost confidence in the future.

On the minus side, we listened to reports in February of a massacre at a funeral in Sebokeng, and there were other horrific mass shootings: in May, we heard of Inkatha supporters rampaging through the West Rand township of Kagiso and killing twenty-two people. In May too Winnie Mandela was found guilty of kidnapping, and in June there was another mass shooting on a train in Soweto. Then in August members of the AWB (*Afrikaner Weerstandsbeweging*, the right-wing Afrikaner resistance movement) were involved in a violent conflict with government troops in Ventersdorp, an Afrikaans town 155 kilometres to the west of Johannesburg.

These stories, compounded with the almost daily revelations of covert operations, double-dealings and subversive actions by various sections of the security forces were horrifying and depressing by turns. Corruption in the police and extremist acts by left as well as right-wing groups made each step towards the end of apartheid seem like a constant series of halts and reversals.

Closer to home, Noordwyk wasn't very far from a major African township on the east side of Midrand. Tembisa was a sprawling settlement that had mushroomed over the most repressive years of apartheid. As people were moved there from Alexandra and Soweto in the 70s, it grew still more. These days, large parts of it have developed into pleasant and respectable suburbs with neat houses and established gardens, but when I drove past Tembisa on the road south to Jan Smuts Airport (now Oliver Tambo), I couldn't help being aware of the dreadful conditions in which many people lived there.

I'd been through the townships outside Pietermaritzbug in Natal many times, but somehow those around Johannesburg seemed worse; more squalid, more desperate. The tin shacks, many with stones on their roofs just to keep the corrugated iron sheets from blowing away were mean dwellings for families, especially in winter when the *Highveld* was so cold at night. A cloud of smoke would hover over the township on winter mornings and the air would be thick with the smell of burning wood and coal. Litter lay everywhere and wrecked cars were heaped up with old tyres and other rotten junk. Amongst all this poverty, children ran about among the goats and pecking chickens.

During the early nineties when we lived in Midrand, I remember Tembisa being terrorised by gangs. Violence was a part of life there; it was constantly in the news, and I saw the army vehicles patrolling the area on many occasions. While I worked for Earl Real Estate, I was glad to be part of the process, if only in a very minor way, of helping black families find homes in more peaceful areas, but we were only too conscious that just a few kilometres away, life was very different for thousands of Tembisa's residents.

All we could do was watch, listen, be aware, and carry on with life. It was the only way to cope and although it might seem as if we were burying our heads in the African sand, there was no way of propelling the system forward without being actively involved in the political process. It *was* moving forward, but for many the process was too slow and anger devolved into terrorism, mostly within the townships.

As for my old home in Richmond, Natal, we listened with appalled dismay to reports of its descent into a war zone of inter-factional killings. Had I remained there instead of spending some time in England, this would have been my reality too. Richmond was small; there would have been no escaping the violence. Johannesburg was huge, and the townships were too spread apart for us to be directly affected by such conflicts, but we lived with the undercurrent of tension.

We got used to roadblocks and car searches and we were constantly aware of potential dangers. As for our relationships with the African people, we helped those around us as much as we could and protected them where possible. The problem was that we were largely helpless in the face of the cumbersome and lumbering moves towards political change. We adopted a policy of spreading small kindnesses but it was precious little in the greater scheme of things. Apart from that, we lived life as normally as we were able to under such abnormal circumstances.

Building works and jobs galore

Talking of help, we soon needed small building jobs done on the house. As often happens, a handyman arrived just when we needed one. I'll swear Africans have ESP although in this case, it was probably just word of mouth.

Wilson appeared one morning looking for work. He was the husband of next-door's maid, and he came with a somewhat faded and dog-eared written recommendation that he produced from his pocket and unfolded several times. He was wearing paint-splattered overalls, a sign of his craft as effective as a billboard ad; that and the collection of paintbrushes and rollers sticking out of his pockets. He was pleasant and soon proved to be hard working and willing.

During our daily chats, he told me he was one of the Shangaan people from the north of the country. Shangaans are a mix of Zulu and Tsonga tribes, the result of the subjugation of the Tsongas by one Soshangane, who was one of King Shaka's warriors. Wilson had moved to Johannesburg a few years back. He and his wife lived in Tembisa, meaning he didn't have too far to come, and Noordwyk was a handy location for building work due to the number of new houses springing up. In addition, there were people like us who wanted alterations done, paving fixed, fences erected and that sort of thing.

The first job Wilson did for us was exterior painting. He set to with a will and before long, our walls were pristine white and our garage door, a metal up-and-over-job, was a gleaming dark green. He made a bit of a mess of the paving where it met the walls, but luckily much of the house was surrounded by grass. Where it wasn't, I scurried after him with old newspapers.

"Wilson, make sure these are against the wall where you're painting. The boss won't like it if there's paint on the ground."

"Oh, okay, madam," he'd say, tucking the opened-out sheets in place and standing his paint pots on them. Then he'd move along the wall, forgetting to move the paper too. The results were predictable.

"Oh Wilson, look! There's paint everywhere!"

"I sorry, madam, I forget the paper."

"I can see that, but we're going to have to get it off there somehow."

"The paint, madam? That's easy. No problem. I just move paper here. You not see it now," he said, pulling the sheets over the offending splodges. That would've been my method too; I'm a typical slob when it comes to hiding my sins, but I knew Bill wouldn't let him get away with it.

"No, no, Wilson. We'll have to get some water and a brush and scrub it clean before it dries."

"Why madam? It go when it rains."

"You're right, I know, but we don't know when it will rain and Bill won't be happy with it now. He likes everything clean. Come on, we'll do it together."

And so Wilson and I wasted half the time he was being paid to paint the garage by scrubbing white wall coating off the paving. Still, I reasoned, he was working and therefore earning his keep; it was a new perspective on the concept of money laundering.

Luckily, he finished painting the walls without Bill finding out about our cleaning efforts, so I set him to a bit of gardening until we had something more constructive for him to do. I'd started a different job then too. My days with Earl Real Estate were always destined to be numbered so before the long-suffering Catherine hauled me over the coals yet again about my uselessness in finding buyers, I handed in my notice.

"I'm not cut out for this work," I admitted.

"No, you're not," she agreed. "But thanks for your efforts, Val." Catherine was a tough nut and a businesswoman through and through, but she also had a sense of humour. "I've never met anyone who worked so hard for so little," she grinned. "You've spent hours taking people around and managed to put every single one of them off buying, while Nathalie here has scooped them up and scored with them all."

Nathalie was twenty-six, sharp, driven and glossy. She drove a BMW and made a heap of money from property sales. She was good. I wasn't.

"I'm just glad I haven't had to pay for your petrol," she finished, rubbing salt into my raw wounds. It was true. No sales, no commission, and the expenses were all mine except for the office administration. Added to that, I'd wasted too many Sundays sitting in houses on show days trying to encourage aimless people to buy.

Show days were open days when prospective purchasers could view houses without appointments. In South Africa, they were always on

Sunday. The house owners would tidy up their homes to an unnatural state of pristine perfection and then go out for the day, leaving an estate agent to sit in bored isolation as hordes of curious neighbours came to poke around and satisfy their inquisitive souls with no intention of buying anything. Well, that's how it seemed to me.

The number of real purchasers was tiny compared to those of the idle curious. If a house had a second show day, I often only saw a couple of people the whole day. All the nosy neighbours had been in during the first one; not that I'm knocking nosy neighbours – I did it myself often enough. All the same, it was the tedious part of an agent's duties and meant I missed the only day when the rest of the family had free time. That aside, the commission I'd earnt on the one and only house I'd sold had all gone long ago and it was costing me money to stay on. Another potent reason for calling it quits.

My new job was another sales position. Looking back, I'm not sure why I thought this would be a good idea after my disastrously short-lived estate agency career, but it might have been because it was local and I could organise my time to be at home when school came out.

The girls were still struggling on at Halfway House Primary, and Tim was selling muffins from a food cart to early morning gym addicts at the business park where Bill was working, but all three of them were home in the afternoons. On the other hand, Bill was busy falling out with the production company. Everything was a bit precarious and we still didn't own our house yet. Things were looking a bit bleak, so I probably took whatever was going.

My employers were a British couple who worked from their semi-built home on a plot in Midrand. Barbara and Tom were very nice and were starting an office furniture business from scratch, which I liked. I felt I was in it with them. Their house was a work-in-progress and the surrounding ground was completely un-landscaped. They needed money to go further, but the business was still in its infancy and costing more than it was earning, which was where I came in.

My task was to slog around the offices in Midrand with brochures. Ultimately, it proved to be soul destroying work even though it got me out and about. All the premises I visited had their furniture already so the most I could persuade them to buy was the occasional filing cabinet and drawer unit.

The big money was in selling furniture for a complete office. As for me, I rarely managed even a quarter of a room, let alone a whole office. I also had to do telesales and I had a quota of fifty calls a morning. Considering Midrand was still a work in progress, there were barely even fifty established businesses to call. My dilemma was whether to phone the same people every day, or start canvassing offices on the East Rand and further afield. If I did that, I'd have to visit them too and that would mean having to drive – at my own expense.

I didn't last long there either.

"Val, much as we like you, you're not selling enough for us to pay your salary or even any commission," Barbara told me, her face pink with embarrassment and regret. She was no hard-nosed Catherine Earl.

"I know," I sighed. "I'm sorry. I've really tried, but I think I just don't have the right personality for sales."

"I'm surprised," Barbara admitted. "I would've thought you'd be good at it, with your background in customer service."

"Well I think that's the point. I'm good at servicing people who are already customers, not at getting them in the first place."

We laughed at that, had a cup of coffee and some cheesecake she'd bought to soften the blow, and then I left Midrand Mobile Meubeliers. Yes. Perhaps it was the name that killed it. I liked to console myself with that thought later on when I heard the whole business had collapsed. It was a pity. I liked Barbara.

Worse news was to come, job-wise. Bill's floundering relationship with the film company came to a dramatic and shuddering end. Always single-minded and with a fiery Scottish temperament courtesy of his parents, Bill had just one too many rows with the director and executive producer. Despite the fact he'd written the script and gained the rights for making the film from the author of the book, the producers found his involvement in the production too irksome and they fired him.

He'd been on a retainer as the script and story advisor, which had been keeping us going. With this regular income gone, the rug was somewhat pulled from underneath us. Bill was hurt, outraged, indignant and furious.

"I can't believe they've done this to me, Val," he spluttered, anger shooting from every nerve.

"Neither can I. It's your story. Your film. Is there nothing you can do?"

"No. They've got it all tied up legally. I don't have a leg to stand on. I gave up my rights in return for a regular salary. But they know what it means to me."

"Do you think they intended to do this all along?"

"Maybe. I'm not one of their group. I'm not in their clique."

I knew what that implied. The production company employees were all members of a particular charismatic church and we weren't. It was possible they'd decided to close ranks to make sure they could make the film their way. And if Bill had surrendered his rights, there wasn't anything we could do to fight it. I resigned myself to the inevitable.

"Okay, so time we both looked for another job."

"Yeah, perhaps," Bill grumbled, but I had a feeling he hadn't finished with this conflict yet.

While Bill and I were busy wasting career opportunities, we made further changes to the house. Wilson started building a wall for us to define the property clearly at the front. This was when we discovered he wasn't really the all-rounder we thought he was. Poor Wilson. He had no idea how to lay bricks and even less idea how to use a plumb line to make them straight and vertical.

His first attempt looked like something a three-year-old might have put up. None of the bricks sat evenly and he just piled them on top of each other with no attention to how they overlapped and lined up. Bill, already stressed by anxiety about his film, was furious.

"Wilson, what kind of mess do you call this?" he raged.

"Sorry, boss. I not know wall building."

"So why didn't you tell me, you stupid moron?"

"Bill, don't shout at him. That's not fair," I butted in.

"I'll shout at him all I bloody like. Look at this!" he jabbed a finger at the wall. I had to admit that even a child with a Lego set would probably have done better.

"Sorry, boss," Wilson tried again, looking increasingly woebegone.

"If you didn't know how to do it, why didn't you bloody ask me, you useless jerk?" Bill spat. "It's diabolical. That's *my* money you've wasted there!"

"Bill! That's enough," I cut in. "Wilson's said sorry. Either let him put it right or let him go. Yelling at him and insulting him do nothing!" I wanted to say 'except make you feel better,' but I thought I'd better not.

"Okay, okay. Come here, Wilson." Bill grumbled. "I'll show you what to do."

And so Wilson received what was probably a very useful and profitable lesson. Since he was married and had children too, I hope what Bill taught him about bricklaying provided him with years of income. He watched, learnt and proceeded to build us a very nice low double wall with four small pillars at intervals and planters in between. I put potting soil in the planters, being the spaces between the two walls, and added marigolds and lavender. It looked lovely.

Indoors, we filled in the hole where the Jacuzzi had been and tiled it. Wilson did the tiling, so it was also what you might call rustic, but it was fine and we used the area as a kind of bar – for breakfast, lunch and otherwise. It was a more convivial place to sit and chat than at the dining table, as well as being handy for the kitchen.

Meanwhile, Jodie and Mo were still at the school in Halfway House but I'd discovered there was another primary school in a suburb called Buccleuch not too far away. It was bigger and more established than Halfway House and it had extensive grounds. The brick buildings looked neat and the sports fields were well-maintained. There was something about its atmosphere that suggested it would suit the girls better. It was also mainly English speaking.

I took them there for interviews and we met the Headmaster, Mr Hayes. He was such a nice man, so kind and welcoming, we immediately knew this was the school we'd been looking for. We decided to send them there in January 1992. For Jodie, it would be her last year of primary school; it would mean new uniforms (mandatory at all South African schools) for them both and more travelling again, but it seemed worth it and it was. Once they started there, they blossomed.

As for Tim, he cut his losses with the food cart. The early starts to get up and make muffins were taking their toll and he wasn't earning enough money from the breakfast customers at the gym to make it worth his while. He applied for a job at a record and CD shop in Midrand and immediately found his niche. Tim's passion was music and as such he added to my education substantially.

South Africa was still burdened with sanctions in 1991; very few musicians came to the country to play and if they did, they only played at Sun City in Bophuthatswana, one of the independent homelands. I well remember the excitement and controversy when Queen broke sanctions and played at Sun City in 1984.

However, the radio, which was mostly all we had, was limited to the big hits and as I'd never been a pop fan as such, I no longer listened to the music stations much. Tim's job was a kind of lifeline for all of us to the rock music of the late 80s and early 90s. Through him, we were introduced to Crowded House, Nirvana, Pearl Jam, Counting Crows, Smashing Pumpkins and Jellyfish, all groups whose music we'd never have heard without his rapidly growing CD collection, courtesy of special discounts at his work and free access to borrowing whatever took his fancy.

Bill bought him a Vespa scooter, or it may have been a Lambretta, I'm not sure. In theory, this was his transport and his independence, but it didn't last long. Tim wasn't what you might call a natural driver and he managed to write it off in record time, leaving him again at the mercy of whoever was prepared to give him a lift.

Recycling the art of cycling

It was at Noordwyk that I learnt to ride a bicycle properly for the first time myself. As children in London, my sister and I weren't allowed bikes, something we were highly indignant about because our brothers were given them. The injustice of it galled and we felt it was grossly unfair, even more so as all our friends had them.

What made it worse was that cycling, I discovered, is a skill best acquired young. Later on in my youth, when my family moved to Dorset in the west of England, I'd had a couple of brief but disastrous attempts to get the hang of it, each time ending up in a hedge because I'd steered straight ahead instead of round the corner. I never did get how that worked and disappointed with my failure I gave up.

In Natal, it had been far too hilly to renew my attempts, but now we were in a bike friendly setting in Johannesburg, I decided it was time to try again. I really wanted a horse, but that was only for the rich and debtless, not for us. I thought perhaps a bike might make a reasonable substitute.

We found my first steed at the Pick-n-Pay. The big supermarkets in South Africa were like the French Hypermarkets. They sold everything. You could virtually set up home with the goods you could buy under their immense roofs, and generally speaking they had a large selection of bicycles at a very reasonable price. Mine was a dark pink mountain bike with twelve gears, knobbly tyres suited to our dirt roads and a good solid frame. It cost the equivalent of around €50 and I was thrilled with it. My first ventures up Francis Drive onto 14th Street were distinctly wobbly. I fell off several times, but I got the knack eventually and then I was away.

There were plenty of dirt tracks to explore in the area with few cars and only walkers or other cyclists to contend with. Most of these were local Africans I greeted with a wave and a cheery 'hello', which was nearly always reciprocated. Regardless of politics and tribe, African people were spontaneous, outgoing and warm and they rarely failed to greet me with answering calls of 'good afternoon, auntie', together with broad smiles and enthusiastic waves.

'Auntie' and 'mama' were common forms of address for someone like me. It didn't matter that I was neither; not to them anyway. I suppose I just looked like that, especially to the youngsters. As I cycled around, I frequently saw schoolchildren on their long trek home.

Midrand was an area still largely made up of smallholdings known simply as plots. They were often run as small farms or businesses, and in these cases the workers would live on site, which meant their children had several kilometres to walk to school. Even with the opening of government schools to all races, it didn't help the children who lived in these rural areas, as there was no public transport.

Sometimes, the girls would cycle with me on my rides out and we'd take the dogs too, but that was much slower going. Sasha and Claude took going for walks literally. They ambled along the sand roads at the sedate pace typical of the older dog. Daisy was the opposite. She charged ahead like a mutt on a mission, and an urgent one at that. While Jodie and I had to keep stopping to urge the elderly couple along and lure them off the smells that needed endless and close examination, Mo would be pedalling off into the future in pursuit of Daisy. We didn't cycle with the dogs all that often, it has to be said.

One downside of my new hobby was the corrugations on the roads. Off the main routes, un-tarred roads were the norm for the area and although they were graded now and then, a smoothing out process achieved by scraping the surface with a long blade designed for the purpose, they developed the same kind of ripples in the surface as we'd experienced in Namibia.

The corrugations form as a result of car and truck wheels rolling regularly over the gravel surface, and they made both driving and cycling pretty uncomfortable. They are apparently unavoidable unless everyone drives at less than three kilometres an hour, and grading is the only solution. Corrugations or not, cycling became my favourite pastime; it was my get-away-from-it-all and eventually, a year or more later, even my transport to work.

The making, breaking and shaping of careers

In the late spring of 1991, I answered an ad in the paper for a position as a claims assessor at a health insurance company in Randburg, the suburb next to Sandton. After three job failures, I'd started missing the security and sense of fulfilment of my work in England. The medical insurance world was one I enjoyed and I felt I knew enough about it to make it worth applying to this one.

Much smaller than the English company I worked for, this one was a non-profit medical aid fund set up specifically for professional people such as accountants, law firms and their ancillaries. Excited to see an opportunity in a field where I had some experience, I sent in my CV. Even though I wasn't much good at calculating claims, I hoped they might have something else for me, and I was over the moon to receive an invitation for an interview.

Dressed in my best, I headed into Randburg to the company offices. They were on the corner of a junction with Republic Road, and at that time, it was a good location. I was impressed. Pulling into the car park, I found a spot in front of the building that was designated for visitors. There was a complete section covered by shade cloth, but that was for staff only. The day was hot, so I resigned myself to getting back into burning seats, but at least it wouldn't matter then. Looking cucumber cool was only important on the way in.

Walking into the building, I found myself at the reception desk being greeted by a cheerful-looking woman sitting behind a switchboard.

"Good morning," I began.

"Are you Valerie?" she asked, smiling.

"Er, yes! How did you know?"

She laughed.

"Well, it's ten twenty-five and I have it on my list here to expect a Valerie for an interview with Christine and Sue at ten-thirty, so it was a lucky guess," she grinned.

"Aah, yes, lucky indeed. You're spot on, but please call me Val," I said, feeling instantly welcome.

"Of course. Would you take a seat, Val? I'll just tell Christine you're here. My name's Beryl, by the way.”

I sat down and watched her as she made the call announcing my arrival and then answered several other incoming calls, transferring them to other departments with practised efficiency. She was professional, yet warm and friendly too. If she was representative of company culture, it boded well for my interview. I hoped I was right.

At ten-thirty on the dot, a pleasant looking woman about my own age walked into the reception area and came straight over to me.

"Hello. You must be Valerie...or do you prefer Val?"

I stood up and shook the offered hand.

"Val, please. If anyone calls me Valerie, I tend to stand to attention. I always think I'm in trouble."

She chuckled.

"Val it is, then. I'm Christine, the Claims Manager. If you'll follow me, we'll go to my office and have a chat before you meet my colleague Sue. She's the Customer Services Manager but also number two in the company."

I followed her up the broad stairs beyond the reception area. Everything about the building appealed to me: its light, its furnishings, its atmosphere. It felt like a place where the people who worked were as important as the professional image. It was nicely fitted and furnished without being luxurious, and it had a human feel to it.

We walked to the end of a blue-carpeted passage and into a spacious office where a functional desk was offset by a comfortable sofa and coffee table.

"Sit down, Val," Christine gestured to the sofa. "Would you like some tea? Or maybe coffee?"

"Coffee for me, please."

"And you so English. I thought you'd be a tea drinker like me."

"I'm afraid I've never drunk real tea," I admitted. "But I do like Rooibos."

"Hmm, I don't think we have that. We're very conservative here, but I'll ask Daphne."

She picked up the phone and ordered tea and coffee from someone.

"No, no Rooibos," she said, "but coffee's on the way."

Sitting down next to me, she began by asking me about my background and why I'd applied to work at the company. Just as I'd launched into the usual 'tell me about yourself' response, a knock on the door announced the arrival of Daphne with a tray. She was a beaming African woman who set the tray down on the table in front of us.

"There you are, Christine," she said. "If you like more, then just call me."

"Thank you, Daphne. I'm sure this'll be fine. How's your little one today?"

"She much better, thank you. I not so worried now."

"Well, you know if you need to, just go home. You mustn't stay here if you're anxious about her."

"I will. Thank you, Christine."

I could hardly believe my ears. Not only were all the employees on first name terms, the tea ladies seemed to be treated as real human beings too. In my experience, they were barely acknowledged in my previous jobs and I doubted if any senior manager would have known that they had children. If the concern was just for show, both Christine and Daphne were putting on a good act. I decided I wanted in on it too.

The problem was, and much as I hated doing it, I had to explain to Christine that I wasn't really much good at claims assessing; that I'd been transferred to Customer Services in my London job because I wasn't fast enough. I left out the accuracy part. No need to do myself down too much. For once, I thought my honesty had paid off. Christine looked at me thoughtfully and then picked up the phone again. She disappeared for a few minutes and came back with a pretty, blonde woman who looked to be the same sort of age as Christine and me. Sue Johnson was the Customer Services Manager.

"Christine tells me you've applied for the claims position, but that you're not sure you're cut out for it," she said. I nodded, a bit worried that I'd talked myself out of a job and held my breath, waiting for the rejection. But Sue went on: "She tells me you worked in Customer Services in London?" I nodded again; so did she. "What I'd like to know, and I want an honest answer, is whether you're any good at handling difficult calls from distressed clients, and also if you're any good at writing letters," she finished.

I breathed again. What a relief to be able to answer positively.

"Yes," I said. "To both. That was the bulk of my work in London."

I explained about my position in Corporate Services and how I'd had the Bank of England as my personal responsibility. I also mentioned I'd been designated the task of writing letters that needed extra tact and sensitivity. I knew it sounded good, and I could see they thought so too.

"Okay, Val," Christine said when they'd finished asking me questions. "It's been lovely meeting you, but we can't give you a decision just yet. The opening we advertised is for a claims assessor, so I think Sue and I will need to talk about you with our CEO, Mr Dixon. Give us a couple of days and then we'll let you know the position," she finished, getting up to show me out.

I swallowed. I'd been hoping against hope they'd offer me something immediately, although I knew I was being over optimistic. Of course it wasn't that simple, but I really needed paid work now and this company felt right. I left the office just managing to keep the smile on my face as I said my farewells to Beryl at reception. Only when I reached the oven my car had become did I allow myself the relief of a frustrated groan. At least anyone listening would have put it down to the scorching heat of my plastic leather seats. I climbed in, winced convincingly, and headed home to Noordwyk.

As I turned back into Francis Drive, I saw Wilson pelting up the road looking as if a vicious dog was on his heels. He was running so fast he never even saw me, so by the time I pulled into our garage, my thoughts were on what had sent him rocketing away rather than on the interview I'd just left.

As I walked into the house, I heard all about it. Bill was raging at the walls, at the dogs and at everything life was throwing at him. The name Wilson came up between a whole series of ever more outrageous expletives. Oh dear.

"I have to assume you and Wilson had a falling out," I ventured when he stopped to draw breath. "What's he done this time?"

"I only caught him here in the kitchen nicking stuff out of the fridge, didn't I?" he exploded.

Before he could go into full rant again, I asked, "But what did he steal? You surely remember I've told him he can help himself to lunch when we're out, don't you? I've told you before!"

"Oh ... have you?"

"Yes, Bill. Wilson has to eat when he's here. I gave him permission to take sausage meat from the fridge for his sandwiches."

"Oh." Bill shuffled.

"What did you say to him?"

"I didn't say anything. When I caught him with his head in the fridge, I grabbed him by the collar and slung him out. Erm ... well ... I might have yelled at him, I suppose. And ...well ... I might have tried kicking him too."

"Kicking him? Oh no, Bill! For heaven's sake! Did you hurt him?"

"No, I don't think I touched him, actually. He was running too fast."

"I suppose you've fired him, haven't you?" He nodded. "I saw him running up the road as if the hounds of hell were after him." Bill had the grace to look sheepish, so I went on. "I don't know. You'll be lucky if he doesn't report you. He should, you know. You can't assault people like that, especially without listening to their side of the story."

"Hmm, well I'm sorry I lost it, but I'm glad to be shot of him," he grumbled.

"Why? He's a good guy. I thought you liked him. He might not be all that skilled, but he's hard working, kind and loyal."

"He's also totally useless! I had to teach him everything, even how to use the hosepipe in the garden."

I sighed. It was no use arguing. Wilson had gone and if he had an ounce of self-preservation, he wouldn't be back. I was sorry. He hadn't deserved to be fired, and I hoped sincerely he wasn't hurt. I also hoped he'd find another job soon. He could build a pretty good wall thanks at least to Bill, and his painting skills had improved under my surreptitious tutelage, but I hated to think of him being so unjustly sent packing.

The next day, our neighbour confirmed she'd seen Bill aiming a kick at him, but she was fairly sure he'd missed. I'd hoped he'd been exaggerating when he told me; he had a tendency to overplay his part, and for once I wished that was the case. It depressed me to find it was true, although I was relieved to know his boot hadn't found its mark. Bill needed to find another project soon; that was clear. The effects of his own unjust dismissal were having a knock-on effect – literally.

Life at home was tense for a few days. We heard no more from Wilson, which was sad as we owed him money.

One of the downsides of such an informal labour system was that we never had addresses or contact details for the people we hired. This was before the days of mobile phones and Internet and most township dwellers didn't have landline phones at home either.

Bill rumbled round the house like a simmering volcano, probably both ashamed and frustrated. But luckily two things happened to relieve the strain.

The first was that he was given the chance to work on another film idea with a young production company based in Bryanston; the second was that I received an offer from the medical aid company. I was over the moon.

Christine, my interviewer, called me and explained I would work in the Claims Department initially, but when they found someone else to take my place, they would move me to Customer Services. The starting salary was good and there was a prospect of pay rises at least once a year and sometimes twice, depending on performance. I would start at the beginning of the month.

The arrangement would also be ideal when the girls moved to Buccleuch Primary in the new year. I'd be able to take my daughters to school and then drive to Randburg on the highway, an easy journey that wouldn't take me too far out of the way. It was all going to work out and I breathed a massive sigh of relief. What was just ironic, though, was that we'd moved to Midrand to make life easier as well as cheaper, and now the focus of our lives was returning to the Sandton area.

To add to the irony, we'd also started spending more time in Johannesburg at the weekends. Bill and I enjoyed the colour and liveliness of the older suburbs like Norwood where we could sit outside a restaurant and drink real Italian cappuccinos with the locals, many of whom were of Italian origin.

We'd also take the family to Rockey Street in Bellevue on a Saturday morning and have breakfast in one of its cosy cafés. It's worth mentioning I had the best toasted sandwiches in Rockey Street I've ever had anywhere in my life. The whole street was a very hip place to be. It was rich in youth culture and an eclectic mix of nationalities. Alternative, multi-culti, call it what you like, we loved the atmosphere of the more integrated society we found there. Architecturally, Rockey

Street was also old Joburg with its covered pavements, colourful shop fronts and thronging crowds.

Another place we liked was Melville, to the north west of the city centre. It was one of those charming old suburbs that attracted the arty types to which we were admittedly also drawn. The whole neighbourhood had a lively village feel with attractive tree-lined streets. Melville was home to Roxy's Rhythm Bar, a club where the live music was guaranteed to be great. Bill and I went there frequently over the years, especially to see Vinnie and the Viscounts, a brilliant cover band all of whose members were well past their prime but could rock most other people's socks off. Their founder and lead singer's day job was as a well-known TV actor. Bill Flynn loved rock music and with his musician friends started playing the clubs as a hobby. They soon became hugely popular and were a regular fixture at Roxy's. The band could perform pretty much any of the 60s and 70s classic rock music, and for us, it was the next best thing to seeing the original rockers of our youth.

Roxy's also hosted many of the up and coming South African bands. It was there I saw a fantastic group called Just Jinger who went on to become internationally popular. Whoever they booked, Roxy's had their finger on the pulse of the best music around, but to my disappointment I never saw the legendary Johnny Clegg there, or anywhere else for that matter. His Scatterlings of Africa, so quintessentially South African, is inseparably tied to my feelings for the country.

At other times, we explored the city further south. Troyeville had some lovely traditional homes with tin roofs, intricate decorative ironwork and deep verandas. Then there was Hillbrow, notorious for its crime rate, but also known for the fabulous Hillbrow Records, a large shop where we could buy both new and second-hand LPs of practically every artist ever known. For all of us, Johannesburg was an endless source of new discoveries. We came to love roaming the city during the quiet Saturday and Sunday mornings and even went to show days to see houses for sale, just out of curiosity.

Knowing only too well how bored the agents on duty probably were, we made encouraging noises and chatted to them with pretended enthusiasm, although in some cases, we didn't have to pretend at all. Many of the older houses had gorgeous Oregon pine floors, high ceilings and moulded cornices. They were often beautifully decorated in vivid colours.

One house we went to see became a genuinely tempting proposition. It was owned by a couple who'd painted the interior in glorious mustard yellows and terracotta reds. With its polished floors, high ceilings and stunning yellowwood furniture, it was exactly our taste. The problem was that Jeppestown, where we found it, was right in the heart of Johannesburg and both too far and too risky (even then) for us to consider as a safe place to bring up two daughters.

Even so, this was still a period of relative safety. We never felt physically at risk in the city and it didn't occur to us to be other than careful with our belongings. Joburg was a large cosmopolitan area with all that goes with it; as such, we enjoyed everything it had to offer.

In the end, it was prophetic that we'd started turning our focus back to the city because along with the thrill of being in work again came a catastrophe that put us in a terrible position.

Adventures in Zimbabwe

Before the next axe fell, however, we went on another adventure filled camping holiday, this time to Zimbabwe. It was the Easter school holiday in 1992 and Tim had agreed to stay at home and look after the animals, which made it much easier to face leaving them behind.

Since we'd never been to Zimbabwe before, we were all excited although we knew we wouldn't be able to go too far over the border as a week didn't give us much time for exploration. Like Namibia, the distances to Zimbabwe were great, but we thought we could make it to Fort Victoria, or Masvingo as it is now called.

We drove the long 550 kilometres north up the N1 through Pretoria to Louis Trichardt and then on to Beitbridge on the border. That in itself was an interesting route. The Northern Transvaal, now called Limpopo, was more semi-tropical than the grassy plains south of Johannesburg. Once past the Magaliesberg mountain range, the land seemed to open up and although there were always ridges and mountains on the horizon, the impression was one of sun baked, rocky valleys rolling ever northwards. However, it wasn't quiet or remote at all. The N1 was a busy road, much more so than its southern counterpart which heads towards Cape Town.

The Northern Transvaal was more densely populated than the Cape for one thing and for another, the N1 was the main route for the annual pilgrimage that African Christians of the Church of Zion made to their Easter gathering at Moria, near what was then Pietersburg (now Polokwane). We drove in company with thousands of buses, minibus taxes, *bakkies* and cars toiling their way to the site where in huge numbers, the congregants made the 1969 Woodstock festival look like a minor event in the park.

A 2016 news report claims the gathering at Moria attracted between three and five million worshippers. I don't know how many there were in 1992, but it must have been approaching the million mark, given the number of vehicles we were trailing. When seen alongside the endless stream of walkers we also saw heading north, the sheer numbers looked something akin to a mass migration.

One of the features of South African churches that made them so colourful was the clothing their congregants wore. On a local level, many of the churches didn't have buildings and their followers usually gathered in fields or parks to hold their services. What made them stand out was that they wore special uniforms. We would see them walking in small groups to attend services on Sundays, and they would be distinguished by the colour they wore. The Zion church's women wore royal blue, yellow or green while the men wore green suits.

Now we were seeing these groups on the long road north. It was vibrant and colourful, but also slow and not without risks. With so many people on foot, in *bakkies* and on overcrowded buses, we had to keep a careful watch out that we didn't run over, across or into any of this massive movement of worshipers on pilgrimage. Add to that the usual collection of straying goats, cattle, dogs and chickens and the numerous broken-down vehicles, and we were greatly relieved to get past Pietersburg in one piece.

As we drove ever further north, the scenery became increasingly African. Gone were the rolling green hills of Natal and the sweeping grasslands of the *Highveld*. Now we had real *bushveld*. Squat thorn and Acacia trees studded the hills over the red earth. It became rocky and the vegetation was sparse.

This was the land of baobab trees, those astonishing contradictions of creation that look as if they are upside down; trees with their heads in the soil and their roots apparently flailing around in the air. Baobabs grow to massive proportions and the well-known Sunland baobab, for instance, has a circumference of over thirty metres and a height of twenty metres; that's about three standard lampposts on top of each other – really incredible.

We stopped for lunch close to the border and picnicked next to one of these giant trees. It made us feel very small and insignificant, especially knowing it was probably more than a thousand years old. The girls chased each other round its massive trunk, enough of a distance to give them a chance to get out of breath and hide from each other too.

To Mo's sorrow, she left a favourite teddy under the baobab tree and apparently still mourns it loss. "It still causes me pain to think of him all lonely under the great African sky," she told me recently, her words imbued with drama.

I just smiled and reached for a large pinch of salt.

Another change we noticed was that it was also warmer than it had been in Johannesburg. Up in the northern reaches of the country, it was rarely cold during the day and summer temperatures could soar. Easter Sunday in 1992 was on April the 19th, which was quite late in the autumn, but even so, the heat up at the border surprised us. It also made our next challenge rather harder to cope with.

The morning we crossed into Zimbabwe, we woke early. We'd stayed overnight at a municipal site with huts, so without too much to load in the car, we left after a leisurely breakfast and arrived at the Beitbridge border control posts around mid-morning. And there we stayed for the next five hours.

As is normal, there were two points to be checked through: the South African and the Zimbabwean. We'd heard plenty of reports about delays at the crossing, so we were pleasantly surprised on the South African side. Our passports were checked and we were through in double quick time. No doubt the immigration officials knew perfectly well what we would be enduring on the other side, but they didn't say anything. All the same, I couldn't help noticing the long queues going the other way back into South Africa.

We drove the hundred or so metres further on to the Zimbabwean post and then everything stopped. As for a queue, there was no sign of one. There were lorries, trucks, cars and *bakkies* parked with no apparent order all over the shabby, pot-holed tarmac area around the immigration shed. Bill squeezed the car into a space between a lorry and a *bakkie* and we got out to join the throngs of people trying to get into the passport office. What followed was a hot and gruelling endurance test.

We'd expected it to be uncomfortable but we weren't prepared for suffocation. The immigration offices had no air conditioning and there must have been at least a hundred people crowded in the stuffy confines of the entrance hall. The smell was appalling, it was hot, we were all sweating freely and it seemed as if the clerks on duty were taking as long as possible to process the documents. We stood and waited. And waited. And waited. A couple of lazy fans whirred ineffectively above us. People shuffled, yawned and grumbled.

Bill held our places each time I took the girls outside for occasional breaths of air. Like a pair of puppies, they needed these breaks to let off steam and amused themselves by hopping to and fro over the official borderline between the two countries. Then they straddled it.

"We're both in two countries," giggled Mo.

"Yeah, we're bi-lateral," said Jodie, raising her arms and flexing her muscles. They collapsed in helpless laughter. For some reason they found it hysterically funny although I suspect they didn't really know what bi-lateral meant. Since it wasn't anything do with biceps, it must have been a phrase Jodie had picked up from the TV news during these times of political negotiation.

At least their good cheer gave us some light relief before squeezing our way back into the queue again. I must say both girls were remarkably patient given the trying conditions. Ideally, one of us would have stayed outside with them, but we knew we all had to be present when we finally made it to the front of the queue. These officious border officials would want to see everyone entering the country. It was a great leveller if nothing else as, black or white, we were all subject to the same torment.

After we'd been waiting for at least three hours, the immigration staff decided it was time for a lunch break. All the desks emptied with no explanation or apology and we were left to practise our skills in patience control until they decided to come back again. Bill, not known for his calm demeanour at the best of times, began to look dangerous.

"I get it," he said, making no attempt to keep his voice down. "It's a petty power game, isn't it? They just love it, don't they?"

"Shhh," I hissed at him. "If you start that we'll never get through!"

"If this carries on much longer, I'm not sure I want to get through. Stuff them! They can keep their pathetic little country. We'll just go back!"

One of the officials on door duty started looking over at us, no doubt alerted by Bill's rather obvious impatience.

"Just cool it for now, Bill. We're nearly there. It'd be such a waste to give up after all this time. Anyway, did you see the queue waiting to go back across the border? It's just as bad. We'd be no better off."

"Hmm. You might be right. What was that song by Stealers Wheel? 'Stuck in the middle with you'? Could be worse," quipped Bill with a flash of his old humour. "I just hope there aren't any wheel stealers out there having a go at the car."

"Oh Bill," I groaned. The worse the pun, the more he liked it.

We giggled, and thankfully, when the staff came back again, things moved reasonably quickly. Once we arrived at the relevant window, an expressionless clerk took our passports, checked we were all there and that our photos matched the faces on our documents, stamped them and let us go. Maybe they too were tired of the game now; it suddenly seemed much smoother.

But that wasn't the end of it. We still had to drive through the Zimbabwe border post and have our car checked for whatever it was they checked for. We never knew, but we had to empty everything out of the interior and the boot before they were satisfied we weren't terrorists or smugglers or traffickers of some kind.

Finally, by mid-afternoon, we were free to go, to drive across the border and into Zimbabwe at last. Bill's sense of humour was restored and we whooped and cheered as we drove away from the nightmare of the crossing, determined to forget it until we had to make the return trip.

The week that followed was a memorable one. If not quite as magical as the Naukluft Desert in Namibia, Zimbabwe made a deep impression on us all. For a start, it was so much more remote and unspoilt than South Africa. From Beitbridge, we crossed the physical border between the two countries at the Limpopo River and pounded along an endless empty road with the sights and scenery of a really African country all around us: rolling hills clothed with thick Acacia bush and ochre-coloured sandy earth. It was like being in a safari park without the fences.

Despite being a major national route, the road to Masvingo was just a two-lane road with dirt tracks on either side. It was in reasonable condition, however, and not too pot-holed, so it was an easy route for us, especially as Zimbabwe, like South Africa, drives on the left. In fact, all southern African countries do, which makes touring in the region quite relaxing for people of British origin.

Our itinerary was a simple one. We'd go to Masvingo and from there to Lake Kyle (now Mutirikwi) and after that to the Great Zimbabwe National Monument, just south of the lake. In our original plans, we thought we'd be outside Masvingo on the first evening in the country but we'd never imagined the wait at the Beitbridge would be so long, so we stopped at a campsite on the way. This was when I discovered I'd left the pillows and sleeping bags at home. Not a good move.

It was a gorgeous site and we'd pitched our tents on the pale grass in the shade of some tall, spreading oaks. The sun shone between its branches and bathed us in the warm afternoon light. It was heaven after the hell of the border. We had a two-man tent for Bill and me, and the girls each had their own tiny singles. It was all very simple. By now we had good groundsheets and sleeping mats too, but still, it wasn't quite enough.

"Val, where are the sleeping bags?" Bill called from the depths of the Uno, his rear end the only part of him I could see. I chuckled at the sudden thought of him talking out of his backside; well, he'd been accused of that before. But then I took in what he was asking.

"Sleeping bags? Aren't they in there?"

"No. And there aren't any pillows either."

"That can't be right. Let me come and look."

But he was. They weren't there. We'd either left them at home or they'd somehow been purloined when we had to empty the car at Beitbridge. Since we didn't know for sure, I opted for that explanation, but later, when we got home, we found them; on our bed.

"Oh heck. We'll have to make do with rolled up coats for pillows and our blankets tonight. Maybe we can find some more bedding in Masvingo tomorrow."

"There's always something," muttered Bill, who then proceeded to give us all a lecture about making checklists.

"Well I hope that includes you too," I bit back.

"Why me? I've got enough to do with making sure the car's in order."

I opened my mouth to retort but then stopped. It wouldn't help. We'd be all right for the night and indeed we were.

Jodie and Mo were experienced campers and knew the drills even down to putting up their own tents and they joined in the chores without complaint. Once we were settled with our tents up and our makeshift beds, we sorted out our food. We had a small gas cooker; we had sausages, tinned vegetables and bread rolls, and we had coffee and juice. After such a long and exhausting day, we were only too happy to eat, wash our few dishes and crawl into bed.

But the following morning, we emerged from our tents to find our small camp in disarray, and our food was scattered everywhere. We'd piled the coolbox and stores in the awning of our tent without taking the possibility of midnight raiders into account – a big mistake, as it turned out.

"What on earth has happened here?" I gasped, dismayed by the mess.

"It's monkeys, Mum," Jodie said, pointing up into the trees. I looked up to see a group of four or five Vervet monkeys sitting above us in the boughs of the oak trees. Each of them was clutching a trophy – packets of seasoning, soup and other dry goods. I could swear they were grinning and if they'd known how, they'd have stuck their tongues out at us. Luckily all our perishable food was in the sealed coolbox, or we'd have lost that too.

"Watch out!" Jodie shouted. Too late. I hadn't noticed one of the monkeys had a packet of rice and with great glee it up-ended it and tipped the contents out in an attempt to shower us. Escaping out of range I waited, picking rice out of my hair, until the packet was empty and then started gathering up the mess. We retrieved whatever we could salvage, meanwhile cursing the monkeys who cackled at us maliciously overhead.

Vervets are attractive creatures with their ash coloured coats, longish hair and black faces. They are common throughout southern Africa, but they are as naughty and mischievous as schoolboys on a field trip and we learnt to watch out for them in our future campsites; we also learnt that we really needed to put our things completely away, as in locked in the car with the windows tightly closed.

Food and supplies were not so easy to come by in Zimbabwe and we'd already lost some important provisions as a result of the Vervets' dawn raid. Order restored and coffee imbibed, we packed up our tents again, loaded up the car and headed towards Masvingo.

Reputed to be the oldest town in Zimbabwe, Masvingo was founded in 1890, but its original location was abandoned after less than a year as apparently it had already fallen into disrepair. I still wonder how that was possible in less than twelve months, but whatever the case, a new fort was built at its current position and called Victoria after the British queen.

Later known as Fort Victoria, it served as a refuge for European farmers and their families during the Matabele raids on the Shona people in 1893, and once established, it grew into the important town it became in the 20th century. In 1982, after the civil war when Rhodesia became Zimbabwe, the name Fort Victoria was changed to Nyanda and when this didn't work with all the local dialects, it was changed again to Masvingo.

When we drove into the centre, we found a pretty colonial style town with tree lined streets and pleasant residential areas. However, it was all quite shabby with most of the shady walkways cracked and the faded shops practically empty. Although we knew things were tough in Zimbabwe, we were shocked to see the scale of the poverty; there was practically nothing to buy and what there was cost a fortune in Zimbabwean dollars.

Having South African Rands was our saving grace as the local people were desperate for foreign currency. Had we had American dollars, we'd have been even better off. We managed to buy some extra blankets of the type we'd usually use for our dogs at home and a few provisions too, but it was sad to see the serious shortage of goods of any sort.

One small supermarket we went into had neat, clean aisles and shelves but with nothing on them except a few lonely tins of spam and some virulent looking soft drinks. What we did find, though, was the orange juice we'd been recommended to buy by Zimbabwean friends in Johannesburg. Mazoe orange crush was famous throughout the region but not easily available, so I was thrilled that we could find it at the source, in Zimbabwe. The shopkeeper was equally thrilled when I bought three bottles of it.

Stopping to talk to a local African trader, I was surprised when he started waxing nostalgic about the former days of the Rhodesian regime.

"We fought for our freedom," he said. "But look at us now. Our country has nothing. We have nothing. Our children have no schools or education. It was better when that Mr Smith was our leader. We were not free, but at least we had food and jobs." He sounded bitter and we knew better than to respond or make any comment, but we wondered how many others might feel the same. The province of Masvingo had a mixed population of Ndebele, Shona and Shagani people, so his views may well have been influenced by whichever section of the populace he came from.

All the same, the deprivation and poverty were visible. There wasn't even any litter in the streets. No one could afford plastic bottles or bags and if they had them, they kept them for re-use. I appreciated the cleanliness, but the reason for it was tragic.

We made our way to the town's municipal campsite richer in knowledge but sad for the people and their plight. What made it even more poignant was that the following day we came across young children begging not for money, but the stationery they needed for school.

They approached us when we were browsing at a roadside tourist craft market where the traders had their hand made wares spread out on cardboard salvaged from old boxes. The three girls, who couldn't have been more than about eight or nine, were dressed in oversized tee-shirts and shorts and were walking barefoot.

"Please mister, madam, do you have pens. We not want money. There is nothing to buy. But we need pens for school."

"And paper," another one said. "We need this also."

"And books," the third child said. "Books for writing."

"I'm afraid we don't have paper or books, but here," I said digging into my bag, "I've got a pen for you. Have you got anything, girls?"

My daughters rummaged through their possessions and came up with a few pencils; we couldn't help with exercise books, but the children were pleased. They smiled their thanks and skipped off.

We then swapped a few radio batteries with a trader in return for some beautifully fashioned wooden giraffes and we bought a carved walking stick for Bill, glad that we could contribute at least something to this community. When we got back in the car, Jodie and Mo both had tears in their eyes.

"Mummy can't we go and buy some things for them?" Jodie asked

"You heard what they said, sweetie. There *is* nothing to buy. We must just remember if we come to Zimbabwe again, we'll need to bring a stack of paper and pens for these kids."

"And batteries, Mummy. We mustn't forget those," Mo chirped.

I didn't like to point out that we couldn't know what kind of batteries they needed without asking them, but the willingness was there; the experience had moved us all.

The next few days were spent camping at the beautiful Lake Kyle, a reservoir formed by an immense dam that supplied much of the water to the area. As I remember it, there were few facilities, but we had a good campsite on the hillside surrounded by indigenous woods and there were tables, benches and barbecue spots. It was enough for our needs and it was a peaceful place to relax in the golden autumn light.

The dam itself was an impressive sight but the lake was desperately low due to the drought that was afflicting the area; yet another trial for the locals to endure. Looking out over the wall, the view was breathtaking. Surrounded by misty hills, the water shimmered as far as the eye could see in spite of its diminished levels. Dams like this serve much of southern Africa. When the reservoirs are full, they are vast, and I always have these 'what if' scenarios about the disaster that would occur if the walls were breached. Even so, Lake Kyle was in a glorious setting.

We then went on to visit the Great Zimbabwe ruins to the south of the lake. There is plenty of literature attached to this special place, not to mention legends and myths. At one time thought to have been built by early Phoenicians as a replica of King Solomon's Temple, more recent archaeology seems to have proved that it was an African construction and probably not the only one of its kind at the time.

Nevertheless, it seems to have been the largest and the fact that its drystone walls were all granite blocks shows what incredible building skills these early people had. According to the items found in its lower soil layers, Great Zimbabwe had its heyday in the mid fifteenth century, but it is said to be quite a bit older.

For our part, we were fascinated by it. As the only people present on the day we visited, we clambered round the 750-hectare site and trod carefully where the walls of the ruins were still in a good state of repair. The conical tower, the circular walls with its chevron detail at the top, the low doorways built for tiny people; these were all reminders that we were stepping over hundreds of years of African history. It made an impact on us all, used as we were to the lack of ancient history in South Africa.

All too soon, our week came to an end and we were heading home, meanwhile promising ourselves we would go back and spend more time exploring the country. I would have loved to go to Bulawayo, Harare and even the Victoria Falls and I regret that we never made it there again. Mo went with friends later on, but none of the rest of us returned.

Apart from the beauty of the African landscape, what struck us was the gentle courtesy of the people. They were unfailingly kind and despite the slump into which the country had fallen, we didn't feel the sting of envy or resentment that we sometimes encountered in Johannesburg.

As for those children and their plea for books and pens (not forgetting the batteries), I told my friends and colleagues that if any of them were going to Zimbabwe on holiday, they should fill a case with school supplies; these would be received with much more enthusiasm than sweets or money.

What goes up must come down, hopes included

After living in the house in Noordwyk for more than a year, and having spent a fair amount of money on improvements, we discovered that we couldn't and wouldn't own the house. Not ever.

With the delay in the transfer continuing, I started asking questions. The conveyancing attorneys admitted they'd had difficulty in pinning the seller down to sign the papers and now they were waiting for the bank to accept the cancellation of the bond. When even that seemed to be taking forever, I started putting the pressure on, and then the blow fell.

The attorneys phoned me one morning while I was at work and asked if I would be able to call in and see them. They had something to tell me that couldn't be discussed over the phone. Not suspecting for a moment how bad the news could be, I duly went to their offices after I'd finished for the day. The attorney I saw was a thirty-something woman, but she occupied an office clearly designed to inspire old-fashioned awe and respect in the clients. Since I wasn't immune to such polished elegance, I sat in silence as I listened to her.

"I've asked you to come here as I'm afraid I have some bad news for you," she began, her face a mask of professional concern and sympathy.

"Oh?" was all I could come up with, worry suddenly crawling up my spine.

"Yes, it is my unfortunate duty to inform you that the bank will not release the seller's bond. Apparently, he hasn't been paying it since you signed the offer to purchase."

"He hasn't? But what does that mean to us?"

"Well, it seems he accepted an offer from you lower than the amount he already owed, and now this has increased due to non-payment of his monthly instalments. I very much regret he isn't in a position to pay the difference ... which is why the bank is refusing to cancel his bond." She broke off for a moment, sighed, and continued. "It now seems he says that under the circumstances, he can't sell the house and he'll have to move back into it himself."

"What? He can't do that to us!" I burst out, horrified, distress stealing my initial composure.

"I'm afraid he can," she admitted. "There's nothing we can do to stop him."

"But we've done so much to the house already. Why has it taken so long to tell us this? Surely the bank knew he wasn't paying? They should have told you!"

"Unfortunately, no one told us and as you know, we've had terrible trouble getting hold of him at all."

"So what do we do now then?"

"I'm afraid you'll have to move out, but you'll have time to do that," she hastened to add. "As I understand it, you'll have about three months to find somewhere else. There are several legal processes to go through in terms of his breach of contract. Sadly, you won't get any compensation as there was no deposit paid, but for now, we'll stop transferring the occupational rent you're paying to him and pay it straight to the bank. That will at least give you some leeway."

I left the attorneys in a state of shock. Three months to find a new home. That was all. We'd lose a substantial amount of money in the alterations we'd made to the house and we had nothing to use as a deposit on another. I no longer worked for an estate agency, so there'd be no opportunity to get help that way either. Bill was going to go ballistic. He hadn't been working with his new partners in Bryanston all that long and I was still under the six-month trial period at my job. Even renting somewhere was going to be a challenge.

I told Bill about the situation when I got home. Surprisingly, he was quite calm about it and other than saying "I knew something fishy was going on," he didn't react as I expected at all.

"I'll have a chat to Jim in the morning," he said. Jim was our bank manager in Midrand. Young, forward looking and supportive, he'd been very helpful in carrying Bill through his last crisis and was instrumental in connecting him with his new film making partners. If miracles were Jim's stock-in-trade, maybe he could pull another one out of the bag.

"Do you think he'll be able to suggest any way round it?" I asked, thinking that maybe he could come up with some extra money to secure the house.

"No idea, but he might have some ideas about what we can do."

I didn't sleep that night, which didn't help much the next day. I was already struggling to keep up with the claims assessing, as predicted.

I sat in a large room with about twelve other women. We had a supervisor, Sharon, who despite being younger than I was, ran the department with all the assurance of an experienced manager.

Every morning, she would lay the batches of claims out on a central table and each assessor would take a batch, sign it off in a book and work her way through the claims. When the batch was finished, the assessor would put the completed claims on another pile. Every item on every claim was coded, numbered and prescribed, but of course, being numbers, I was not in my comfort zone at all.

I was visibly slower than all the other girls and where they would get through three or four batches in a day, I would manage one, which was not good. It was all too obvious and couldn't be disguised, as the signatures in the book told their own story. On this particular day it was worse for me than usual.

"Val," Sharon said gently, "you really will need to work through these batches a bit faster. The others are doing three times what you do."

"I know, Sharon. I'm slow. The trouble is if I go any faster, I'll make mistakes and that will be worse."

"Hmm, you're right there. Well, do your best to speed up," she said and left me to it. Nevertheless, she must have said something to Christine, because an hour later, I was upstairs in her office explaining. I told her about the house and all the problems we'd had with it.

"The thing is, Christine, I know I'm slow and I'm really sorry, but I can't afford to enter the wrong numbers and today it's taking even more of my concentration to keep at it."

"It's okay, Val, I understand. Actually, what I wanted to ask you is whether you're happy here with us. The point is I've found someone to take your place in Claims, but I need to know now if you still want to move to Customer Services."

I could have wept. I was so sure I was going to lose my job and now I felt I'd been granted a reprieve. But I didn't cry; I smiled. A Cheshire cat kind of smile.

"I take it that's a yes then," she said, laughing. "I had to ask, though. You haven't been here quite six months yet and we normally only do these appraisals at the end of the trial period. You can thank Sharon for this, by the way."

"Ah yes, I thought she might have had something to do with this conversation. But I was afraid it was to get rid of me, not move me. I'm so grateful to you both."

"Well, we always felt you'd be better off in Customer Services, so it was really the plan from the outset."

"That's a very kind way of confirming I'm a useless assessor," I grinned. I could afford to now.

"Since you put it that way," she said, seriously. I was uncomfortable for a second until she laughed again. I was to discover this was very much her way. Christine liked to tease.

"When will I be moving departments?" Changing the subject seemed like a good idea.

"Next week, I think. I just have to check to see when the new girl's starting, but I think the sooner we kick you sideways, the better for all of us." This time she winked.

Since I'd heard about the catastrophe with the house the day before, I'd been in a state of sick anxiety. My transfer to Customer Services, or CSD as we called it, was a glimmer of light on the horizon. I was happy at the company. I'd found what I was looking for: a good job with some stability. Added to that, my colleagues were great, the management were considerate and kind and even Mr Dixon, the CEO, was a character – of a sort.

Typical of an old-fashioned gentleman, he had perfect manners. It was his custom to do the rounds of the departments every morning, greeting each member of staff by name and shaking hands with everyone. He sometimes exchanged a few words with us too, asking after family or children.

The trouble was he had his favourites among the ladies and to me he seemed a bit creepy. At that time, there were very few men working for the company, and most of those were in IT or Accounts. If not, they were management; that was just the way things were. In the Claims Department we were all women, and it wasn't long before I twigged Mr Dee (as we called him) had taken a shine to me.

During the morning handshake, he'd hold mine just a little too long and his look was just a bit too lingering. It made me cringe. Mr Dee was a divorced man in his fifties; he also bore a strong resemblance to all the images I'd seen of Mr Micawber in my Dickens' books. I was thirty-seven. Enough said.

Later on, I managed to avoid his morning tours. I'd get someone to warn me he was on his way and then disappear to the loo or find an excuse to call a customer; anything rather than have to try and extract my hand from his limp, slightly clammy clasp. Still, it gave me something to laugh about with the other girls and we were all in on the conspiracy to avoid him when we could. I wasn't the only object of his attention and since it never went any further than the hand clasping, we all endured it with good humour. Mr Dee was essentially a decent and honourable man; in hindsight, he was probably just lonely.

I'd soon realised there were certain formalities that were observed just because he wanted them that way. All female employees had to wear skirts; tee shirts were forbidden and we all had to look respectable. Inappropriate dress, make-up or piercings were not only commented on, they weren't accepted and offenders had to go home and change regardless of where they lived. Tough.

The men had to wear shirts and ties and smart slacks at least. The reason? I didn't know, but the excuse was that we were the medical aid for a top profession and had to present ourselves accordingly, even employees who never saw the public or even so much as an occasional Board member. It was all quaintly conservative and quintessentially English. On that subject, although we had Afrikaans clients, the company language was English and we weren't expected to be able to speak anything else.

Nevertheless, even allowing for the rose-tinted hue of hindsight, nearly everyone was happy and the atmosphere was good. There was plenty of laughter in the office, some of it pretty ribald, and we all sat together for our tea breaks, usually around the trolley wheeled in by Daphne or Tina, our hard-working tea ladies.

Birthdays, on the other hand, were celebrated each Friday with cake and a gift. The money for such luxuries came from a birthday fund to which we all contributed and all the week's anniversaries (if that's not a contradiction) were celebrated at once.

For this, we gathered in the staffroom. Mr Dee would make a speech, a gift from the staff was handed over to each birthday girl (or occasionally, boy) and we had half an hour to chat and mingle.

Altogether, old-fashioned as it might have been under Mr Dee's direction, it was a relaxed organisation despite some inevitable grumbles and inter-office spats. The company also had a good reputation and I was grateful I could take myself to work there every day and escape some of the dramas on the home front.

As a result, my drive home that evening was much happier than it might have been. I drove down Republic road as the sun was beginning to set and thought how marvellous the horizon looked in the late afternoon light. My route took me down the hill and then up onto Hans Strydom Drive (now renamed Malibongwe) where I turned right and followed the road until I reached the intersection with the N1 Western Bypass, locally known as the concrete highway because of its pre-formed slab surface.

Down the ramp onto the highway, I normally sped round past Rivonia and Sunninghill and through the intersection with the N3 and M1 before heading north to Midrand. It was an easy drive once the rush hour traffic was over. Being concrete and laid in sections, the road surface had its own noise, a kind of roar interspersed with clicks every time the wheels crossed the joints between the slabs, but it was a fast-moving road most of the time.

This particular evening, it was locked solid. There'd been an accident just past Rivonia and the traffic was at a standstill, a frustration for me as I wanted to get home and tell Bill the news about my job. There weren't any car phones yet so I just had to be patient. It's strange now to think about how we simply accepted that no one could contact us then. We didn't expect to be in touch with our colleagues or family twenty-four hours a day and it didn't do us any harm either.

That said, there was one particular time a little later on in my career when I was going to fetch the company chairman from the airport and I was caught in another traffic jam on the highway somewhere near Bedfordview on the East Rand. I'll admit I was in a total panic on that occasion, but there wasn't a thing I could do. The worst part of it was that he, the chairman, was due to give an opening speech at one of our office functions. My being late would hold everything up. And he was the top of the pile when it came to the company dignitaries; the head honcho himself.

Lips were very tight when I finally made it back to the office, very late, with a smiling and serene chief in tow. He'd been all charm and forgiveness but Mr Dee took a long time to absolve me, although that had its upside. He didn't come and see me on his morning rounds for weeks.

I eventually saw what had been causing the tailback after we'd been inching along for half an hour or so. An old truck that should probably have been in the scrap yard years before had been in a collision with a *bakkie* in much the same state. Bits of both vehicles were scattered across two lanes of the three-lane section. The remains of the truck straddled the Armco railing that ran down the middle of the highway, and the pick-up had broken through the barrier on our side and was half way down the ditch. Neither vehicle was blocking the road, but of course, road accidents were a spectator sport if ever there was one and when drivers slowed down to peer at the damage in passing, everything ground to a halt behind them. Predictably, it wasn't an uncommon occurrence.

In South Africa, an annual roadworthiness check was not required and we only had to have it done when we bought a vehicle and registered it. This meant that many vehicles were never 'roadworthied' (as we called it) since large numbers of them were sold but not registered and the owners would drive them without being checked until they disintegrated, bits falling off at regular intervals until the end came – usually after impact with another car.

The death rate on the roads was horrific when I think about it. With pedestrians making a dash for it over the highways, as they often did, and the multitude of seriously dangerous cars, trucks and *bakkies* on the road, the only reason driving was a pleasure at all was because there was relatively little traffic compared with European roads. Within a few years, though, it became much more congested because of the influx of new residents to the urban areas; it developed into a daily nightmare, not just an occasional inconvenience.

I got home eventually, brimming with excitement and full of my stories, but Bill wasn't listening. He had other news.

"You're not going to believe it," he fumed. "That scumbag excuse for a human being, Roy, has done a runner and left me with a heap of trouble."

My heart sank. Roy was the new partner Bill had been working with. If this was true, he'd only lasted a few months. According to Bill, he'd realised all his big ideas of fame and fortune in the film industry were just that, big ideas, and skipped off to England with his wife and new baby.

"No!" I gasped. "Not him too! What is it with these people? Is there no one decent in the film world?

"Dunno, seems not, doesn't it? But thank heavens Jim was his bank manager too. It means he's doing his best to help me out of the mire again. It's his job on the line as well."

I felt sorry for Jim. Having met him by this time, I knew what a nice man he was. It wouldn't do his reputation much good to have a client he'd financially supported doing a duck. What hurt me personally was that I'd lent Roy's wife the shawl a favourite aunt had knitted me for my babies and they'd taken off with that too.

I know that to have worried about something so minor when they owed Bill thousands of Rands in unpaid work seemed petty of me. But it's true to say I no longer remember how much money was involved; the loss of the shawl was personal, and it stung.

Disaster averted

In the end, Jim, the magician, did some juggling and offered us a solution to the situation, dire though it seemed at first. Before doing his bunk, Roy had been in the process of buying an old house in Bryanston, which Jim suggested we might like to take over to avoid a bank repossession. The house was in a recently built-up area and was said to be the original farmhouse that belonged to Reverend William Nicol, the man who gave his name to the road we used so frequently as a route from just about anywhere in the northern suburbs to everywhere else.

Reverend Nicol was quite controversial for his time. Despite being appointed Administrator of the Transvaal when apartheid was introduced in 1948, Dr Nicol believed that children should be educated in their own language. He was a great supporter of teaching African children in their mother tongue with English as a second language for general communication, not Afrikaans. He also worked with African religious leaders to translate the bible into Zulu.

Given that the 1976 Soweto riots were sparked by protests against enforced Afrikaans education, it suggests his ideas didn't find favour with the government. But regardless of his championship of black education, the name of his road has been recently changed. It is now Winnie Madikizela-Mandela Drive after the erstwhile wife of Nelson Mandela. She was also controversial, but for different, and rather more unconventional reasons.

In any event, the house in question certainly looked the part of an old homestead and probably was the main house in the area when it was built, which makes it possible the story was true. When Jim told us we might save both his bacon and our own by agreeing to buy the property at a much reduced price, we greeted the idea with enthusiasm. That we might be rescued from the teeth of disaster by moving upscale to such a glamorous suburb as Bryanston seemed too good to be true; we had the kind of 'how did we get so lucky?' feelings. That was the problem: it wasn't true and we weren't lucky.

All my excitement changed to despair the first time we went to see the house. Surrounded by a newly-built cluster complex, the quaint charm of the old thatched homestead looked somewhat out of place, but I could imagine how graceful it must have been in its glory days, standing in open parkland amongst beautiful mature trees. Swamped as it now was by smart, up-market modern homes, it wore its age like a shabby coat. All the same, we remained excited until we opened the front door. It was then that I froze.

"Oh my word," I breathed, but not in pleasure; it was more like horror.

"Blimey, what on earth is that?" Bill gulped beside me.

From the spreading lake of water on the quarry-tiled floor of the hallway, we looked up to see a gaping hole in the roof with what looked like half a tree hanging through it.

"Bill," I squealed. "We can't live in this!"

"Umm, well we don't have a choice."

"What do you mean? No choice?"

"I've already signed to say we will."

At that point I burst into tears.

It might have been better if the rest of the house had been in good condition, but it wasn't. The whole place was a tip. There was no kitchen, the bathrooms were old, stained, and quite frankly, fairly disgusting and the bedrooms were basic in the extreme with no cupboards and cracked glass in the windows.

I couldn't believe we'd be giving up our house in Noordwyk with its garden, its view and the children's pool to live in this hovel. Its only redeeming features were that it had a good address and it was thatched, well most of it was.

In the end, we moved because we had to; there was no other option. It was either that or being rendered homeless with three kids, three dogs and three cats. In other circumstances I might have found that liberating, but not just then.

Our residence in Noordwyk covered just over a year and a half, and our move marked the end of an era for us all. Life was about to become much more confrontational as the country moved towards the end of the apartheid era and we came into closer contact with the reality of an urban environment.

We'd arrived in Noordwyk early in 1991; we packed up and moved to the house in Bryanston sometime in the spring of 1992, this being September to October. Fortunately, the girls were both at school in

Buccleuch where they were happy and doing well. Another plus was that thanks to Jim's contacts and amazing skills at casting safety nets, Bill started working on corporate training and promotional videos for a number of banks and insurance companies. He was also planning another feature film, which would come to be a major factor in our lives. As for Tim, he was still at the CD shop in Midrand, where it seemed he'd found his niche for the foreseeable future.

For my own part, I'd transferred to the Customer Service Department at the medical aid in Randburg, an important step for me as this was the start of my first real career in South Africa. Our house would be nearer to my work and I hoped it would take us onward and upward again.

I'd had enough of crises for the time being, but little did I know they were set to follow us around for a while yet.

BRYANSTON

Righting the wreck

L iving in Bryanston brought us closer to the hub of Johannesburg life, but at the same time, I felt it took us further away from much of what I loved about South Africa. Due to the separation of the city's residents, both legal and economic, we inevitably saw less of the African people and mixed increasingly with Europeans. We also saw less of the sweeping scenery now we'd moved further in to the urban jungle, and we became less aware of the natural rhythms of African life.

In KwaZulu Natal we saw the hills turn from emerald to gold as summer gave way to autumn; we felt the suffocating heat of the *berg* winds against our faces and witnessed the lightning fork across the sky. We watched fire breaks being burned and the smoke lingering over the parched winter landscape; and sometimes, we saw snow on the distant crags of the Drakensberg. We knew drought, faced *veld* fires, experienced an earthquake and the aftermath of Cyclones Imboa and Domoina. Always in close contact with our Zulu neighbours, many of them became dear to us.

Now, however, it seemed ironic that the closer to the new non-apartheid South Africa we came, the less we felt part of it; we lived a city life, albeit an African city, which meant all that came with it; the good and the bad. The pace was faster; the stress was greater. We exchanged driving down the mountain leaving clouds of dust behind us for ducking and weaving through the hordes of minibus taxis that honked and hooted their way along Johannesburg's arterial routes.

Another factor we became much more aware of was the tension between all the parties involved in the political processes, and we witnessed the inevitable results of the differences between the affluent suburbs and the poverty-ridden townships. It was during the two and a half years we spent in Bryanston that we suffered break-ins and encountered violence for the first time; not first hand, but unnervingly close. All this aside, there were compensations to life in the fast lane, and it was an exciting period from a number of perspectives.

The house, or rather wreck, needed substantial renovation, and it wasn't only because of the tree growing through the roof. Luck in the shape of our guardian angel, or rather bank manager Jim, made sure we had some extra funds to repair the thatched roof. What had happened to create the huge hole, we didn't know, but further investigation made it clear the whole roof was rotten. It needed to be replaced urgently, so that was the first job.

We hired a small company to do the work, a process I found fascinating to watch. The way the hanks of grass were laid looked easy, but I knew the young men clambering about above us were highly skilled so it was probably much more exacting than it looked. They did a section at a time, covering the open parts with tarpaulins until they were complete. Within a month or so, we had beautiful, smooth, and pristine thatch. I loved its golden colour when it was new, but this didn't last very long and it soon developed the typical dark beige hue that we all associate with the cottages in Beatrix Potter illustrations.

Gorgeous though the roof undoubtedly was, we realised we would also need some substantial lightning protection for both insurance purposes and for our own peace of mind. After some research about the requirements, we had two twenty-metre conductors erected at strategic points in the garden. They didn't do much for the property aesthetically, but they helped reduce our anxiety levels given the number of thunder storms we were subjected to on the *Highveld*.

The next job was to sanitise the house. It was probably the largest property I've ever lived in as an adult; it covered four hundred square metres. Built in a U shape, it was also quite a distance from end to end, and all of it was filthy. In fact, taking the volume, length and floor area into account, there was an awful lot of house in urgent need of cleaning.

We started by painting all the walls white with a kind of lime wash that would apparently kill all the germs. Then we got down to the floors. They were quarry-tiled, which I liked at first, and reminded me of the basement floors we'd had in my childhood home in London although we didn't have four hundred square metres of those to clean.

After scrubbing the floors from one end of the house to the other, it took me a while to regain my appreciation for them. It was a huge and back-breaking job and I spent several days convincing my spine that being bent double wasn't normal. When we'd finished, we hired an electric polisher and waxed them. The effect was magnificent and my fondness returned. The old floor glowed with its infusion of polish and I was sure it hadn't looked so good since the worthy Reverend Nicol had paced it from the bedroom to the Jacuzzi.

But then I haven't mentioned the Jacuzzi before, have I? This house had one as well, although it probably wasn't installed by its illustrious former owner. Luckily, it was in a much saner place than the one we'd had in Noordwyk. Tucked into a charming addition on one end of what I called the living wing (as opposed to the sleeping wing), it was tiled in pretty blue mosaics and was altogether a more appealing proposition than our previous, moulded plastic model. To prove its worth, we had more than one Jacuzzi party at our home in the months after our move.

Following the cleaning and whitewashing, we replaced the broken glass in the windows. As luck would have it, they were all what we called 'cottage-pane', so each piece of glass was small and could be easily and cheaply renewed.

Then we had to think about a kitchen.

Essentially, there wasn't one, so we initially placed an electric stove in what should have been the breakfast room and the sink was in the extension purported to be the kitchen. It was a step down from the eating area and consisted of a collection of decrepit old Formica cupboards. Beyond this ramshackle arrangement was a kind of lean-to shed, which was probably intended as a utility room. It was all a horrible mess, but once we'd cleaned it, we had to use what we had. By the time the roof was finished, we'd run out of funds anyway; it was a case of 'make do and mend', at least for a while.

I must say the greatest advantage of having such a large house was that there were plenty of bedrooms and bathrooms. Bill and I had what was clearly the master bedroom with a fireplace and our own *en suite* bathroom – of a very rudimentary sort. Jodie took the room at the end of the same wing and which was separated from our room by another simple, old-fashioned bathroom. She had French doors that opened out onto the garden, a feature she liked very much – at first. Mo had a bedroom on the other side of ours and Tim had his in the middle of the same long passage. He had a toilet next door and a built-in shower (again, very basic), so he could be quite independent. On the other side of the passage, there was another small room that I earmarked as a sewing room. In short, we didn't have to live on top of each other and that was a significant advantage with a growing family.

The biggest disadvantage, however, was that even though we were essentially broke, we were now in one of the most affluent neighbourhoods, and we would certainly be perceived as rich by any canny robbers in the area. Within six months of moving in, we had our first confrontation with the need for vigilant security. Despite having Daisy and Claude (Sasha had returned to Anna before we moved) and three fearsome but insufficiently armed moggies, we had a break-in.

It should be said that Daisy rarely barked; she just rumbled. She slept in Mo's room and that night, if she rumbled at all, Mo didn't hear it. Claude was simply deaf. In any event, we woke the next morning to find most of our more expensive possessions missing as well as a new hole in the roof. The robbers had cut a section in the thatch over the Jacuzzi room big enough to feed one person through. Since this room also happened to be where Bill had his office set up, all his precious technical equipment as well as some old and valued cameras that had belonged to his father were there.

The robbers took the lot as well as our stereo equipment, TV and other assorted items. And we hadn't heard a thing. With the benefit of hindsight, it was probably a blessing as we might have been faced with loss of life as well as loss of property. Bill owned a gun at the time, but he kept it in the bedroom overnight. The upside of that was firstly, the robbers didn't find any weapons to harm us or others with and secondly, Bill didn't get to shoot anyone. I'm not sure how pleased he felt about that but I was.

It was a shock, though. We'd lived in South Africa for more than ten years in total and this was the first time we'd been faced with an intrusion into our home. On the farm in Natal, we'd left doors unlocked and windows open with no thought of risk. In Byrne and Richmond too, we'd never had anything stolen, nor had we lost anything in Noordwyk either. I suppose this was the price we were paying for that 'good address'. Since I personally didn't care what kind of address I had, I couldn't help wondering if it was worth it, especially when I saw how the loss of his heirlooms affected Bill.

"I don't give a toss about the TV and stereo," he fumed, his voice breaking on a sob. "It's my dad's old cameras. They meant the world to me."

And it was true; they were worthless items from a burglar's point of view. They had no monetary value, but they were steeped in emotional significance for Bill. I knew how he felt; the loss of my shawl still hurt.

We had another break-in later on, but that happened when we were all out. I'd gone to work and Bill had taken the girls to school. As was usual, the dogs went for the ride too, so it was an easy matter for the burglars to prise open the garden gate and the office doors. Once again, they helped themselves to all our home appliances and stereo equipment. Our insurance company sighed and paid up again, but they took their revenge by increasing our premiums.

These trials aside, we were growing to love our quirky house, although we clearly needed to be more careful. We also needed a more effective dog alarm. Daisy was just as likely to invite the burglars in as deter them, so we set about looking for a noisier companion for her. Enter Polly the Collie into the picture.

Polly was a rescue dog. We saw her at the Randburg branch of the SPCA when we went to the big hardware and builders' merchants we frequented during our renovating operations. The SPCA was close by, so we decided to go and have a look despite my reluctance to go to animal shelters; they always break my heart. Polly spoke to us immediately and I don't mean barked. Everything about her made us want to take her home. She danced, rather than ran. She also had very pretty, symmetrical markings and Bill, who had a thing for watching the sheepdog trials on TV, decided a Border Collie was just what he needed. The fact that she was desperately thin added to her appeal. She needed us.

We asked about her history and apparently her previous owner complained of having trouble keeping her at home; in a farming area, that was not handy. She was lucky she hadn't been shot. The problem was she was a great jumper and would clear his four-foot fence without even scraping the top. We smiled. We had a six-foot wall. Let her try that, we thought. So once we'd been approved and all the administrative details were concluded, she too moved up-market and came to live in Bryanston with us.

Initially, her escape skills weren't the problem. It was our own survival that was at risk from her jumping capabilities. Polly was very nervous when we brought her home. In fact, we soon wondered if we'd done the right thing in taking her on. She was fine with Daisy and Claude, but nothing in the kitchen was safe.

In the first few days she was with us, we repeatedly had to clear her off the kitchen table where she'd jump to grab food from our plates, and I even caught her on the cooker one day stealing chicken out of the frying pan. I was stunned. I'd never had a dog so starved that she would risk burning her paws to snatch food cooking on the stove.

It was a serious fire risk too with our thatched roof and wooden furnishings. Polly had to be watched and attended with vigilance until she settled down. Luckily, she was endearingly sweet-natured and in spite of these early trials, she rapidly became a much-loved member of the family. Bill made it his mission to train her, which gave them both something to focus on other than the rest of us; always a plus. On the downside, she didn't bark all that much either, but she was more alert than lazy Daisy.

When one night someone tried to force open the French doors to Jodie's bedroom, it was Polly's warning bark that woke us all and presumably scared the intruder off. After this, Jo wasn't quite so keen on her romantic room and made doubly sure the doors were locked and barred every night. She also took to keeping her bedroom door open and having Claude in with her overnight. He too would rumble if the noise was close enough to penetrate the fluff over his ears, and that in turn would wake Polly. Daisy, bless her, continued to snooze undisturbed.

The house gradually took on a more noble appearance the longer we stayed there. Bill loved a project and the old thatched farmstead became his greatest 'oeuvre'. When we both started bringing more money in, he went along to one of the spots where labourers gathered waiting for casual work and hired a new gang of builders. Together they built a carport with another thatched room over it into which Tim moved as soon as decently possible. It was his own den and he loved being up there. None of us dared to intrude and he could do whatever he wanted without interference.

Together too we built a new kitchen with fitted pine cupboard units we bought from a large warehouse. It was the same business I'd seen several years before near the Oriental Plaza during my first foray into Joburg, but it had grown substantially. Because we had to renovate everything on a DIY basis, we did our measurements and then selected whatever units would fit the space. The finishing was also something we did ourselves, but that suited us as we could varnish them a warm teak colour to match the other old furnishings we'd picked up.

After that came the tiling, and I made my first attempts at grouting both on the walls and on our beautiful new terracotta paved floor. It was fiddly and messy to begin with but very rewarding, especially when all the dust was cleaned and mopped away. With the spotlights Bill fitted in the ceiling, a new electric hob, and a large oven, the whole kitchen looked wonderful and was completely in keeping with the house.

Between the breakfast area and the kitchen was a large archway that became the next family project. We all felt it needed some adornment and since the style of the room was like an Italian café with the colours in the kitchen and the quarry tiles, we decided to make a hand-painted border round the arch with a sunburst at the top.

The girls, Tim, Bill and I sat round our scrub top kitchen table together and painted a swirling design of vine leaves on some plain terracotta border tiles we bought. We'd traced the pattern from the decor at a local Italian restaurant and transferred it to the tiles using a soft pencil. This creative collaboration was a special time and perhaps the closest we'd ever been as a family.

The children, and I include Tim here, giggled together and we all groaned at Bill's corny stories and jokes. Puns flew around the table at lightning speed, each one worse than the last. Mo often started the contest; she loved punning.

"My vine's branching out here," she'd say, the gleam in her eye warning us. What followed was probably predictable. Bill and the others would take up the challenge.

"I'll take a leaf out of your book."

"Have you twigged it yet?"

"I haven't got to the root of the problem."

"It'll sap your energy to keep up with them."

"Now you're all going out on a limb."

"You're all barking mad."

We wept with laughter. How we managed to finish the tiles without any mishaps, I don't know, but we did and it was Jodie who painted the stylised sun on the square tile that fitted at the top of the archway. It was exactly the finishing touch we wanted.

From both the passage and the breakfast room there were doors into the official dining room. Then the lounge was another couple of steps down and took up most of the living wing of the house. The thatched roof looked correspondingly higher here and since it had no ceilings, the sense of space and volume was liberating. It was a glorious room. There was a massive open fireplace, opposite which was a wide bay window with its own deep window seat of polished oak; a place I loved to sit and read in the winter. It caught the sun and where the rest of the house remained chilly, this spot collected warmth and was the best place to relax. I could easily imagine Reverend Nicol enjoying it too and I loved the African atmosphere of the room; without ceilings to conceal the thatch, it was reminiscent of the more spacious Zulu huts on the farm in Natal.

As time went on, we settled still more into our gracious old home, spreading ourselves out to fill its embracing spaces. Apart from the kitchen, we did no other modernisation, partly because we no longer had the funds, but also because we didn't want to spoil the intrinsic character of the house. Eventually, the lean-to shed on the kitchen became a proper laundry room, but we did no major improvements to the bathrooms.

Instead, I spent hours refurbishing our somewhat rustic *en suite* by chipping cracked and broken tiles off the walls and simply replacing them with new ones from old stock I found under the kitchen sink. In addition, I re-painted the double basins and the bath with white enamel coating and made new matching curtains to cover the open fronts of the cupboards and the windows. The fabric had a kind of 'Laura Ashley goes autumnal' print, with yellow rosebuds on a background of browns and greens. With all the floor tiles and taps polished to a bright shine, it looked great and gave me much more satisfaction than having an expensive modern bathroom installed.

Unlike most other older homes, there were no servants' quarters next to the house, probably because it was once a farm and any such workers' rooms would have been outbuildings separated from the main homestead. For once I was sorry not to be able to employ a live-in maid; the house was so large. Having a fulltime job meant I didn't have much time for housework and although the family all helped with washing-up, cleaning their own rooms and general tidying duties, I still needed help to keep the rest of the house in reasonable order. The solution was to have a 'daily help', and we had a series of these.

The first disappeared after our first burglary; we could only conclude there was a connection there somewhere. The second got her marching orders for being too much of a liability. The first hint that I'd got a helper with butter fingers was when I found not one, but three ceramic ornaments stuck together with Prestick, the South African version of Blu Tack. She'd dropped them when dusting but instead of telling me, she'd made a hasty attempt to mend them. The same evening, I happened notice they weren't in their normal position and when I tried to move them, they fell apart.

"Mavis, why didn't you tell me you'd broken my ornaments?" I asked her the next time she came.

"Sorry, Valerie, I not want you to be angry."

"But now I *am* angry because you didn't tell me."

"Yes, I very sorry."

"Well, okay, but if it happens again, please let me know. I won't be cross, I promise, unless you try to hide it. Alright?"

"Okay, Valerie, thank you."

A month or so later, I wanted to do some ironing, but the iron was missing. I found it in the rubbish bin.

"Mavis?"

"Yes, Valerie."

I ranted.

"Sorry, Valerie."

I forgave.

The last straw was when I found the Hoover full of water. It wasn't a wet and dry vacuum cleaner. I'm not sure if they were even available at the time, so unless she was a visionary, Mavis had done it again. It was a sad goodbye; she meant well but she had to go. I couldn't afford her. To help her on her way, I gave her a glowing reference for her next job. "A good, hard worker, adept at cleaning, and creative in solving problems." I avoided saying what kind of problems and could only hope she found another post where her skills were better appreciated. After all, the creative part was true.

We had other cleaners after Mavis, but because we couldn't offer them accommodation, they didn't stay long. Being the area that it was, most Bryanston homeowners could offer better conditions than we could.

Housework aside, the worst of our discomfort was the cold in winter because heating was difficult in such a lofty house. Any warmth we could generate tended to disappear up into the rafters. Bill and I had a small open fireplace in our bedroom, but keeping it alight at night gave us both headaches so we stopped using it. The girls had electric heaters in their rooms and we used a portable gas heater to warm ours before going to bed. Even so, we had to be very judicious with our energy as it was an expensive commodity and didn't help much anyway. But as everyone was quick to remind us, winter was only a short three months. It was a test of my endurance all the same. I wasn't good with cold.

Developments of a social and anti-social kind

L ife in the complex was much more social compared to the community we'd lived among in Noordwyk. Now I come to think of it, we barely knew our neighbours in Francis Drive. By contrast, our immediate neighbours in Bryanston were open, friendly and warmhearted. Granville and Annette quickly became good friends and we spent many an evening with them either on their beautiful veranda or on our patio.

Theirs was a lovely home; modern but welcoming, classy but informal. I developed a close relationship with Annette and it was marvellous to have someone I could just drop in on for coffee, or a glass of wine and a chat. We'd sit at her kitchen counter, joking, giggling and sharing dreams for hours. We did plenty of 'girl talk' in those sessions too, something I'd missed in our previous two homes where I barely knew anyone, and I valued her friendship deeply. Granville was very dear to me too; kind and generous, he was endlessly cheerful. I became very fond of them both.

The road into the complex made a complete loop around all the properties, and further along was a family with a little boy who became great friends with the girls. The three of them played in the street, cycling or kicking a ball around. They decided to start a newssheet for the residents and collected stories by conducting interviews and drawing pictures to illustrate their small publication. They ran it off on Bill's office photocopier and delivered it to all the houses. They took their journalism quite seriously for as long as it held their interest.

Another enterprise the children started was making fresh lemon squash to sell. The three of them made up litres of lemon drink in the kitchen, using a mix of commercially made juice and real fruit. They then stood on the street corner with their tray of cups on a small table and offered their thirst quenchers for ten cents a-piece.

This was generally a good time for the girls. They were happy at school and enjoyed being part of the community. Since most of the residents were sociable and friendly, Bill and I also relished the new sense of belonging we felt.

Our only real problems in that first year were Polly and water. The two weren't connected, but they both presented us with ongoing challenges. Although Polly settled into the family pack, her new confidence combined with a full tummy meant she no longer felt compelled to steal. Instead, she reverted to her escape artist tendencies.

So much for our conviction that the two-metre wall would be too high. Polly was able to scale it with all the dexterity of a squirrel on a high-speed setting. She would then prance along the top of the wall waiting for a suitable victim on which to pounce, usually a neighbour's cat. If we caught her at it, we called her down and she came without question. Unfortunately, we didn't always see her and the resulting hisses, indignant yowls and scuffles told their own tale. Polly would then reappear with bloody scratches across her nose. I decided that it served her right, especially as she seemed completely unrepentant.

And then she developed a hate thing for the paper-boy.

Well, it's true he drove a very noisy moped, and I actually sympathised with her feelings of outrage about it. Since it sounded more like a disturbed wasp than a useful vehicle, I could readily understand why she wanted to kill it. Nevertheless, it wasn't good for her or our reputation.

The poor lad used to come round during the afternoons, presumably after school. His practice was to ride round the block on the moped and hurl the relevant rolled up paper towards each customer's door. It wasn't a terribly accurate method and sometimes we got the wrong one, not that Polly cared about that. No, it was probably a combination of the manic buzzing of the bike combined with the flying missile that got to her.

The first time, it happened when the paper boy came screaming round the bend one afternoon. Polly, who'd probably heard him coming long before he arrived, launched herself off the wall where she'd been dancing and charged. He, of course, in trying to avoid attack, swerved, skidded and came off his bike with an almighty crash. Bill heard the ruckus and rushed out to see who and what had been damaged.

One look was enough to give him a pretty good idea of who was at fault.

"Polly! Come here!" he yelled at his errant Collie. Now she'd felled her victim and the wasp had stopped buzzing, she just stood there with her tail waving looking pleased with herself.

"Polly! Inside!" Polly trotted inside. Remorse wasn't needed as far as she was concerned.

Bill helped the paper-boy to his feet.

"I'm so sorry. Really. I can't apologise enough. She's never done that before," Bill grovelled, visions of thousands of Rands in damages giving his words extra conviction. The fact she'd already been leaping over the wall for some time suddenly seemed to escape his memory

The paper-boy muttered, shuffled onto his now scratched and less than pristine bike and sped off, without a word of criticism or complaint. Bill watched him leave with a mixture of relief and incredulity.

For the next few days, we kept Polly in during the afternoon. Bill was working from home and was able to manage the situation, but then the inevitable happened. He had a meeting with a client and forgot that the doors were open. Polly was outside in the garden when the paper-boy came. As soon as she heard him she was up and over the wall hurling herself at the evil-monster-angry-wasp before Bill even had time to stand up. This time, the bike's mudguard came off, but once again, there was no complaint and no criticism. Bill was mystified.

"If I'd been him, I'd have lodged a charge against Polly for assault and battery," Bill told me.

"Or at least against us for letting her assault and batter him," I pointed out. "Maybe it's going to come. We'd better do something more serious about keeping her in."

But of course, it happened again. Either a door was left open or the paper-boy came earlier, I forget which, but it resulted in further damage to the bike, if not the boy. Bill, fearing an uproar, grovelled again, yet there was still no complaint. We couldn't figure it out at all. Why wasn't he upset, or even angry? There was no logic to it. Our dog was a menace, but it seemed he refused to blame her.

What *did* happen, however, was that our paper deliveries started coming by car, and Polly's flying activities were duly curtailed.

The boy, whose name we never learnt, must have persuaded his mother to save him from the constant attacks. From that time on, she drove while he hurled the papers out of the window.

But perhaps that's what he'd been angling for all the time.

Then there was the water, our other problem. One of the rules in South African towns was that where homes were built on a slope, the lower houses had to 'accept' rainwater flowing down from the houses on the upper slopes. It was just the way it was, and probably worked fine as long as the property builders took the implications into account.

In our case, they hadn't, or maybe it was us who didn't. Our house was at the bottom of a slope and there were two or three homes above us. This in itself wasn't a problem, but the fact that their gardens were mostly paved was. What it meant was that storm water didn't soak sufficiently into the soil on their properties; with nowhere else to go, it flowed unchecked into ours.

Again, most of the time it was fine and our own drain systems could handle it. We also had grass almost all the way around the house which absorbed the normal intake and gave us wonderfully lush growth. But every now and then there'd be an exceptional cloud burst; one of those humdingers we had in Noordwyk when the Jacuzzi popped out. Close to the end of our first year in Bryanston we had one of these storms, and on this occasion our beautiful new laundry room was flooded.

We hadn't long finished it. The walls were plastered, the floor was tiled, there was a new roof and new windows and altogether, it had become a real utility room and not just a lean-to shed. But then the rain came. It thundered down in sheets so heavy we couldn't even see out of the windows. It found leaks where we'd never had them and didn't have again. Water crept under the doors, through the window frames and down the chimneys.

The dogs and cats tucked their noses under their paws, holding on to whatever they needed to do until it was over. And it poured, and poured, especially from our neighbours' gardens into ours. I only noticed it when I went into the kitchen. There was something wrong with what I was seeing. Water was lapping over the step that led down into the laundry.

"Bill," I called to my husband, who was as usual lying out the storm on the sofa. "Bill, I think we need to do some bailing out here!"

"What d'you mean, bailing?"

"Bailing as in boats, you know. Bailing water!"

"Why?"

"Come and see. The laundry's suffering from a tsunami!"

That moved him. The laundry had been his pet project and now it was at risk. This was personal. He bounded through to the kitchen and took one look through the door.

"Oh no!"

"Oh yes," I said. "What shall we do? My washing machine's going to cast off in a minute and make for the Pacific."

"Oh very funny," he grunted. "We'll have to get the door open this side and let it drain out. It's probably coming in through the other door."

The laundry had two doors, one on each side of the room, and the garden rose a little higher on the side furthest from us. For that reason, there was a drain there to take the first rush of water, but it obviously wasn't doing its job.

We both took off our shoes and waded into the shin-high murky depths covering the whole of the laundry floor. The washing machine and the freezer were standing in it too.

"The outside drain must have got blocked," Bill muttered.

"Or else it just can't cope with this level of inundation."

Bill grunted again and pulled open the door closest to the kitchen step. It was hard work with all the pressure up against it, but with enough of a gap to let the water gush out, the level quickly dropped and he managed to open it completely. I ran to pull up the garage door and the flood washed out into the street where it ran out into the main drains. Once the laundry was more or less empty, we checked the drain outside the other door. Sure enough, it was blocked with debris and mud that had come down with the water, but even so, this proved that in extreme conditions, it wasn't going to cope.

"We'll just have to hope there's always someone here when we have one of these torrential downpours," I remarked.

"Yes, well, that's quite a tall order, isn't it?" Bill grumbled. He wasn't happy. "I'd better dig out a trench round the outside of the laundry just in case."

Which is what he did, or rather he hired some casual labour to do it. For the most part, it worked although it wasn't entirely the end of the problem. Fortunately for us, the crunch only came sometime after we moved out a year or so later.

Several months following our move, we heard that during another torrential storm, the entire laundry collapsed. It seems likely that the water we 'received' from further up during subsequent storms had made its way under the footings and damaged the foundations. The deluge in question happened to be the final straw and the laundry room was no more. We felt twinges of guilt when we heard about it. Perhaps Bill's trench wasn't such a good idea after all.

Working out and about

A s far as our lives outside the house were concerned, the Bryanston period was also a mixed bag. My work was going well; I loved being in Customer Services and it wasn't long before I was also visiting member firms on service calls. It all happened quite suddenly. My boss, Christine, who was now the manager of Customer Services too, approached me about this potential new role one morning.

"Val, have your ears been burning?" she asked me, her eyes teasing.

I narrowed mine and peered at her. This sounded suspicious.

"Not since you last pulled my leg," I replied. She laughed.

"Well, they should have been. You must have lost your antenna for trouble."

"Christine, stop it. What have I done now?"

She roared with laughter.

"Nothing, Val. Nothing at all, but we *have* been talking about you. Mr Dee and I thought you might like to take on some of the firm visits, the smaller partnerships that is. You'd come with me at first, but once you've got the hang of what we do, then you'll be able to do them alone. That'll free me up to focus on the larger firms. What do you think?"

"Wow, I mean yes! I'd love to."

"We'll also expect you to give presentations now and then too."

"Oh. Will you?" I wasn't quite so keen on that idea. I still lived with memories of the stage fright that paralysed and silenced me when I was social secretary at my university's student union elections. Christine must have sensed my reluctance.

"What's the problem? Don't you like that idea?"

I explained about my fear of audiences.

"Oh don't worry. We'll send you on a course first. We won't send you out there with no training. Once you've got your confidence, you'll be fine," she finished with unnerving ease.

I wasn't so sure, but since I liked the idea of getting out and about, I nodded my acceptance.

And so it started. I vividly remember my first company visit. I went with Christine to a firm in the centre of Johannesburg. Their offices were on Commissioner Street in one of its older blocks, all of which were tall and varying shades of sandy brown. With the city traffic being organised in a one-way grid system, it took us a few block circuits to find a suitable parking garage. We then walked along the busy streets wending our way through the mix of African hawkers and jostling throngs of office workers to reach the firm's premises.

We did our best to stay in the shade of the overhanging shop awnings that covered most of pavements but it wasn't always possible. There were trees that cast welcome shadows, but it was difficult to avoid the sun completely. It was a hot day and I was dressed in my smartest: a maroon two-piece business suit with a calf length flared skirt. Luckily, I wasn't obliged to wear anything on my legs. Mr Dee's dress code didn't extend to obligatory nylon tights; that would have been too much, but even so, I was sticky with both nerves and heat by the time we arrived at our destination. This was my very first outing as a representative for my employers and I didn't want to mess it up.

Which of course I did.

Instantly.

Walking into the senior partner's office, I followed Christine's lead and held out my hand to greet the man getting up from behind his desk. He was tall and bulky and he had a mop of rather improbably red hair.

"Good morning. Johan Visser," he said with a smile, gripping my hand firmly. "Good to meet you."

"Good morning, Valerie Poore speaking," I gushed. "How can I help you?"

Mr Visser's eyebrows shot up. And then I realised what I'd said. I couldn't believe I'd just managed to put not one, but both feet in my mouth without drawing breath. I'd just come out with the standard patter I used when picking up a phone call.

Flushing beetroot as I felt rather than saw Christine catch her breath, I sat down in the seat offered. Our host gave me an odd look; I couldn't blame him. He must have thought I was a very strange creature, but I'd been so nervous I just went into default mode. Not a very propitious start to my visiting career.

My mind went numb for the rest of the visit but despite being crippled with embarrassment, I gave my party piece about the firm's medical insurance usage. I'd swotted up on it enough beforehand so it was a case of pressing my internal repeat button and out it all came. This statistical information was the main purpose of these visits. They were primers to prepare the companies for increases in their premiums, which at that time depended largely on what was called the 'loss ratio'.

In layman's terms, if the firm's staff had used more in medical aid funds than they'd contributed, they were likely to have an increase. Since just one major surgical procedure could make all the difference to a small group's usage, it was fairly predictable that firms with, say, four or five members of a more senior age would pay the highest premiums. Of course it was smoothed out somewhat over the rest of the membership, but there was definitely a price to pay. Never good news for them and difficult for us to deliver. But it was my job and I'd got used to explaining such issues over the phone. However, this was the first time I'd had to do it in person. Mr Visser took the news with apparent equanimity, but perhaps I'd shocked the poor man into silence.

Once we were in the safety of the lift descending to the ground floor, Christine poked me in the ribs.

"You do know what you said in there, don't you?"

"I'm surprised I managed to say anything at all after that classic piece of foot in mouth," I replied, pulling a face to match my shame.

"That's what I meant. Oh Val. How do you do it? I nearly disgraced myself by snorting. It was hilarious."

"Did you see Johan Visser's face?" I giggled.

"Yes, I thought he was going to lose his eyebrows in his wig."

"Is that what it is? I thought his hair was a bit red for reality. Oh dear, can you imagine what he thought. He'll never want me back again. Any more gaffs like that and he'll lose it completely."

"Actually, you were fine once you got going."

"I was?"

"Yes, you explained the firm's stats really well."

"Did I? I don't remember any of it," I confessed. "I was so embarrassed I must have just blanked out."

"Well, maybe you should do that more often," Christine laughed. "It might save you from making a fool of yourself."

We were almost hooting with laughter as we exited the lift and walked out into the heat of the Johannesburg afternoon. The temperature hit us like a wall and we kept in the shade as much as possible while we negotiated the street sellers once more. A thin African woman sitting on the pavement was selling some tired looking bananas. She had them on a plate. I stopped, fished for some change in my purse and bought them from her. They were only just edible. The skins were spotted and they were soft at the ends, but I wanted to celebrate my first steps into this new phase of my career. It seemed right to be passing some of my success on, especially as she didn't seem to have anything else for sale.

"*Ngiyabonga,*" the woman smiled at me. I recognised the Zulu word meaning 'thank you'.

"*Wamukelekile,*" I answered, hoping it was the right word. I wanted to say 'you're welcome' and I thought I'd remembered this from when I lived in Natal.

She smiled again, so I guessed it was at least close enough. For some absurd reason I wanted to hug her. She was a reminder of my beloved Natal, but I didn't, of course. I'd probably have split my skirt bending over for one thing, and shocked the poor woman rigid for another.

Instead, I caught up with Christine and offered her a banana.

"Erm, no thank you," she shook her head, but her expression said more.

"They don't look that great, do they?"

"They look fit for the bin if you ask me," she muttered.

"You're probably right, but I'm going to eat the good bits. I'm starving."

"It's all that nervous energy you've expended."

"Probably a week's worth of calories," I laughed.

"Well stock up then. We've got other clients to see now."

I did my best with the bananas although I couldn't stomach more than half of each one; they were too far gone. As celebratory fare, they weren't up to much, but perhaps equal to my performance. I reasoned it was only my first outing as the company rep and it would surely improve, which it did.

It didn't take long before I couldn't wait to get out of the office and head into the city even if it wasn't without risks

Looking back, I sometimes think my employers were a bit negligent about my safety. Before leaving the office, I would remove any neck chains, earrings, watches or bracelets. I then drove into the centre of the town stripped of all valuables and bare of any adornment, making sure I had nothing of worth on me at all. The city streets were known to be dangerous, and I had to walk, briefcase in hand, from one firm to the next without drawing attention to myself.

Altogether, these company visits took place between 1992 and 1998, some of the most turbulent years in the transition from apartheid to the new South Africa. On one occasion, I drove into the multi-storey parking garage at one of the 'big five' accounting firms and saw a sign saying: 'This is a gun free zone' with bullet holes in it. I must say it didn't give me much confidence; particularly as I didn't own a gun, nor did I really want one. But I'd have been completely defenceless if I'd come up against anyone wielding anything other than a rolled-up newspaper and a mouthful of abuse.

All the same, my managers sent me off with no protection and no phone either. By 1992, mobile car phones had emerged onto the market, but they were largely unaffordable for most people although Bill had one for his film work. It was the size of a small suitcase and fitted in the centre console of his car. He loved brandishing it about as it was quite a status symbol. By 1994, though, the first hand-held cell phones were being sold. Motorola, Nokia and Alcatel were the market leaders in South Africa and our senior managers all had one of the newest models as a staff perk. But not me; they were considered far too expensive an investment for a member of staff of my rank. It was just the way it was. I was the one who went into downtown Johannesburg alone, but the risks were simply accepted, and I accepted them too. More or less.

In the course of these appointments, I travelled the entire *Highveld* from Pretoria in the north through to Vereeniging in the south; in fact, anywhere that was within a day's return drive. But the main concentration of my work took place in and around central Johannesburg. It was my town and I knew every nook and cranny of its busy streets after a few months of visiting clients, most of whom were small partnerships with just a few articled clerks and a secretary or two. Following these calls, I had to write reports, a part of my job I relished as it gave rein to my love of writing. Apparently, the managers liked them too, despite (or maybe because of) the fact I sometimes took some chances with the content.

"Ooh good. Another heap of reports for me to read with my coffee," beamed Joyce, the Finance Manager as I handed her a stack of files. "I always enjoy your descriptions of the partners."

"Thanks, Joyce. I know you don't get to meet them, so it's fun to give them a bit of life."

Joyce laughed.

"Well, you do certainly do that. I think I'd know them all on sight. I loved how you described Denis Smythe. What was it now? 'Mr Smythe is short, round and bald. He looks like an egg in a suit,'" she quoted.

"Oh dear," I winced. "Maybe I shouldn't have written that. It's a bit on the edge, isn't it? What do you think Mr Dee will say?"

"I think he'll be highly amused," she grinned. "I was."

He must have been because the only comment I ever received was a hand-written note saying 'Do not let partner see this!' next to one of my more flippant remarks.

The accountants I met were a fascinating mixture of characters. Apart from the red-wigged Mr Visser, there was Mr Rosenblum, whose unlikely mop of rich brown hair was betrayed by his bushy white eyebrows and a pair of snowy wings above his ears. Apparently, going grey gracefully was not to be countenanced in the accounting world; or maybe it had to do with giving some colour to what might otherwise have been grey lives. I wouldn't know, but accountancy didn't strike me as the most stimulating of professions. I'm the first to admit I might have been biased, given my aversion to numbers, but even so there must have been some desire for difference, or maybe deference, in their displays of hairy individuality.

Anyway, other than these two, there was the 'beak', Mr Vermeulen, a tall, ascetic man with a predictably long pointed nose and of course the rotund Mr Smythe whose 'eneggmatic character did not match his eggcellent shape' as I also mentioned in my more than usually irreverent report.

In nearly all cases, the clients were men, mostly older and often mildly eccentric. However, that isn't to say there were no women in the profession; female articled clerks and qualified Chartered Accountants were quite plentiful, but most of them worked in the large practices where there were more opportunities for advancement. There weren't many in the small firms I visited and perhaps this was because women didn't stay in practice for so long and often moved out into the corporate world. There was little room for growth in a small firm. There were also increasing numbers of Indians and Africans working their way up the ranks during the 1990s, which was another healthy development, but again, I didn't see them at the small one and two man practices.

On that subject, there was not much diversity in our company when I started there either. We had one Indian computer programmer, Jared, who joined at the same time as me. He was much too good-looking and far too nice to be true, but I never found any cracks in his facade, so it was all genuine. He had the looks of a film star but he was kind, funny and thoughtful. Needless to say, half the girls in Claims and Customer Services had a crush on him.

By dint of the fact we'd started together, he and I became great friends and it gave me a sneaky smugness knowing how envious the other girls were. I was both older and married; I was therefore safe, which suited me just fine. Apart from the tea ladies, Jared and our general factotum, Symon were the only non-white employees in those early days before the 1994 elections.

Symon was magnificent. Of all the employees, he was Mr Dee's most trusted assistant and undoubtedly his right-hand man. He knew the daily operations of the business better than all the managers and organised post, deliveries, diaries and logistics. He liaised with caterers, florists and stationery suppliers, not to mention managing the practical arrangements around events. If we wanted to know something on an operational level, Symon was the man to ask. Deeply religious, he belonged to the Church of Zion and would quote scriptures to us in the way others might dispense small wisdoms. He also seemed to have a personal hotline to God.

"Symon, do you know when the flowers will be arriving for the Board meeting?" I asked him once.

"The Lord knows, but I do not, Val," he smiled. "But do not worry. I will ask."

"The Lord?" I smiled back. He laughed. He had a lovely, rich laugh.

"Not this time, Val. This time, I will phone the suppliers, but that is only because you are in a hurry. The Lord might be busy. It is Friday, you see." And he laughed again.

It says something about Symon's status that he was one of the first staff members to be given a cell phone. When I last went back to visit the company in 2014, Symon was about to retire. I would like to believe his long service award was something very special.

In the meantime, Bill was working hard on a project to finish a trailer for a film he was hoping to make. He'd been told a good clip could work as well as a proposal, and this particular story seemed guaranteed to succeed. The subject of the film was all South African. His name was André Stander, a policeman who'd turned from enforcing the law to breaking it by becoming a bank robber in the late seventies and early eighties.

André Stander was white and Afrikaans, and his father was head of the prison services. Accounts of the time report that when taking part in a riot control incident in Tembisa, already known for its dismal living conditions, Stander happened to shoot and kill a black youth. This incident apparently affected him deeply and, disillusioned with the apartheid government system, he changed his attitude to the service that employed him. Not only this, he developed an aversion to the entire system that represented the privilege of the white Afrikaans male - and this included the banks.

The story goes that one day, on the spur of the moment, he flew to Durban, went into a bank and robbed it. He then flew back to Joburg for an afternoon's work. The thrill of his spontaneous exploit was liberating, and he started on a series of robberies that were breathtaking in their audacity. In fact, in one reported case, he was the investigating officer at his own crime. All of this is on public record although the Tembisa incident may well have been Stander's own fabrication to garner sympathy. That part isn't clear.

Nevertheless, André Stander became something of a folk hero before he was caught and imprisoned, but later, his legendary status increased when after escaping from prison with two of his fellow inmates, Lee McCall and Allan Heyl, he embarked on a spree of robberies of quite astonishing proportions. Sometimes, the Stander gang would rob as many as four banks in a day. Their modus operandi was speed: no fuss, no noise, in and out as quickly as possible. The idea was to make the events so mundane, customers would barely notice them. Despite using guns to threaten, they did not shoot or hurt people, and bank customers were even heard to boast about being robbed by the Stander Gang, as if this was something to be proud of.

I remember reading the reports in the papers of the time and being fascinated by this man and his friends. They drove around in a yellow Porsche Targa (a sign of their gradually increasing audacity), but no one seemed able to catch or arrest them. Stander's family must have been mortified. Here was their son, the image of bright, educated Afrikanerdom, shaming and humiliating them. For sure, his image has been polished somewhat and, in reality, he probably doesn't deserve the sort of Robin Hood status he achieved, but this is what happens when people step out of the mould and do something of immense daring.

Inevitably, the Stander gang were all caught in the end. The first to go, Lee McCall, was killed in a police shoot-out when the gang's safe house was surrounded. The other two escaped. Allan Heyl, the only surviving member today, spent some nine years in a UK prison after being arrested and tried in Winchester. He then spent another dozen or so years in a South African prison following his extradition from Britain.

André Stander himself escaped to the US, where he was finally caught after being stopped by the police in a road check. He presented a forged driving license and this event led to him being recognised as the notorious South African. His apartment was surrounded, but he was not in it at the time. He arrived home on a bicycle during the siege of his home but, unluckily for him, was recognised by an officer on the perimeter of the stake-out before he could sneak away. Stander was fatally shot in a struggle to wrest the gun from the officer and died before the ambulance arrived.

And so ended the Stander Gang's story, an episode that had captured the imagination of the public vividly. I think it's true to say there was a collective sigh of regret at the news he was dead. Bill too had been captivated by the story and had great plans to make a film or even a TV series about Stander. But first he needed sponsors, and before that, a five-minute clip to lure them into negotiations.

The upshot was perhaps one of the most interesting and thrilling periods of my own involvement in Bill's film world, even though the enterprise ultimately generated financial problems for us again.

What Bill needed to do was make a collage of short scenes that would represent the style and character of the eventual feature film. Bill had long been a fan of the producer, Michael Mann, known for the 80s Miami Vice TV series, and he wanted to produce his trailer with the same style and feel that had made the series so popular. Being in the film world and knowing a number of the right people were advantages he capitalised on. With the help of a casting director friend, he managed to recruit some well-known actors in the South African television and film industry to play the parts of André Stander and his gang.

My job prevented me from being closely involved, but at the weekends, the girls and I went along to help out. In my case, that meant acting as general 'gofer'. I arranged the lunches and sandwiches, the coffee on tap and the snacks. I also saw to the general well-being of the crew who were all friendly, professional and incredibly focused.

On one of the shoots, the girls took their knitting. The scene was at a bar in the downtown district of Hillbrow where the Stander gang were discussing their next heist while playing pool. My daughters sat out of the way as much as possible although I think they enjoyed the buzz as well as being part of the whole 'scene'. They were surrounded by gaffers (lighting technicians), sound technicians, boom operators (the people who place the microphones) and grips, (the 'builders' who construct the lighting and build the camera tracks and cranes). It was sometimes exciting, vibrant and bustling, but it could also be very long and tedious; hence the knitting. Somewhere in the family archives, I have a photo of my daughters sitting in the crowded bar with film crew all around them. The incongruity of two school girls with knitting needles and wool in amongst the apparent chaos of a film set in action was a sight to behold. Blasé took on a whole new meaning when demonstrated by my youthful offspring and their apparent insouciance.

Given that scenes would be shot several times over, I could imagine it was mind numbing for the actors. They didn't even have craft hobbies to keep them occupied while waiting for yet another take of a five-second shot to be set up. Still, I suppose anyone who's a seasoned actor is used to it. I enjoyed watching the process, but I was glad I didn't have to stand around and do nothing as much as they did.

Some of the scenes had to be filmed very early in the day to escape interruption from the general public and to avoid having modern 90s vehicles in view. One such shoot involved going to a lonely road near the Tembisa township around six o'clock in the morning. The dawn was grey and chilly, the landscape brown, bare and forbidding. Smoke coiled into the sky from the shacks nearby. A dirty yellow cloud hung over the horizon. It wasn't a vision to inspire good cheer. The crew huddled into their jackets, yawning and stamping their feet. I realised we'd have a mutiny if there was nothing to drink and eat, but we'd forgotten to bring anything.

"There's a tea room back at the junction," I told Bill. "Shall I go there and get something. I think I saw it opening as we came past."

"Great idea," agreed Bill, somewhat relieved he wouldn't have a riot on his hands. Film crew only run effectively on vast quantities of coffee and food. "Will you get some toasted sandwiches too? I'll never get this lot to do anything without it," he laughed. The crew laughed too, but it was a bit forced. Bill had a point.

A tea-room in South Africa was really a small supermarket, the difference being it usually had a few tables and chairs so that customers could buy a drink and something to eat as well. They were standard throughout the country and every village, suburb and neighbourhood usually had one. Most of them baked their own bread and we nearly always bought our fresh loaves and Sunday morning rolls from the local tea-room. They also sold hot pies, sausage rolls and other delicious homemade baked goods. Best of all, they tended to open early so workers who didn't have time for breakfast could grab something nourishing and vaguely healthy while picking up their newspapers, cigarettes and chocolate bars.

I set off back to the junction where I pulled into the pot-holed tarmac in front of the store. Behind the regulation bars that covered the grubby windows, garish posters advertised hot dogs and hot drinks. This was just what we needed. I walked up and pressed the buzzer to open the security gate, a precaution most retail outlets took in these semi-urban areas. Burglaries were part of life and caging themselves in was about the only way the proprietors could prevent robberies.

A few minutes later, I'd made the shop owner's day.

"Are you serving toasted sandwiches yet?" I asked as I approached the sleepy looking man poring over the morning paper spread out on the counter. He looked up slowly, his flat, pudding-faced countenance staring back at me.

"Yes, lady. What can I get you?"

"Can you do six bacon and cheese and six ham and egg please?"

His eyes popped.

"Twelve toasted sandwiches? Are you sure about that, madam?" It was funny how I suddenly earned a promotion in respect.

"Yes, thanks. Actually, add another three with just cheese and tomato," I smiled. "And I'll need twelve coffees to go too, please. I've got a film crew to feed."

"Right, madam, *ja*, sure, no problem, see," he beamed, all signs of sleep vanishing. "You sit over there, and I'll bring you a complimentary coffee, *ja*?" Every syllable of 'complimentary' was enunciated separately.

"Thanks again," I nodded, gratified by what the prospect of a whole morning's takings could do to a person's attitude.

"Ben? Jo?" he shouted through the door behind the counter. "Come on guys, get to work, we've got a big order for toasted sarmies here."

And so the machine went into operation. Ten minutes later, fifteen toasted sandwiches in a box and twelve cups of coffee in another were carried out to the car for me by the delighted proprietor. I thanked him warmly. The free cup of coffee had been good. He beamed again. It wouldn't have surprised me if he'd shut up shop and gone home for the rest of the day. What I'd bought was a good score for a small enterprise on the edge of the township.

Back at the location, the crew fell on the food with a will and it wasn't long before it had all vanished. It was just as well shooting didn't take too long or I'd have been scouting round for more snacks. It never ceased to amaze me how much these people could eat, but it was fun to be involved and when things went pear-shaped later on, I remembered these shoots with affection.

Apart from the Stander project, Bill was working continuously on corporate information and training videos. The money these brought in was good, but even so, we had to put up funds to make the trailer for the film that would bring Bill the recognition he so badly wanted. He agreed with Jim that we would take an extra mortgage on the house. I had a sinking feeling about his decision, but he was convinced it would all be worthwhile. He was earning regularly; I had a good salary; the film was a shoe-in with the cast he had. What could go wrong? Everything, I thought.

The day after I heard about the second mortgage, I was driving to the southern suburbs on firm visits, my destinations being Benoni, Boksburg and Vereeniging. The weather was perfect. The sun was bright in a cloudless sky and the gardens were rich with flowering shrubs, vivid splashes of colour against the gradual browning of the grass.

I visited my clients in Benoni first, a quiet neighbourhood of charming old mining houses with tin roofs, wide verandas and gracious high rooms, most of which had lovely moulded detail on the ceilings. It was a conservative area, but I liked visiting the unassuming partners and staff there; the same applied to Boksburg, albeit a less attractive area.

And then I went to Vereeniging, a town that leans against the banks of the Vaal River. This is the waterway from which the Transvaal of historical fame derived its name. In former times everything across the river was the Transvaal and if not, it was the Northern or Eastern Transvaal; it encompassed a huge area that is now split between Limpopo, North Western Province, Gauteng and Mpumalanga. As things stand now, the Vaal River defines the southern borders of the latter two modern day provinces.

I headed for the road closest to the river and sat watching the water meander past on its lazy route south west, wondering what life was going to hurl at us next. It was beautiful there, quiet and restful and Vereeniging became a special place for me; far enough from the city to be an escape, but also part of my working route. Each time I went there, I would sit for a spell in one of the many parks, or next to the gentle river and relish the solitude. I often think it was prophetic that it meant so much to me as many years later I would buy a barge of the same name: a boat that became my home and another kind of refuge.

As far as the town itself was concerned, I should say that the offices I called on in Vereeniging were nothing remarkable. The accountants who were members of our medical aid were housed in functional office blocks with nothing particular to distinguish them, so this was not the attraction. It was the river first and the parkland second; these places were where I could go to absorb the timeless serenity that only trees and water can give.

Looking at the face of violence

At the beginning of 1993, Jodie started high school. Our Bryanston home was central to a number of schools but we chose the school at Fourways, mainly because it was where the children from Buccleuch naturally went. Jodie had done exceptionally well at Buccleuch but even so, we were surprised to learn that she was the top pupil, the *dux scholae*, of her year. Sadly, I didn't know this until after the final prize-giving evening.

On that date, December the 3rd, 1992, Bill and I had tickets to see Jean Michel Jarre's Legends of the Lost City show at Sun City. It was to be a rare and special performance, so we'd arranged for Bill's mother to come up from her home in Grahamstown to attend Jodie's prize giving on our behalf. Nanny, as she was known, had moved to South Africa about a year previously and was thrilled to act *in loco parentis*. The concert was phenomenal, the setting magical, but I would have given anything to have known about my daughter's success and to have been there when she received her award. There's no doubt which show I'd have attended given the choice.

That disappointment aside, she began going to Fourways in January, the beginning of the South African school year. For the past two years, increasing numbers of black and coloured children had been attending the previously white only schools, but because my daughters had been at school in London before we moved back to South Africa, they were used to multi-cultural environments and for them, it was condition normal. Nevertheless, it was quite a change for the other children.

Fourways had formerly been what was known as a Model C school in that it was partially fee paying and was run by a school board made up of parents and administrators. It was a relatively new school too, only founded in 1988. Jodie enjoyed it and I enjoyed seeing her grow in confidence. She used to cycle on her own in the mornings riding her new and very smart mountain bike from our house to the school, an independence that was another new development in her life.

Meanwhile, Mo was still at Buccleuch and I still drove her there every morning for quite some time. It was a circuitous route, but quite straightforward and it always tickled me that she had no clue where Buccleuch was in relation to home. On one occasion a friend offered to fetch her for me, only to be flummoxed when she asked Mo the way home. "I don't know," said my daughter. "Maybe we can phone my mum and ask her," which is what they did.

The school run started early. Mo had to be at school at 7:30 and I needed to be at work at 8:00. We would leave home around 7:00 and I would generally kiss my child goodbye well before she needed to be there. Then I hit the Concrete Highway and followed it back past Rivonia until I reached the Randburg exit. At this point, the traffic stopped and the tailback into Randburg and Sandton started. It happened every day and I needed to be early to be sure of reaching work on time. As I sat in the traffic at the top of the off ramp, I would watch the informal traders canvassing for business from the waiting cars. There were the usual sellers of sunglasses, sunshades, fruit and flowers, but there were also other small impromptu businesses.

One of these was a welder who kept his gas bottles and welding gear in a shopping trolley along with two small adjustable ramps. I often watched cars pull off the road and onto the sandy verge so they could drive their front wheels onto his ramps for a quick welding job. It reminded me a bit of Formula one pit stop – although not quite as fast, I'll admit. The welder adjusted the ramps, positioned his tools and crawled underneath the car with a fluid ease of someone well practiced in the art. It wasn't unusual for me to see a complete job done in just the time it took me to inch forward to the lights. I liked watching and admired the young African's enterprise.

One morning, though, things went badly wrong. I'd just stopped behind a car at the junction when I saw our welder crossing the road. He was pushing his shopping trolley crammed with his tools and gas bottles. The tarred surface at this point wasn't well maintained and before he could get the wheels up over the curb, he hit a small pothole.

What followed was inevitable. The trolley tipped and his gas bottles slid out and hit the car as they fell. I don't think they did any harm, but it infuriated the driver. He leapt out of his vehicle, ran round the front and began throwing punches at the welder, who fell sprawling over the curb. The man then started kicking him with mounting viciousness.

I was horrified. I couldn't believe what I was seeing and couldn't bear to sit and watch, so I too leapt out of my car. In my feeble attempts to pull the assailant away, I grabbed at his arms, but it made no difference. The poor welder was by now curled up in a foetal position, taking the beating meted out to him.

"Leave him alone!" I screamed. "Get off him!"

I tugged hard at the man's sleeves trying to haul him away from his victim, but he was big and bulky and swearing like a maddened bull. He barely noticed me. So much for my attempts at heroics.

I then tried putting my arms round him middle and pulling, but he just carried on kicking.

"Let him be!" I shouted again. "If you don't, I'll call the cops!"

That seemed to make an impression, but not the one I was expecting The man turned round with an angry snarl, and before I could step back, he smacked me hard on my face, marched to his car and got in. Stunned, I rubbed my cheek as I watched him drive away, screeching his tyres in the process. He stuck a very pointed finger up at me. My anger flared. What a foul, rotten human being. He'd not only been trying to kick the life out of someone who'd done him no harm, he'd then thought it was okay to hit me as well. Unbelievable. I wished I had a phone. I could have made good on my threat.

Ignoring the drivers hooting at me to move off the highway exit, I helped the welder drag his trolley and gas bottles to safety before climbing back behind the wheel and pulling over onto the verge to let the others pass.

I walked over to where he was setting up his ramps. Mercifully, he didn't appear to be hurt.

"Are you going to report that man?" I asked him. "Did you get his registration?"

I'd hoped one of the other traders might have seen the number.

"No, madam." He lowered his eyes, not wanting to look at me.

"Why not?" I was bemused. "He could have injured you really badly."

"No, madam. I'm okay. It's nothing."

I ran back to the car, found a pen and a scrap of paper. I wrote my name and phone number on it. Walking back to him, I handed it over, but I could see he'd already lost interest.

"Here, if you change your mind, call me. I'll back you up with the police," I said, but I knew he wouldn't.

By the time I arrived at work, I was shaking. The anger had given way to shock. Any display of violence is upsetting, but the sheer injustice of the car driver's rage was beyond anything I'd experienced and I found it deeply disturbing.

During the morning, I talked it through with some of my colleagues who were also shocked, but not as much as I was.

"I can't help thinking about how long this kind of treatment has been going on and the bitterness it must have caused." I said to one of my friends.

"That's true, Val, but you know how short people's fuses are at the moment. The political unrest and the violence are getting to everyone. Maybe he just snapped."

"That's no excuse for kicking the living daylights out of the guy. His gas bottles only hit the car's bumper. I doubt if there was even a dent."

"No, it isn't an excuse, but these aren't good times and people aren't acting normally. If you think of all the carjackings and murders, it's not that surprising there's so little tolerance."

"Even so," I said, "the poor guy's just trying to make an honest living. It's so unfair."

She was right, though. Everyone was stressed without even being aware of it. I didn't know if such aggressive behaviour from individuals was all that widespread, but it must have occurred frequently enough to prompt the resigned look in the welder's eyes – as well as the knowledge that complaining would get him nowhere. I was also aware no one had come to support me either; another sobering thought. It was an incident that has remained with me ever since.

After taking Mo to school the next day, I followed my normal route to work and noticed the welder wasn't at his usual spot. Nor was he there the following day. As a matter of fact, I didn't see him at the off ramp again, which was sad; I'd enjoyed watching his and his fellow labourers' activities. However, a couple of months later I had to go to the Builders' merchants and saw him at the crossroads next to the store, working away at welding the underside of a minibus taxi. I recognised him from the shopping trolley and the ramps, and a weight lifted from my mind. He was all right, and that was good.

On the subject of tension and violence, 1993 was no better than the previous years had been. The most active aggressors at this time were the Azanian People's Liberation Army, the APLA, whose main targets were white civilians. Their belief was that there was no place in the new South Africa for European people at all since they'd invented apartheid. During the year, the APLA claimed responsibility for four attacks on civilians in different parts of the country in which altogether 23 people were killed and a further 50 were injured, the latter being during an attack on a church congregation in Cape Town. They also killed four police officers in Soweto. Such killings were bound to increase the fear and insecurity. In addition, there were further clashes between the ANC and Inkatha and early in the year, Chris Hani, the leader of the South African Communist Party was assassinated. Not a good year.

It was around this time that we also started worrying about what my friend referred to as carjackings but which were more generally known as hijackings. It was quite a new phenomenon but it was to become a scourge in later years. We heard reports of people being held up in their cars, being forced to hand over the keys and any valuables, and then being taken elsewhere and dumped, sometimes alive, but often dead. It was an alarming trend and we all made sure we drove with our doors locked and windows closed, particularly in urban areas. We didn't stop unless we had to and drove from one place to another with our eyes peeled, careful to avoid places where hijackers could conceal themselves.

Coming from the heartlands of rural Natal where we rarely locked anything, such vigilance was hard to maintain and added to our unconscious stress levels. But we got used to it; we adjusted and adapted. It was just another aspect of the emerging new South Africa; it was also part of urban life, but it never made us feel we should leave.

On one occasion, though, Bill shook me with his gung-ho attitude to the deteriorating situation. We were going home late after visiting friends in town and we were heading north along Louis Botha Avenue, one of the main arterial routes out of the city. As is typical of Johannesburg's old main roads, Louis Botha is a wide, dual carriageway lined with a variety of retail outlets, interspersed with old tin-roofed homes and low-rise flats. It's always been slightly scruffy, an impression emphasised by the numerous garish hoardings and billboards on the shop and building fronts. In any event, it was dark on this particular evening, and we were approaching some red lights. As we slowed down, a minibus taxi roared up, overtook us and screeched to a halt in front of us, forcing Bill into an emergency stop. He was livid. Outraged, in fact. His Scots temper flared and he yanked the car door open.

"Bill, just leave it," I begged. "We're all right!"

But I might as well have told a bull my red rag was blue.

Then I realised with horror we were right next to the notorious Alexandra Township, or Alex as it was better known. If our taxi driver had friends nearby we were done for. It had a bad name as a hotbed of crime and murder.

But Bill was already at the minibus door trying to pull it open and have the driver out for a full on fisticuffs in the street. He was hopping up and down with fury and hammering on the door. It would have been comical if it hadn't been so frightening.

"Get out, you fat, arrogant, worthless scumbag," he yelled, yanking at the door. "You're just a pathetic, snivelling, lowlife coward! Think you're so clever, do you? Get out and meet me like a man, you skellum!"

Oh come on Bill, I thought. Don't be ridiculous. In spite of myself, I laughed, one of those tremulous, bordering-on-hysteria types of laugh. Trust Bill to challenge the man's masculine pride. How could he know the size of his girth anyway? But I was also watching the side streets closely just in case. This could get serious, and when my fuming other half started kicking at the taxi's door, I began feeling sick with anxiety.

Thankfully, the driver must have locked himself in tight on seeing the small raging dervish spitting all types of fury at him. Bill could be terrifying in a temper and he was in a big one this time. I could only hope the object of his wrath was as worried as I was.

Seconds later, the lights turned green, the taxi driver floored the accelerator and shot off, almost dragging Bill, who hadn't let go of the door, with him. As the minibus roared away, Bill hurled abuse at its rapidly departing rear. A hundred metres further on, it turned right and headed into the depth of the township. I couldn't hear what Bill was yelling into the darkness, but I had no doubt it was peppered with colourful expletives.

He got back in the car with a truculent look on his face.

"I'm going after him," he said.

"No," I cut in. "No, you're not! And don't you ever, ever do that again. Do you know where we are?"

"Sure I do."

"You mean you know we're right next to Alex?" I asked, incredulous.

"Oh, err, no. Are we?"

"We are. And that was totally and utterly irresponsible of you. Do you have any idea of the danger you put us in by blowing off like that? You're just a loose cannon, you are. No sense and no control! What if he's now gone to collect his mates and comes after us? What are we going to do then?"

Relief made me angry, and it was my turn now.

"You can get yourself killed if you want, but don't put me at risk too."

Bill didn't answer, but he didn't argue either. We drove silently home. As quickly as possible.

Alexandra's reputation for violence was underscored by the tales we heard from Bill's driver, Andries. He'd replaced Nicky who'd remained with the first film company Bill worked with. Tall, bespectacled and mild, Andries was a dear soul. He had a gentle, academic air and we were all fond of him. He often collected the girls from school if it was raining or Bill couldn't, and he'd take them to the nearest tea-room to buy fresh baked bread, ostensibly for himself. By the time they reached home, half the bread was usually gone. It was so delicious none of them could resist tearing lumps off the end, and chewing on the soft, warm hunks. Andries was as guilty as the girls; it was a bond between the three of them.

His affection for my children was heart-warming and I imagined his own children loved him even more. He lived with his wife and three little ones in Alex in a small cement block home. Since Andries always arrived at work clean and neatly dressed, I expect his home was much the same. Nonetheless, most of Alex was shabby, scruffy and wretched. Tensions ran high, crime was rife and the political or partisan divisions were frequently played out in the streets with guns.

One morning, Andries turned up looking unkempt, exhausted and worried.

"What's up, Andries? You look knackered," my husband said, to the point as always.

"Ah, boss, I have a bad night, very bad. Me, my wife and children, we all sleep on the floor in our house."

"Oh? Why was that?"

"There is a lot of shooting in Alex. Bullets, they come through the window, break the glass, break our china. We lie under the table, but we get no sleep."

"That's terrible, Andries. Really sorry, man," Bill said, putting an arm round Andries' shoulder. "Tell, you what, if you need to be at home to sort things out, just go."

"Thank you, boss." Andries put his hands together and made a small bow.

I saw Bill slip him some money.

"Get your windows fixed, and don't come back until you feel it's safe to do so. We'll manage."

Andries climbed gratefully into his old Ford Escort and drove away. This was the most terrifying incident he had to live through, but he told us of others. Pitched battles in the streets, murders, shootings, all of it horrific. It must have been a kind of hell to raise a family in such an unstable environment, with the fear of violence a constant undercurrent in their lives.

But Andries and his family survived and he remained working for Bill until 1995. It was only when Bill could no longer afford to keep him on that he found another driving job, which was probably a relief to them both. They'd been too loyal to each other to end the working relationship even though Andries could have been earning much more elsewhere and Bill was battling to pay him. The eventual parting was sad; Andries was the only employee Bill had that he really trusted and the affection was mutual.

One other occasion served as a reminder of how volatile the situation could be, and this time it happened right next to our home in Bryanston. It was a sunny weekend afternoon and we were doing normal chores when there was a knock on the garden door. Bill went to open it and since I was close by, I heard the conversation that ensued.

The caller was an African man.

"Hello, sir," he greeted Bill. His 'sir' sounded more like *sair*. "Sorry to trouble you, sir, but may I use your telephone."

"You can," Bill answered, "but will you tell me why?"

"I need to call the police, sir," came the response.

"The police? What for? Can I help?"

"No, sir, it is for my wife."

"Your wife? What's wrong with your wife?"

"She is dead, sir. I kill her."

"You what?"

"Yes, sir, I kill her. I get angry and I hit her with an axe."

"Oh no."

"Yes, sir. And the axe, sir. It is still in her head."

Bill turned and looked at me, disbelief and horror in his eyes. I was equally dumbstruck, but somehow we managed to communicate mutely and agree that he could use the phone.

Bill stayed with him while he made the call and then our murderer left, thanking us politely and returning to where his wife lay until the police arrived.

From the direction he took it was evident this incident had occurred where we regularly walked the dogs. At the side of the complex a track ran down to a stream, alongside which was a pleasant grassy stretch lined with trees and a profusion of flowering shrubs that spilled over the back walls of the complex. We went there almost daily to give Polly and Daisy a run, but it was a few days before we could face going again. The image of what must have been a gruesome death unnerved us and we chose other paths until we felt sure there would be nothing to see. What happened to the man we never knew, but from his behaviour we felt sure he would accept whatever fate deemed fit to bestow on him.

The effect the proximity such a shocking event had on us was to make us aware that there was a limit to negotiation possibilities in South Africa. At any point, reason could swiftly be replaced by explosive anger that could destroy every effort at compromise. Subsequent to his release from prison, Nelson Mandela had been striving to reconcile the different parties involved in the political process. His message was firm in that all races needed to participate in free and fair elections, and he inspired a spirit of cooperation, not conflict. He knew full well that when the elections were ultimately held in 1994, he was certain to become president and his actions, speeches and stature generated confidence.

Even so, culture and cultural behaviour cannot change overnight. Our axe-murdering visitor brought this home to us quite forcibly: he was a pleasant and polite man who minutes before arriving at our door had cleaved his wife's head in a fit of anger. I loved the African sense of humour, the wit, the sheer unrestrained ability to enjoy company and conversation, but that very lack of restraint could flip so swiftly to violent anger. It was cause for caution at the very least.

Leisure time at home and away

By the end of 1993, Bryanston had become more of a home than either of our previous two houses. We all cherished its old-world style, its African farmstead atmosphere and its calm space. I had my sewing room where I made clothes, curtains and covers for numerous cushions. It felt such luxury to have this small area to myself. Fitted with a mushroom coloured carpet, it had a cupboard for my materials, an armchair and a table for my sewing machine; it was all I needed.

The casement window looked out on the garden and the sun slanted through the jacaranda tree, relieving me of some of its heat but brightening the floor with pools of light. It felt almost sinful to have such a cosy corner all to myself. Not that I was always alone. The girls would come and sit with me while I sewed, chattering, giggling and telling jokes. A favourite pastime was to talk in foreign accents and they had me at it too. The sillier and more ridiculous we sounded, the more we laughed.

During this time, I'd also started cycling to work, leaving the school run to Bill and Andries. My fondness for my bike had been steadily growing. I was having thoughts of doing the gruelling annual Argus cycle tour, a 105-kilometre race sponsored by Cape Town's Argus newspaper which took place in the Cape peninsula in March every year, so I needed to improve my strength and endurance.

The run to work in Randburg was only about eight kilometres, but it had some fairly serious hills, so it was a good start. I was terrified at first. The traffic zooming past me was fast, dense and not all that considerate of the lone cyclist. There were many occasions when I dived into the bank to avoid being side-swiped by someone's wing mirrors.

Minibus taxis were the worst as they would swerve into the emergency lane and screech to a halt to offload passengers. I lost count of the number of times I nearly hurtled into the back of them. The scorch marks on the road and the smell of burning break rubber were all too familiar.

Eventually, I learned to trust myself and hold my own, but it took much longer to gain a respectable speed. I was mortified one day when, puffing and sweating up the hill to Bryanston on my way home, I was overtaken by an ancient African man on an equally ancient delivery bike with no gears. He drifted past me effortlessly, bidding me a cheery 'good afternoon' as he sped away. He was eating an apple, just to add insult to injury; these days, he'd have been texting for sure. The point was that I had twelve gears and I was struggling. My confidence plummeted. I kept at it though, enjoying the challenge as well as the ribbing I received from a growing number of my friends at work.

I also started jogging gently round the block when taking the dogs for a walk, a new hobby that led to my participation in the odd fun run and company relay race, but this didn't become serious until later.

Another call on my time was acting as chauffeur for the girls' social sprees. They had gathered more friends around them and I often found myself taking them to parties in suburbs I didn't know; a wonderful opportunity for getting lost, but we got there in the end.

Tim was still resident above the carport. He spent his time listening to increasingly desperate music by Nirvana and other such bands, which drove his father mad – although that could well have been why he listened to it. Tim's relationship with his dad was like that of many teenage boys and their paternal parent: turbulent.

The end of year summer holiday was the only time we went away together as a complete family with Tim included. No border crossings this time, though. We decided to do a long triangular road trip firstly to Grahamstown to spend Christmas with Bill's mother and then to follow the coast west along the famous Garden Route to Cape Town. The final stretch would be the direct route back to Johannesburg. The round trip was about 3500 kilometres, but since we added in a couple of extra diversions, the reality was closer to 4500 kilometres by the time we'd finished. The distances were always impressive when tallied up.

Our transport was interesting to say the least. Bill had bought himself a 1970s BMW motorbike, which was his therapy when life was stressful. He spent hours tinkering, cleaning, polishing and fixing the bike. It gleamed under his meditative attention. We'd done a few breakfast runs out to the gorgeous Hartebeestpoort Dam north of Pretoria where the mountain roads of the Magaliesberg range gave bikers a chance to 'stretch' their wheels, but we'd never done a long run with it, so Bill decided he and Tim would travel on the bike, while the girls, the dogs and I would follow up in my Fiat Uno. We also took our mountain bikes with us on a special roof rack made for the purpose. This was our convoy and as usual, the car was crammed with camping gear.

The trip to Grahamstown was uneventful except for one stop we made in the Free State. We drove out of Joburg on a bright sunny morning and headed south on the N1 highway. Once away from the city outskirts and suburbs, signs of habitation started falling away. The road beyond Vereeniging and Vanderbijkpark opened up to the great Free State plains and we drove for what seemed like endless kilometres across bare farmland with only the occasional small copse of trees indicating a house was nestled amongst them.

The sky was a steely blue and it was easy to understand what people meant when they said 'in the Free State, you can lie on your stomach and see into next week.' The landscape is not palette board flat, but it is empty: largely bare of trees, outcrops and any other hindrances to the eye. With its rolling undulations, the traveller can rise to a crest and see forever. It is magnificent, vast, remote and slightly forbidding. And dry. The grass was blonde rather than green. About 400 kilometres from home, we reached the provincial capital, Bloemfontein, but we didn't stop there, not this time. Instead, we travelled another 120 kilometres before we decided we needed some petrol. My Uno could do hundreds of kilometres on a tank, but the BMW bike needed to fill up quite regularly, so we pulled off the N1, and drove into Trompsburg, a small town by anyone's standards, although smaller in other ways we hadn't anticipated.

We found the filling station on the way in. Stopping to see if we could serve ourselves, we noticed it only had old-fashioned manual pumps, and there was no one there to help us. This was when we noticed it was lunchtime. Anxious, we drove further into the town to see if there was anything else. The streets were surfaced with sand, every house had its own windmill and there were no power lines. All this could only mean one thing. There was no electricity and probably no mains water; in other words, no modern conveniences of any sort.

They must have had boreholes and generators – if they were rich enough – and gas. It was like a film set for a western, a town held in the grip of a time warp. The attractive old houses looked bleached and faded, their tin roofs rusting. Some of the inhabitants were sitting on their front steps. They stared at us as we passed. It was distinctly creepy. I had a 'get me out of here' moment and was intensely relieved when Bill turned the bike around.

"Let's head back to the filling station. We can wait there until it's open," he called.

"Good idea!" I nodded eagerly. "It's nearly two o'clock. There'll surely be someone there soon."

And so I followed him back the way we'd come, happy to pull into the filling station forecourt.

"What did you think of it back there?" Bill asked as I got out of the car.

The heat, the atmosphere, the disconnectedness of the town, the vacant looks in the people's eyes; that was what I felt and saw. I didn't know what I thought.

"A bit weird," I answered cautiously. "Did you see all the windmills?"

"Yeah," Tim cut in, "and those people too," he giggled. "They were something else. Like Deliverance, the movie."

"Maybe it was just the heat," I said, "and maybe it's because we're obviously strangers, but yes. It was all a bit odd, I agree."

At that moment a couple of old cars drove onto the forecourt followed by a big, battered Dodge pickup, just to complete the movie scene. A young man leapt from the Dodge and walked over to us and nodded.

"*Goeie middag.* Good afternoon. Petrol?"

"*Ja. Dankie.*" Bill answered.

"Fill them both up?" He gestured to the Uno as well.

"Thanks."

We watched while he pumped for all he was worth till the bike was full and then he started on my car.

"That must keep you fit," Bill laughed.

"*Ja, boet.* Now and then I change arms, you know, else I'd end up like Mr Universe on one side, and Mr Punyverse on the other," he grinned, proud of his English pun. As Afrikaans as they come, he probably learnt his English from travellers like us. We all laughed as required, but I expect he'd entertained many another English-speaking driver with the same joke. I couldn't help noticing it sounded well-rehearsed.

As we drove towards the highway, I was glad to be on the way again, but I thought of Trompsburg many times over the years. In some ways, I would like to believe it remained the same. Technology and progress aren't always accompanied by wellbeing and happiness. But I hope for its residents it has grown and developed. It couldn't have been easy living in such an arid area with only boreholes for water. We'd been fortunate all those years before on the farm in Natal. We'd had the dams to fall back on during the drought, but these people could only have relied on the water table below ground, and if that fell, life would have been tough.

Back on the road south, the landscape glistened with the harsh beauty of the great Karoo: eternal horizons, occasionally broken by jagged outcrops of rock; scrubby sparse yellow grass growing in clumps among the red earth; vague outlines of mountains in a hazy distance; and peace. The peace was almost tangible.

Stopping by the roadside to give Tim a rest, we marvelled at the silence, its all-encompassing stillness punctuated only by the call of a bird far above us, or the whoosh of a passing car. But then came other sounds. Small, scattered flocks of sheep nibbled constantly, chewing the last vestiges of goodness out of the ground. The solitary windmill, a tall steel tripod with a rusty many-bladed wheel on top, whirred and creaked in the heat. We stood and listened, gazing at the barbed wire fences with their cracked wooden posts marching overland in ever diminishing steps.

Another 120 kilometres further, we stopped again at Colesberg for some refreshments and a petrol top up. At that time, there were fuel and food service stations on the N1 at fairly regular 250-kilometre intervals and on earlier trips to see Bill's mother, we'd stopped at them as a routine; it forced us to take a rest, stretch our legs and swap driving places, but this time, there was no relief for either Bill or me as drivers, so our stops became more frequent. Another consideration was that Tim was finding pillion riding quite tough. He'd never travelled far on a bike, so this was a baptism of some burning, if not exactly fire, especially where his rear end was concerned.

From Colesberg, which was a bit more than halfway to Grahamstown, we left the N1 and cracked on across country. There were few places to stop on this stretch, but we managed to find fuel in Cradock and Adelaide, luckily with normal modern petrol pumps.

Amenities aside, I had to wonder what people did in these quiet country towns. Beyond a few shops and a modest town hall, there appeared to be nothing to offer employment to the residents of the houses lining the streets. Being in the middle of nowhere began to have real significance.

We were moving into the Eastern Cape and the terrain changed from flat open plains to hilly, arid, semi-bush. It was even more remote and even had we possessed cell phones, they wouldn't have been any use. There was no signal between Colesberg and Grahamstown, a situation that not even ten years more development changed. In 2001, I did the same trip and was still unable to make contact with the world throughout this section of the journey.

It was a very long drive. The heat was intense and we kept the windows open for the dogs – for us too if I'm honest. I had air conditioning in my Uno, but it added to the fuel consumption and slowed us down. As far as possible, I tried not to use it.

The girls were patient as only children who've grown up with such huge distances can be. They roped me in to playing 'I spy' with them and other guessing games to while away the time.

"I spy with my little eye something beginning with T," Mo started.

"Telegraph pole?"

"No."

"Tortoise?"

"No."

"Tree."

"Yes!"

"No way," scoffed Jodie. "There aren't any trees out here."

"Yes there are. I saw one. Back there," Mo said, defending herself vigorously.

It was telling that Jodie thought seeing a tortoise was more likely than spotting a tree, maybe a little bizarre too. Of course, there were some trees, but they were rare in this beautiful, barren landscape. And as chance would have it, we'd seen a tortoise crossing the road only an hour or so before and we'd stopped to urge it out of the road. It was large, labouring and somewhat stubborn, resisting all our attempts to steer it to safety in a fit of tortoisy pique. But we were determined it should obey mainly because we were afraid other drivers wouldn't see it in time. While the tortoise was in danger itself, it was also a safety hazard to other vehicles. We were delighted and very excited to see it, though. It seemed like a great privilege to have encountered one in the wild.

Live entertainment apart, there were no video or computer games then. The only other option was to read, which both girls did. Polly and Daisy too were incredibly patient, but like most dogs, all they cared about was being with us. As for Claude, we'd left him at home in Andries' care. By this time, he was old, blind and more than a little incontinent. It would have been unkind to subject him to such a long journey.

Eventually, we wound our way down into Grahamstown. It had taken us a full day: eleven hours of driving to complete 1000 kilometres. It was a long haul to do in one stretch, but we'd become accustomed to distances such as these. When we summed it all up, we could say quite truthfully that the roads were good, there was little traffic and the scenery was awe-inspiring. All in all, it wasn't so hard.

Grahamstown was a South African gem; it was also an educational centre of repute with its highly respected Rhodes University and several nationally renowned schools. There was much of the English country town about it, but it had its colonial influences too in the porticoed pavements of its streets and the wide verandas of its older homes. The town hosted a major arts festival every year which drew artists, academics and literary types from all over the country, many of whom lived in the area too.

The fact that Bill's mother chose to make Grahamstown her home also encouraged her daughter and son-in-law to move there with their children, so we had a proper family to visit. Christmas was therefore familial and enjoyable for young and old alike. At least that's how it appeared, but I may be spreading my rose tint around in hindsight.

We explored the area and visited East London, Port Alfred and Kenton-on-Sea. The latter two boasted fabulous beaches of such breadth the dusky yellow sands seemed to stretch beyond the horizon. The Kowie River flowed quietly out into the Indian Ocean at Port Alfred, ideal for the adventurous to canoe inland up deep gorges lined with dark, dense bush. While the sun soaked our limbs with its warmth and the salty sea air whipped through our hair, we revelled in the South African summer. The girls cycled, the dogs pounced at the waves and the rest of us watched the girls cycling and the dogs pouncing. All good fun and very relaxing.

After fond farewells to the cousins, aunts, in-laws, in-laws' offspring's friends and the inimitable Nanny, we packed up the Uno, loaded down the BMW and headed west, firstly to Port Elizabeth, a city that was just a stop-over and earmarked for a later visit. Next, we made a diversion to hot and historic Uitenhage where we met some impressive but unimpressed ostriches on a farm, and then we resumed our journey along the famous Garden Route to Cape Town.

We also stopped at the Tsitsikamma National Park, but only to gaze in awe at the famous Storms River Bridge, a 77-metre suspension bridge that crosses the deep Storms River gorge at its mouth. Not being fond of heights, I didn't look down too long but the outlook was phenomenal. I would have loved to spend more time there. The forest is dense and wild but it's possible to have guided walks, something I would have relished. Having two dogs and a family to keep amused curtailed my dreams on this occasion, and we travelled on along the tree-lined roads to the pretty towns of Knysna and George.

The scenery was lovely and we hugged the coast as far as Mossel Bay so as to make the most of it. With the ocean to our left and the mountains of the Swartberg ranges to our right, the views were frequently breathtaking. It's no wonder that the Garden Route is so often ranked among the most beautiful drives on earth.

The N2 highway we followed is the longest in South Africa and follows the general outline of the country from Cape Town to St Lucia in northern KwaZulu Natal before turning inland to Ermelo. Apparently, it is also one of the most dangerous roads in the world. I don't know when it gained this reputation, but we were certainly aware of the hazards as we proceeded westwards from Grahamstown. The number of broken-down trucks, overturned mini-buses and crashed cars made driving a nerve-wracking and exhausting business at times, especially when travellers from the afflicted vehicles milled around at the edge of the road, their belongings scattered across both lanes.

As the follower in our mini-convoy, I watched carefully as Bill steered the bike through the debris of one such calamity.

"Mum, why have those people left all their stuff on the road?" chirped a voice from the back.

"Because they've had an accident, sweetie. See that minibus on its side there? I suppose there was luggage and stuff on the roof rack and it's all fallen off. I'll just have to drive round it but I need to wait for a gap in the traffic."

"Look, Mum! There's a big bus down the bank there too!"

"Oh dear, is there? I hope there's no one hurt," I said, keeping my eyes firmly on the road. I didn't want us to join the statistics.

"I don't think so. There are lots of people walking around it. I can't see any bodies."

I was a little taken aback at my child's prosaic attitude, but thanked everything that there were no fatalities this time. Had there been any bodies, as she put it, it would have been infinitely more disturbing.

South African roads were mostly very good, but the vehicles on them often weren't. The number of rusting bus and lorry shells resting in the valleys was testament to the frequency of serious accidents that took place all over the country. What often made things more dangerous was that buses not only pulled huge trailers behind them, they also sported end-to-end roof racks that were usually overloaded. With the speed at which they travelled, the trailers were prone to jack-knifing and then it was an 'everything all fall down' situation. The resulting chaos usually caused still more accidents.

On this part of our trip we were camping, and on the second night after leaving Grahamstown we ran out of luck in finding a campsite. Every place we tried on the road past Knysna and George was full; it was that or they wouldn't accept the dogs. As the light faded from the sky, we no longer noticed the stunning scenery we were passing through. Anxiety replaced delight and we considered smuggling the dogs in anywhere we could find under cover of darkness.

Even the usual jokes about being dog tired and having a black dog day (Daisy was a very black Labrador) didn't help and I could imagine Tim was feeling particularly saddle sore. Eventually, long after darkness had fallen, we managed to find a campsite whose managers reluctantly let us pitch our tents as long as we promised to keep our furry friends under control.

That was never going to be difficult with Daisy, unless of course she scented snacks anywhere in the vicinity. Polly, on the other hand, had to be kept under constant surveillance. Both diligence and vigilance were needed. One glimpse of any creature that gathered in numbers of more than two (and that included humans) required herding as far as she was concerned and she was ever watchful for an opportunity to exercise her 'gathering' skills. If there were rabbits, that was bad enough, but given the possibility of buck, *dassies* and a variety of other African night wildlife, a short rein was essential. We put them to bed in the car overnight.

The following morning, we started out again with our goal set on reaching Cape Town. We'd been aiming for South Africa's Mother city since we left home and we were finally in sniffing distance of reaching it. There was one stop we had to make on the way, though, and this was to fulfil our mission to look for whales.

We knew the coastal town of Hermanus was well known for whale sightings and it was there that we made for, hoping we'd be in luck. It was a cloudy, cool day when we pulled into the parking area at Hermanus beach.

To our great delight, we didn't have long to wait and were thrilled to be granted a glimpse of two Southern Right whales out in the bay. We only just spotted them, but the sight of their huge bodies surging and rolling through the water was part of the real wow factor of the trip. I don't know what it is about seeing whales and dolphins; I always feel privileged to witness their displays. It made a profound impression on all of us then. Satisfied and smiling, we continued on towards Cape Town.

Cape Town has a number of satellite towns, one of which is a place called Kommetjie, which translates as 'small bay'. It was here that we decided to pitch camp at a site that mostly consisted of long-term mobile homes but also had space for holiday campers. There was something mildly eccentric about the whole place. Many of the caravans had awnings, small gardens and a variety of ornamental features. One had gnomes; another had a small fence around it enclosing a tiny garden crammed with plants. It also had an even tinier lawn, for which the owner had a huge lawnmower that would have been fit to care for the whole campsite and probably the whole neighbourhood too. We liked the informal atmosphere, and even more, we liked the path straight down to the small stony beach. Well, the dogs did.

As on previous camping trips, the girls had their own tents and now Tim had his too. The added fun this time was for the canine crew. Waggling in and out of tents was huge entertainment, although Jodie didn't think so for long. Both girls had brought their favourite toys with them, and we were all electrified when out of the blue, Jodie's clear voice issued from her tent: "Daisy, no! Leave my pussy alone!"

Tim's eyes nearly sprang out of their sockets and Bill looked momentarily horrified until they realised she was talking about a fluffy white toy cat. They hooted with laughter, much to Jodie's disgust and Daisy was henceforth banned from her tent.

We spent the next few days exploring Cape Town and its environs. We did it all: the city centre, the wine estates, the new Victoria &Albert Waterfront (a renovated dockside shopping and restaurant complex) and a trip around the bay to see the seals for which the harbour is famous. Polly was overcome with excitement in the boat. She stood on the bench seat at the side with her front paws on the rim, neck stretched out and her glossy coat blowing in the breeze. She yapped. A lot.

Seals lay everywhere: on old tyres hanging on the harbour walls, on rocks, on quays. Like overweight mermaids, they rolled, lazed and lolled in the sunshine, their heavy bodies lumbering with the tired effort of being out of the water. But as soon as they slid off their perches and into the harbour, they assumed a fluid grace that was a joy to watch.

Then there was Table Mountain. To our pleasure, its cloudy tablecloth was absent the morning we decided to walk to the top. It was a lovely clear day and we wound our way up the path through the *fynbos* (fine bush), the heather-like, incredibly varied fauna that is unique to the Cape. The scents were subtle, the flowers multi-coloured and varying substantially in size shape and hue; it was beautiful. At the top, we walked and gazed and walked some more. The dogs snuffled busily, excited by all the new smells, among which were rabbits just to add that extra *soupçon* of canine delight.

The view is worth every step to reach it. Looking out over Cape Town spread below and then to Signal Hill and Table Bay is simply phenomenal. I cannot imagine there is any more uplifting a panorama anywhere. From our lonely heights (surprisingly, there weren't many people there on that day), the city below appeared to glow with reflected sunlight while the sea beyond was a mass of glinting sapphires. I have been there many times since and my impression has never changed. It is not only the Mother City of South Africa, but also the loveliest.

To descend, we took the cable car. Not my idea, I should add. We climbed in with some other passengers who looked as nervous as I was. In truth, I wasn't at all keen on setting my trust in a small cubicle suspended on what looked to be absurdly thin lines that would hurtle us down the mountain. As I saw it, there was nothing between us and total destruction except a few inadequate looking pulleys. So when Jodie piped up: "Did you see that movie where the cables broke?" I don't think I was imagining it when I say everyone in the cable car stopped breathing. Life more or less went on hold until we reached the bottom when normal inhalation was resumed.

"Thank you for that, Jodie," Bill said through gritted teeth.

"Why? What did I say?" she asked, all innocence.

Everyone explained at once.

Each evening of our city sojourn we headed back to our campsite in Kommetjie, and it was good to be there. The tranquillity it offered after the hectic activity of the day, the ability to walk down to its small stony beach and watch the sun setting over the ocean, the quiet murmurs of the campsite residents as they, and we, prepared the evening meal, all this made the holiday more relaxed. Kommetjie was a quiet corner of peace and we loved it. But eventually it was time to pack up and head home.

The road north was the N1 we'd left at Colesberg on the way to Grahamstown. The second longest highway after the coast road, the N1 runs from the Zimbabwean border to the heart of Cape Town, almost 2000 kilometres in total. In 1993 most of the distance was just a two-track road with an emergency lane on each side, but there were stretches where a third lane was added to facilitate overtaking on hills when slow trucks and buses would otherwise hold everything up.

What often happened as well was that on the two-track sections, slower vehicles almost always pulled into the emergency lane, indicators flashing, to encourage us to overtake. It was a courtesy that seemed to have become a habit, as was the customary flash of lights to thank the slower driver. I liked it. It showed a consideration by road users that crossed all barriers and divides.

From the depth of the Western Cape, we wound our way up through the mountains towards the Great Escarpment. The drive was jaw-dropping in its beauty, especially between Paarl and Matjiesfontein. The mountains were wilder and the scenery more barren than the Garden Route. They reminded me strongly of Scotland, but on a grander scale in both size and temperature, the latter being almost off the scale.

We stopped at Worcester for a leg break. Far from the metropolitan rush, the town was quiet; almost hushed. Wrapped in the intense forty-degree heat of the summer afternoon, we tiptoed round the streets of Cape Dutch houses and whiter than white buildings. Its setting against the backdrop of the dramatic, craggy mountains gave it an atmosphere of gracious charm and genteel civilisation. Worcester was definitely taking an afternoon nap when we arrived. And why not? It was far too hot for anything more taxing than desultory conversation over mint tea.

Up on the great plateau of the Karoo, Matjiesfontein was even more of an old-world jewel. In this unique one-street village, palm trees graced the gardens of houses decorated with fine wrought-iron work on windows, gates and verandas. Originally established as a railway station on the line from Cape Town to Kimberley's diamond mines, Matjiesfontein developed into a settlement thanks to James Douglas Logan, superintendent of this particular stretch of railway.

Afflicted with a weak chest, he found the clear Karoo air beneficial to his health, so he bought himself some land near the station and moved there. Having done so, he started a business selling refreshments, which proved so successful a community grew up around it. The village maintained the integrity of its Victorian colonial style into the 20th century and in 1975, it became a national monument with the station and cemetery following suit in subsequent decades.

Matjiesfontein marked our farewell to the Cape. We were all sad to be leaving and heading home. It felt as if we'd been abroad, to another country altogether, and even the people had been different. Oddly, despite its history and connections with the British Empire, most of the inhabitants of the Western Cape were Afrikaans speaking, as many of the town and village names confirmed.

The population too was not what we were used to. Our neighbours in Natal were predominantly Zulu. In Johannesburg, there were mostly Tswana, Venda or Shangaan people. The majority population in the Cape, however, was the result of a melting pot mix of Khoisan, Bantu, European and Asian peoples. They used the term Cape Coloured to distinguish themselves until relatively recently. I'm not sure what the correct term is these days, but it has probably changed along with general perceptions of what is politically correct.

Physically, Cape people tended to be small, fine featured and light skinned reflecting the dominant ethnic background of the Khoisan and Asian mix. For us, it was a bit like travelling from the Netherlands to Spain (and about as far); from tall and robust to tiny and delicate.

I felt it was a pity we didn't meet many locals while we were on holiday. This time we were too busy being tourists and sightseeing in the city, a type of travel that didn't lend itself to exploring villages or seeking contact.

Like Johannesburg, Cape Town was too big, too cosmopolitan and too urban for the intimacy of making instant acquaintances. It had both affluence and poverty, grace and squalor; the extremes of both stood out, something I never felt at ease with. That said, of all the cities I have visited in my life, it remains the diamond.

The rest of our return journey was much as it had been on the way down and we crossed the Karoo with a feeling of familiarity. It is a harsh, unforgiving region, but it is the South Africa I always think of when I have fits of yearning and nostalgia about the land I have left. The image of that endless parched landscape gives rise to the strongest of emotions.

Soon after our arrival home, we noticed Polly was listless. She was off her food and seemed to have no energy. Worried she'd picked up a parasite or tick fever from the *fynbos*, we took her to the vet, who examined her thoroughly.

"Well," he said. "I'm a bit mystified. I can't find anything wrong with her. Her temperature's fine, her glands are normal, there's no sign of anaemia or biliary."

"There must be something. She's not eating and she's just been lying around sleeping all the time since we got back," Bill persisted.

"Oh? Got back from where? Have you been away? Did you take the dogs with you?"

Bill told the vet about our holiday, where we'd been and what we'd done.

"Polly was fine until we got home," he said. "She was having a great time. You should have seen her in Cape Town. Seal watching, climbing Table Mountain, going in the cable car. She loved it all."

The vet looked at Bill thoughtfully.

"Well, there's nothing physically wrong with her, so there's only one thing I can suggest,"

"What's that?"

"I think she's got post-holiday depression."

"Huh?"

"Yes, that's the only thing I can think of. She's been over stimulated and now she's got the blues."

Bill shook his head, laughing, but the vet was probably right. A few days later, Polly recovered her spirits and came back to life. She'd got over her dip and found her equilibrium again. We were naturally bemused but Bill was never one to waste the reward of a good laugh. The tale of our Collie's depression kept him going in party stories for the next few months and probably longer.

Changes both national and local

Back in Johannesburg, 1994 was upon us and what a momentous year it would turn out to be. Two events marked it for us: the first was the election of Nelson Mandela to the presidency of South Africa on April the 27th; the second was the realisation that our gamble on the Stander film hadn't paid off.

In the early months of the year, the political machine moved haltingly towards the first national elections that would include all races. Given the diversity of the people, country and terrain, it was a huge undertaking. Polling stations had to be established in remote areas and townships; observers were needed to ensure that polling was fair and that everyone voting was registered. For us, the easing of the process made it possible for everyone with permanent residence to take part. That meant Bill and I could vote too. We weren't South African citizens yet, but given our long-term establishment in the country, we would be entitled to make our choice alongside every other South African. We were thrilled. I was in my late thirties, but this would be the first time I'd been able to go to the polls since I was twenty-three, the last time having been in England in 1979.

Nevertheless, it amazes me now that the elections managed to take place at all. The violence and upheaval prior to the end of April escalated sharply and the deadlock between the ANC and the Inkatha Freedom Party was only broken a week before election day. There were bombings, murders and threats of independence declarations by both the Zulu King, Goodwill Zweletini, and the AWB, the Afrikaner *Weerstandsbeweging* (resistance movement). Negotiations were feverish and two key players had emerged in Pik Botha and Cyril Ramaphosa (the president of South Africa at the time of writing). These two, together with Mandela and the other few who saw how essential a peaceful transition was, seemed to be the glue that held the process together.

The day we went to the polling booths together was one of those lifetime moments. We all have them, don't we? The day JFK was shot (for those old enough to remember), the moon landings (likewise), 9/11, royal weddings, births, deaths; all these are memories we share with millions of others, and for me April the 27th, 1994, was one such.

I remember vividly the morning Bill and I walked to the polling station in Bryanston.

We queued in the same line as everyone else, regardless of colour; we held hands with neighbours, maids, road workers and gardeners and we were free to cast our vote for the candidate we favoured, irrespective of race. It might not sound all that momentous to those for whom this is normal, but in South Africa, it was an occasion of great celebration. The sense of unity we felt is forever imprinted in my memory.

I imagine it helped that it was also a beautiful day and the sun beamed its benevolence on the proceedings. There were some unavoidable disruptions; there were also allegations of voting irregularities, but all told, it was a surprisingly peaceful election and everyone I spoke to felt the optimism. The outcome was predictable, inevitable even, and Nelson Mandela was inaugurated as president two weeks later.

On the home front, our situation was not so good. Bill's film trailer had not generated the funding to make the Stander movie he'd hoped. Despite pitching it to several film companies, none of them was in a position to make such a film at that time. They loved the style, feel and approach of the five-minute clip, but no, they couldn't see a market for it. Maybe it was bad judgement on Bill's part; maybe Jim should have foreseen this too, but with the eyes of the world on a new South Africa, no one wanted to make a film glorifying those who were perceived as members of the old regime.

Even though the angle the film would take was Stander's disgust with the system, the industry didn't want to take the risk and it was nine years before the movie was made – by someone else. It didn't even help that during the making of the trailer, Bill won an industry award for his earlier film script, a bonus that had given him and Jim some false expectations.

Despite the kudos attached to the prize, the production companies weren't willing to commit to his new film. The result was that the extra mortgage we'd taken to make the trailer became unaffordable. We couldn't meet the payments. Simple. The bitter truth was clear. We'd have to sell the house.

To cut a sad and sorry story short, Jim broke the bad news to us at the same time as telling us he'd been fired from his management position. His superiors judged that he'd handled our business badly and he was demoted; transferred to another provincial bank where he couldn't do any harm. We were devastated at the suddenness of the falling axe.

Although I'd had my misgivings earlier and I'd been uneasy about the extra mortgage from the outset, I thought we would have had some warning that the rug might be pulled from under us. Upsetting though it was, there was nothing we could do, and the house we'd come to cherish had to go on the market. It was a shattering blow and meant we'd have to rethink our lives all over again.

"I'm sorry, Bill, Val, I've done my best to ask for some leniency and more time," he said, "but my neck's on the block now too. I'm in trouble for sanctioning your extra funding for the film. Okay, it's not just you; my boss says I've been reckless in supporting new businesses in general, but he's using you as an example of my misdeeds. Apparently, I should never have let you buy the house or take the extra mortgage."

"That sucks, Jim," Bill objected, indignant for both himself and his friend. "You were just doing what bankers are supposed to do, weren't you? And anyway, we saved the bank from losing money on the house in the first place."

"I thought so as well, but the powers that be don't see it that way. It would have helped if you'd been able to get a contract for the film, of course," he finished with a sad shrug.

"Yes, well. I'm still hoping, but that doesn't help us now."

"No, although the upside is you've done so much to the house, you should be able to cover both the mortgages with the proceeds. As long as it doesn't take too long to sell, that is."

I hoped Jim was right, but we felt wretched about losing our beautiful home. Bill, in particular, had grown to love it so much. It wasn't quite as bad for me, although I knew I'd miss my sewing room; it was the first and last time in my life I had the luxury of a 'me' room, and I'd revelled in making it my own. I would also miss Annette, my neighbour, and the convenience of cycling off to work every day.

Sadly, there was no way round the problem and we called in an agent to give us a valuation and advertise it. Bryanston was definitely a good address. The downside was that interest rates were showing no signs of dropping, which didn't help when selling a higher priced house in a higher priced neighbourhood. In 1994, they hovered around 16% and were on the way up. We could only hope for the best.

In the meantime, we would need to look for somewhere to rent as we were in no position to buy another property at this stage.

Since Jodie was well established at Fourways High and Mo would still be at Buccleuch until the end of the school year, we started looking for a new home in the less expensive areas of Randburg. At the same time, Tim decided he was going nowhere fast in South Africa and announced his intention of going back to England. He wanted to study, he said, and he couldn't do what he wanted in South Africa. Although we were all sad to see him go, it made sense and also made it easier to find a house to rent. If we didn't need a fourth bedroom, our options would increase.

Eventually, we signed a one-year lease on a house in a suburb called Olivedale, which was in the greater municipality of Randburg. It wasn't too far from anywhere that was important to us, namely the girls' school and my job, and from my perspective, it had the added advantage of being just round the corner from one of my closest friends at work. Given that I'd be leaving Annette behind in Bryanston, I was relieved I'd still have someone nearby. As things turned out, I would become even more grateful for my office friends.

The crashing disappointment of his failure to gain support for his film and the consequent loss of our home had an effect on Bill's attitude to life. In the coming months, my work became ever more important to my wellbeing.

OLIVEDALE

Suburban simplicity

We lived in Olivedale for a year. It was a pleasant suburb and the house was quite similar to our Noordwyk home. A standard three-bedroom, two-bathroom, single-storey home, it was built on the regulation 1000 square metres of land. Unlike Noordwyk, though, it was in an elevated position on the plot and the front garden sloped up as opposed to down. It was also quite far up a fairly steep hill and the road that passed the end of our close ultimately ended next to a large private hospital.

The house had no front fence, the windows only had burglar bars on the opening sections, and there was little other security. But this was Randburg, not Bryanston. It was middle-class, middle-income and middle-everything else, meaning it wasn't as attractive to thieves and therefore wasn't such a risk. Unlike the areas where developers were cramming flats and maisonettes into a kind of jigsaw fit, Olivedale had space between the houses and was attractively green and quintessentially suburban.

We had no burglary problems while we lived there, although we used to hear gunshots in the distance at night, being high up as we were. At first it was unnerving, the kind of background noise that unsettles, but we became accustomed to it. From crossing fingers that no one was being hurt, we eventually failed to even notice it.

It seems callous in hindsight, but robberies, carjackings and violent crime were not yet showing signs of diminishing as they did in the coming years and we had to live with it without being paranoid. Olivedale was comparatively peaceful and had the house been ours, we might have stayed longer, but it wasn't and we always felt that.

We mourned our Bryanston home. More accurately, Bill mourned it. That was the problem. I missed it too, but where we lived wasn't so important to me, I suppose. What made it easier for me was that the girls seemed to adapt well to our new environment. The house was in a cul-de-sac at the end of which was a circular turning point. They took their roller skates and practised their moves up and down the road, using the circumference of the circle as a kind of skating rink. The road's verges were wide and grassy, so they had good soft landings as and when they fell.

By the time we moved, Mo had also started school at Fourways and it was close enough for them to walk home. Since much of the route was downhill, it wasn't too taxing on foot. Cycling was more difficult with the gradient of the hills and I had to give up pedalling off to work. There were no showers at the office, so in the interests of my professional image and my colleagues' olfactory senses, I had to confine my passion for two wheels to the weekends.

Fortunately, we were close to the Jukskei River, next to which was a long, narrow park that quickly became known as the 'Sniffy Bum Club'. We walked the dogs down the hill every day to run by the river, meet their furry friends and have a dip when it was hot – the dogs, that is, not us. There we met many other local residents with their canine companions; hence the club name.

As was often the case in South Africa, the park was also the location for a dog training school. Many dog trainers had no premises of their own and conducted their classes on patches of bare ground or informal parks, which I found both handy for observing tips and entertaining to watch. Seeing the misadventures of the earnest owners having rings run round them by their happy, unruly dogs was much more fun than taking part. In any event, our three were well beyond the stage or age for any kind of obedience education; not that we'd have had any success if we'd tried.

What was noticeable about our life in Olivedale was that we felt relatively safe in our suburb. I didn't worry about my daughters walking home from school; neither did I hesitate to go running early in the mornings or for long cycle rides at the weekends, usually alone. We weren't fenced in, nor were we in a gated community and in general, we took no measures against crime other than making sure we locked doors and cars. Overall, we had no sense of being imprisoned in our community. That's not to say there weren't plenty of burglaries, but they were mostly somewhere else, in the richer areas, an experience we'd had twice in Bryanston. Some of the break-ins reported were horrific, involving murder, mutilation and rape; even more took place in the townships as Andries had testified. In Olivedale, it felt as if we could breathe more easily.

Generally speaking, the suburbs were becoming more mixed and this was quite noticeable in our area. Professional and higher paid people of all races were buying into the tranquillity of this green, established neighbourhood. There were those who mistrusted this development but it was quickly visible and hardly surprising that given the opportunity to live in a clean and calm environment, everyone, no matter what their skin colour, wanted to maintain it, and we regularly saw maids and gardeners turning into the driveways of our new Indian, African and coloured neighbours. As far as I was concerned, this could only be a positive change.

Having grown up in London where I lived in a multi-cultural area and was at one time the only English child in my primary school class, I wasn't at ease in a mono-cultural world. In Natal we'd managed to avoid confronting apartheid, seeing ourselves more as transplanted foreigners living a country life; we lived with the African people rather than over, above or against them. I was glad of the change in Johannesburg that the 1994 elections initiated, but only time would tell whether there would be equal opportunities for all in the new South Africa, newly dubbed the Rainbow Nation.

Affirmatively active at work

Bill continued working in corporate video production and made numerous fifteen-minute programmes for the banks. He also made clips for MTV, the music station, as well as a Canadian current affairs company who wanted short film inserts about life in South Africa.

Despite the ongoing commissions, his disappointment about the Stander film and what it had cost us weighed on him heavily, a gloom not helped when the Bryanston house sold for less than anticipated and barely covered our debt. Life at home was consequently strained, so I threw myself still further into my work and career.

I also saw much more of Moira, the friend from work who lived just around the corner, and we forged an even stronger friendship as a result. Moira and I shared everything: secrets, frustrations, jokes and confessions. We took to playing squash together at lunchtime and gave our squash balls names depending on who was currently giving us cause for complaint. It might have been our bosses, our partners or our colleagues; whoever it was got a thoroughly good whacking and we felt curiously exhilarated, cleansed even. Real murder was avoided and we vented our displeasure in an activity we considered to be a fair, and much healthier, substitute.

With the new post-election policy of affirmative action, which made it mandatory for employers to hire black people rather than white when qualifications matched, companies like ours also started employing more non-white staff. By this time, I was the assistant manager of the Customer Services Department, and one of my assisting roles was to interview applicants for our expanding call centre. The first to join us was a lovely woman from the Cape who made me appreciate that truly good service staff are born, not made.

Myriam walked into the interview room and within thirty seconds I knew she would be perfect for the job. A former nurse, she proved to be one of our best and most knowledgeable team members. She was bi-lingual in Afrikaans and English and had a soothing voice that would appease the grumpiest of clients while delivering the worst of news.

Others joined the department soon, and we added men to the mix too, a further radical change. Suddenly, the company gained a new vibrancy and life. Gone was the slightly stodgy atmosphere of a single culture, mostly single sex organisation. In its place, we had a new group of employees who shook the dust out of the corners and breathed fresh air into the corridors.

Another innovation, which had nothing to do with people but affected us all dramatically was the introduction of the Internet and email into our working lives. We'd seen it coming, but the day in 1995 when we were all switched on to the world wide web and we could send emails not just to clients but to each other made a major difference to the way we worked. There was no Facebook or other social media in those very early days, but even so, the management made strict rules about surfing, emailing and online shopping. I remember the excitement of creating my first private Hotmail account, which incidentally, I still have and use today. Although the use of email made life much easier in most respects, its effect on the quality of the company's communications was not so good and ultimately caused some bad feeling.

One of my pre-email jobs had been overseeing letters sent out by the department. In practice, all letters responding to members' questions were typed up and passed through to me for checking. If there was anything that needed revising, I would correct the text and it would come back to me again before being sent out. Most of the time, I wrote the more difficult letters myself. However, with the advent of email, employees were allowed to answer members' email questions immediately.

To help them, I devised a manual of tips for good email writing and gave them some training, but even with these guidelines, members started complaining about tactless replies, lack of courtesy and bad spelling. Unfortunately, one of the worst culprits was the supervisor of the Finance department, an Afrikaans girl who was excellent at her job, but not at English. It didn't go down very well when she was told she had to send all her emails to me for approval.

I felt sorry for her, as I was well aware I'd have had an even harder time writing in Afrikaans. I couldn't, in fact, so it was with some reluctance that I agreed to monitor her mails. Being in charge of external communications wasn't always an easy job, especially when so many of the staff had different home languages.

Luckily for me, most organisations opted to use English for their communications after the elections, rather than trying to produce information in all eleven official languages of which Afrikaans was now just one. By this time, I understood it but still couldn't speak or write it other than on a very rudimentary level.

Most of the time, it wasn't an issue. When Afrikaans clients called, they would speak to me in their own language and I would answer in English. In our job, the questions were usually predictable, so it didn't take great language skills to learn the terminology and know what they were asking. They were mostly along the lines of, "When will my claim be paid?" "Why won't you cover pregnancy?" or "Why haven't you paid all my expenses?" I only needed to know the key terms and questions to know what answer I should give.

If things became complicated or the client was upset, I called in help from a bi-lingual member of staff or asked the distraught member to come and see me. It worked ninety percent of the time. When it didn't, it was usually because the caller had some personal axe to grind about the increasing lack of bilingualism.

In all such cases I worked on a policy of 'honey tastes sweeter than vinegar'. One of my colleagues once asked me why I kept being pleasant to people who were so rude to me. "Because in the end, it makes life easier," I said. "Conflict is hard work. Being pleasant diffuses conflict. I'm just being lazy, really." Essentially, that was true. I hated friction and the energy it cost.

Another of my jobs was to write the company newsletter. This was probably my favourite of all my tasks. It involved liaising with our advertising agency, Saatchi & Saatchi, whose Sandton offices were quite close by. I'm sure Mr Dee appointed them because of their rather top-drawer reputation in the advertising world, but it was well deserved and I liked working with our designated account manager and the artistic team.

They did the layout, visuals and design for the text I produced. I interviewed staff, wrote profiles on senior partners, prepared information articles, added quizzes and designed competitions. It was a mixture of news, views and clues all wrapped up in a colourful production called 'Heartbeat'. I had great fun working on it. Even better, the employees liked it and the members, to whom it was sent four times a year, gave us good feedback about it, which helped me to enjoy it even more. It ran for several years until eventually it fell victim to a cost cutting exercise and was reduced to an extended email that no one ever read.

The South African advertising industry was one of immense creativity and talent. The TV commercials produced were among the best in the world and regularly won international awards. Often funny, witty and sharp, they were also beautifully filmed in wonderful locations, a feature ably enhanced by the country's stunning scenery.

As one of Saatchi's valued clients our company received tickets to go to the screening of the top 'Ad awards' every year, a perk of my job I looked forward to with unashamed eagerness. The motor industry often won the top awards, probably because they had the money to fund the most expensive campaigns but the originality of the ads was a credit to the agencies that produced them. One that will be well remembered was the series of VW 'Volksie bus' ads starring the popular folk singer, David Kramer. Slapstick and comic, they were filmed as a series of mini-stories in some of the most beautiful parts of the country.

The company's association with Saatchi & Saatchi also included producing brochures, flyers, benefit and tariff leaflets and the Annual Report, all of which fell under the marketing budget. Because my boss, Christine, was both Marketing and Customer Services Manager, I was part of this production process as well.

There was less creative input here and more of the tedium of proofreading and checking, the result being I wasn't so fond of these duties. Proofreading was a minefield and when one year I overlooked a spelling error in our address on customer information packs, I came close to losing my job.

Mr Dee called me in, a thunderous look clouding his face.

"Val, is this your doing?"

"I'm sorry, Mr Dee, but is what my doing?"

"This," he said, pointing to the tiny, miniscule, pale yellow print at the bottom of the small folded brochure.

I squinted at it.

"Erm, that's our address, isn't it?"

"Since when did we include a 'c' in the Hendrik of Hendrik Verwoerd Drive?"

"I don't know. Hasn't it always had one?"

"Are you telling me you didn't know? That you've driven in here every day and failed to see the name of the road on the front of the building?"

I looked at him with interest.

"Is it?"

"For heaven's sake," he groaned. "Are you blind? Anyway, that's not the point, or maybe that's just the point. It's your job to check these things!"

"I agree, Mr Dee, but I thought it was correct, so it didn't occur to me to change it. And anyway," I said, drawing breath for the risk I was about to take, "you were the last person to approve the copy. You could have checked it too." In for a penny, in for a pound, I thought; if I'd blown it now, so be it.

Mr Dee glared at me for far too long before his mouth twitched.

"Touché," he laughed. "You're right. I should have seen it. I never thought to proofread something so routine as our address. I'm also to blame."

I breathed again but thought it best not to mention that being so small, it was more than likely no one would notice the printing error. I'd been outspoken enough and had too close a call. But it was an important learning curve and I paid special interest to these minor details from then on.

My place at work was by now well established. It was home from home and I was never reluctant to get up and go to the office. Instead, I looked forward to it. Weekends were important for spending time with the family and the animals, but I valued my job not least because I had so many good friends there, and the quick-fire banter between us all was non-stop.

South African humour can be quite on the edge, very sarcastic and often tasteless, but the worse it was, the more we laughed. One morning, I was climbing the stairs to my office and listening to all my colleagues greeting each other.

"Morning, Les (or Ann or Jan), how are you?"

"Fine and you?"

"I'm fine too. Have a nice day."

It always went like this. Every morning. It was the standard South African greeting formula and it simply wasn't possible to avoid it, which I have to say became just slightly repetitive. On the phone it was even worse; a conversation couldn't get underway until we'd been through the 'how are you?' routine. On this particular morning I decided to try something different.

When Pamela, a cheerful woman with a guaranteed sense of humour, started with the usual patter, my response wasn't what she was expecting.

"Hi Val, how are you?"

"None the better for seeing you," I smiled sweetly.

"You what?" she spluttered, shocked. "What d'you mean?"

In her eyes I wasn't playing the game at all. Then she saw my face and started laughing.

"Well, Val, you had me there, didn't you? Talk about rocking the boat … I nearly fell overboard with that one."

She got me back the next day, though. I was wearing a loosely fitting flowing dress that I thought was rather elegant and was pleased when a friend complimented me as I walked in.

"That's a lovely dress, Val. It really suits you."

Pamela looked up from what she was doing.

"You call that a dress? It's more like a tent. Actually, no, it's not a tent, it's a marquee!"

The wave of sniggers was audible.

"Good one, Pamela. I'll think again before I tease you in future," I chuckled. "Your kick's twice as hard as mine."

"No, don't do that, Val, please carry on."

"Oh, why?"

"The revenge is so very sweet," she grinned.

The laughter and camaraderie cheered me up no matter how I was feeling. It made the stresses of the job so much easier to cope with too. Medical insurance combines two highly emotive subjects: health and money. We often had to deal with quite severe crises, especially when members didn't have the financial cover they needed to pay for costly treatment. In extreme cases, it could mean loss of essential assets and even their home; in others, it meant being transferred to a state hospital, and no one liked that idea much. That's not to say the treatment they received was bad. In many cases, the medical and surgical specialists were the same as those at the private hospitals, but the conditions on the wards were quite grim: bleak and shabby were the best that could be said. We didn't like having to sentence a patient to a state hospital stay. It distressed us all, so our office humour was a way of coping.

Given the closeness of our team, it wasn't surprising that we often socialised together too. Staff lunches, parties, drinks evenings, weekend *braais* (barbecues), we willingly spent time together outside work. The ultimate social occasion for Bill and me was when Jared invited us to his Hindu wedding in Durban.

Like many Indians, Jared and his wife had known they were destined to be married since they were teenagers. Theirs was an arranged wedding, but it wasn't an unhappy arrangement. They'd known each other since childhood and seemed to be genuinely in love. In any event, it was a special day and an experience I wouldn't have missed for the world.

Bill and I arrived at the wedding venue in Verulam near Durban not having any idea what to expect.

"D'you know anything about Hindu weddings?" Bill asked me.

"Well, no. I didn't actually ask except to find out what we should wear."

We both wore light, smart and colourful clothes to suit the summery weather that Durban had all year round and to fit in with the vibrant Indian traditional dress.

"I have a feeling it's a bit of a show," Bill said. "I've seen photos of the weddings my Indian dealers went to when I was down here, and it seems that everything happens on a stage with the guests looking on."

Bill was right. The wedding took place in a huge hall filled with round tables, each of which seated about six people. There was a large stage lavishly decorated with yellow and green garlands and a kind of set that made it look like an idyllic garden with a gazebo. All the guests sat at the tables and watched the proceedings while eating and drinking and generally having a social time. It was beautiful, but for us, used as we were to the formal solemnities of a European wedding, it was quite strange.

The performance of the wedding ceremony was stunning, almost like a choreographed ballet. It seemed to go through several symbolic steps that were necessary for the couple to complete their vows. The gorgeous rich saris the women wore were works of art, while the men had equally vivid satin coats and pantaloons. Meanwhile, we sat at our table eating curry and drinking mint tea while we watched the various stages of the couple's pledge-making process.

We didn't know anyone else as our fellow guests at the table were local friends of the couple, so we only managed to make small talk with them. It didn't matter, though. I was mesmerised by the wedding ceremony. As I recall, there was no alcohol available, and when we left, we were given a small packet of Indian sweets wrapped in bronze coloured cellophane as a thank you gift for attending. We didn't see Jared and his new wife at all on the day, but when he came back to work after his honeymoon, I told him how much we'd enjoyed it.

"That's good to hear, Val. I'm sorry we didn't see you, but as you now realise, a Hindu wedding isn't really an interactive affair."

"No, it isn't, but it's amazing to witness. I'm so glad we came."

"Well, there's no way I can deny I'm a married man now, is there?" he chuckled. "We had more than enough witnesses to the whole thing."

"That's for sure. How many guests were there in total?"

"I don't know exactly, but I think, give or take a few, there were about five hundred."

"No wonder I didn't see any of our other friends there."

"Actually, I don't think anyone else from the office came," he said with a sad smile. "It was probably too far for them."

"Their loss, then. I wouldn't have missed it for anything. Thank you so much for inviting us!"

Jared gave me a hug that told me more than anything how pleased he was we'd made the trip. We were already firm friends, but this cemented the friendship completely. Metaphors about concrete foundations would be appropriate, but suffice to say Jared and I remained good buddies for the duration of my life in Johannesburg.

Relay races and rugby

Work also offered more opportunities for the fitness training I was busy with in my drive to compete in the Cape Argus Cycle Tour. Determined to do it before I turned forty-one, I knew I had to take part in March 1996 or I'd be too late, but I needed to be more than just cycling fit; the Argus (as it was usually referred to) was an endurance test; it needed strength for those long-haul hills, so I stepped up my running as well to increase my stamina.

The incentive I needed was handed to me on a plate. Every so often, the company put up teams for participating in corporate sponsored relay races and although I'd never been much of a runner, I'd put my name down for first one in 1993, then another and so on. In Bryanston, I'd been a kind of round-the-block jogger, never doing more than about three kilometres and never pushing myself on speed. It had also been a way of walking the dogs, meaning that my progress was often hindered. Daisy and her smells were not easily parted.

For my first relay races, I'd only done the short distances, but now I offered to do the five-kilometre leg. The sections of the races started at about one kilometre for the faint-but-pursuing couch potatoes among us and then increased incrementally in length to around eleven kilometres. In total, the entire relay race was the length of a standard marathon, namely forty-two kilometres.

The point of these events was to raise money for charity and by having several participants in a team, the chances of increasing the contributions improved. We each signed up sponsors who pledged whatever they wished for us to complete our part of the race. As a challenge, I thought it wouldn't be too hard to push myself up from three to five kilometres, and so the early mornings thus saw me pounding up and down the hills of Olivedale. To make myself easily visible in the dawn light, I wore a red shirt but I think my red face was just as much of a beacon. It took a major amount of effort to convince my forty-year old body I could do this.

Race day itself was always a Sunday and began at the crack of dawn. Even though most of the runs took place in spring and autumn to avoid the main summer months, it could still be sweltering by midday and even hotter in the afternoon. Beginning at six in the morning made it possible for the event to be finished before the highest temperatures of the day kicked in.

As a rule, the first runner's stretch was a long one and then the distances varied. Each of us had to wait at our allotted hand-over point for our predecessor to arrive with the baton, which resulted in some anxious moments. We could only guess when our team-mate was going to come charging towards us, baton thrust forwards like a bayonet in battle. It was all pretty chaotic, but luckily we all wore corporate T-shirts, otherwise it would have been even more of a shambles than it already was.

The atmosphere was terrific. Supporters lined the streets, cheering us on and giving us the extra boost we needed to push ourselves to a personal best. One of my friends, a girl who admitted that the extent of her normal exercise was raising the remote control to switch channels on the TV from her reclining position on the sofa, shuffled her way up a steep hill near the SABC (the South African version of the BBC) in Auckland Park in a noble effort to complete her two-kilometre stint. She had to spend the next day off work to recover, and she made more mileage out of garnering sympathy for her aching muscles than she ever did running, but she was over the moon she'd done it.

I was pleased to finish my run without too much pain, so when the next race was planned, I signed up for a seven-kilometre leg. Once again, I staggered up and down the hills in Olivedale in the early mornings but when I wasn't hammering my knee joints, I was cycling in ever increasing circles further afield to prepare for the Argus.

For training purposes, Johannesburg was exceptional. Not only were the hills seriously demanding, the altitude of the city made it an ideal location to train for any kind of sport. Joburgers were supposed to have the advantage when it came to endurance tests as we were used to the oxygen starvation.

That said company runs were fun but they weren't without risk. During one of the races, my part of the route took me up into Houghton. It was a very hot morning and the hills around what I remember as the Wilds, a beautiful natural park, were steep. I was taking it gently as I knew the heat would win if I tried to fight it, and I was shocked when a much more middle-aged man ran past me puffing and wheezing. He was overweight and struggling, labouring to put one foot in front of the other.

Ten minutes later, I reached a spot where a number of people crowded round a recumbent figure on the ground. It was the man who'd so recently overtaken me and from the way he was lying, I knew he was dead. A race official waved me past and I jogged on sadly; there was nothing I could do for him anyway, but I wished I'd told him to slow down. He'd pushed himself to the limit and beyond and it was a sombre reminder that the line between perceived and actual fitness was a fine one.

On a more cheerful note, 1995 was the year South Africa not only hosted, but won the rugby World Cup, an event that did much to unite the country further. Still basking in post-election euphoria, the fact that the World Cup was scheduled to take place in South Africa and was being supported by the president himself already had the population in a state of heightened bliss. The president had called publicly for the whole nation to get behind the Springboks (the team name). He'd taken a risk as African people were, and still are, mostly football supporters; they saw rugby as the white man's sport. Mandela rallied support from all the country's citizens by wearing a Springbok hat and rugby shirt, and by doing so, he endeared himself to millions on both sides of the colour divide. So when in the final match, and against all expectations, the host nation pulled off a win against the mighty All-Blacks from New Zealand, the entire country erupted.

It didn't seem to matter whether we were rugby fans or not, whether we were black, white, yellow or sky-blue with pink spots, everyone, regardless of race, celebrated the win with unprecedented elation. Nelson Mandela attended the match and beamed with pleasure as he presented the cup to what had become his team. For the president, it was the culmination of a dream to unite the people through a major sporting event, and in that he succeeded magnificently.

Even the minibus Taxis sported the Springbok symbol alongside the new South African flag and hooted their way down William Nicol Drive, rejoicing in the rugby team's win. As for our family, we weren't rugby fans either, but it didn't matter. I personally preferred cricket, but I was more than willing to wave my flag out of the car window, while Bill joined the hooting party on the road and the girls hollered in the back.

In retrospect, it was just the spur the country needed to get on with the process of reconciliation, a process that would take many years. However, it had to start somewhere and Nelson Mandela's was the political genius that ensured it had a future. The rugby World Cup, said author, John Carlin (who wrote the screen play for the film Invictus), was an incredibly important political event. We weren't conscious of its significance at the time, but we knew how much it did to improve relations between the races.

Killing time in Krugersdorp

Still on the subject of sport, it was during this year that my daughters took up ice-skating. Of all the sports I could have listed that would appeal to them both, this was the last one I'd have thought of. What's more, I never even knew there was an ice-rink in Johannesburg until clients of Bill's introduced us to it.

A Swiss family, Heinz and his wife and children had a fabulous architect designed house on a rocky ridge bordering Krugersdorp, a self-contained town on the West Rand. We became quite close to them both socially and on a business level. Part of the cement that set the relationship was that Jodie started helping their young son with his English reading and became friends with their daughter too. She was taking skating lessons at the rink and invited Jodie to join in. An added incentive cropped up when two of Mo's school friends turned out to be taking skating lessons as well, and within a few weeks, Mo was also asking to go along. Before long, Saturdays were given over to ferrying the children over to the Krugersdorp rink from Olivedale.

I scratched my head over this new passion of theirs. It involved spending hours in a darkened hall where the sun never shone, where it was cold, and where they shared the ice with hordes of other people all skating round and round with no apparent purpose; a sort of endless follow my leader, or tail chasing exercise. There was a beautiful world of sun, nature and fresh air outside and they wanted to immure themselves in what amounted to a huge fridge.

It was beyond me. I tried it once myself, and only once. I spent most of the hour I'd agreed to endure on the ice either clinging to the edge of the rink or on my backside with my legs stuck out in a graceless 'Y', not my favoured position to appear at my best. Nevertheless, the girls loved it. Skating took over their lives and, in the intervals when we waited for them to finish their lessons or other entertainment at the rink, Bill and I started exploring Krugersdorp.

Historically, the town was significant in that it was named after that 19th century thorn in the British side, the intransigent President Paul Kruger. It was under his leadership that the Afrikaans Boers became such a prickly force. Having said that, other reading suggests Kruger's wife was more than a little instrumental in stimulating his bull-headed obstinacy, so maybe she provided the thorn while he wore the horns.

Anyway, the town was originally called Paardekraal after the farm owned by its founder, Marthinus Pretorius, but the local government later changed its name to that of the Boer leader.

Essentially, Krugersdorp was a mining town. The Witwatersrand Goldfields were first discovered in the area and later, the town's mines were the first in the world to extract Uranium as a by-product of gold refining. Apart from these questionable claims to fame, Krugersdorp was the hub of the Afrikaner initiative for independence; it was also the site of a British concentration camp for the Boers during the second Boer war. With all this history in mind, we cruised its quiet streets with increasing interest.

Many of the houses in the northern parts (unsurprisingly called Krugersdorp North) were traditional in style and wore their corrugated iron roofs and pretty wrought-iron work with great charm; rather like elderly ladies with neatly coiffed hair and a touch of lipstick. They reminded me of Grahamstown, although its mining background meant that Krugersdorp's houses were more functional and didn't put on quite such a show of genteel colonialism as they did in the more tourist-focused university city.

That said, we'd been told that Krugersdorp had a growing population of artists and creative people, a suggestion supported by the colours some of the other older houses were painted. There was no denying that purple or blue walls matched with contrasting trims of mustard or red on window frames and doors made quite a statement. The lack of subtlety was striking, but we were very taken with it. The vibrant colours suited the style of the buildings and when embellished with climbing wisteria, or overgrown with bougainvillea, the effect was glorious.

Krugersdorp's centre was typical of a small South African town. Slightly shabby with badly maintained roads and cracked paving, it was home to numerous small businesses that seemed to survive on local trade. Although there were bigger supermarkets out of town and a huge shopping mall at Westgate on the Ontdekkers Road leading back into Johannesburg, we saw people of all backgrounds and races frequenting the high street shops.

There were stores selling cheap household items and furniture; others sold shoes or toiletries, cosmetics or vegetables, car parts or cigarettes. They were miscellaneous but clearly useful and the centre was busy. The streets were wide, a legacy from the days of ox-wagons that needed a very large turning circle. Now, they had parking spaces down the middle separated by tall and well-established trees that gave natural shade to the cars beneath them.

While we waited for our offspring to skate themselves into dizzy exhaustion, we browsed through the shops, had coffee at the small, friendly Wimpy and became increasingly fond of this off-beat but unusually cohesive town.

As time went on, I suppose it was inevitable that we started thinking it might not be a bad idea to live closer to our daughters' new obsession. After several months, their enthusiasm showed no signs of diminishing and while the forty-kilometre drive to Krugersdorp was pleasant, it was quite a distance to travel and then spend much of our free time waiting for the skating day to finish. The dogs usually came too and we took them for walks around the area, but although this increased our interest in Krugersdorp's leafy streets, there were other things we knew we should be doing. Inevitably too, we started scanning the classified ads for houses that might be for sale in the area. Krugersdorp North was close to the ice rink and had many of the older style houses we liked. It seemed a good place to look.

Having been both a conveyancing clerk and an estate agent in my past, I'd never lost interest in the subject even though I wasn't so keen on the selling side of the property business. With a new goal in mind, I went into the search with a will and found myself looking forward to our weekend ferrying as it gave us an excuse to find the houses I'd earmarked during the week and decide whether they were worth viewing.

We'd paid our debt on the Bryanston house, but we only had a twelve-month contract in Olivedale, so we needed to sort ourselves out before the end of the year. It would mean moving yet again, however, which wasn't something I ever looked forward to, but if it gave Bill a project to take his mind off what had happened in Bryanston, we would all think it was worth it.

One of his frustrations in Olivedale was that he couldn't do anything to the property. It wasn't ours, so he couldn't even paint it. Finding a modest and preferably old place in Krugersdorp would quell his DIY withdrawal symptoms – and mine too, for that matter.

It didn't take us very long to find it. After spending one entire day seeing several properties that were either too modern, too expensive or too well renovated in a style that didn't suit us, our last call found us parked by a low wall behind which was a wide strip of bare earth separating the public walkway from a small white house.

In shape, it reminded me forcibly of something a child might draw: square (although the front wall was slightly slanted on both sides) with an arched doorway in the middle and two windows on each side. Built on quite high foundation walls, it had a pyramid shaped green corrugated iron roof, or to be more accurate, it used to be green. Much of the paint had come off and there were large areas of rust showing through.

Towards the back was a separating wall, which connected to a garage and maid's room on the left and to the neighbours' wall on the right. Behind this, we decided there must be a small garden. The whole place looked a bit bleak. The front garden was non-existent apart from a small palm tree, and the whole impression was one of neglect.

It needed us more than any other house we'd seen, but that wasn't what we initially said.

"Crikey, it's a bit sad, isn't it?" Bill muttered, peering through the security gate into a large vestibule, at the back of which was the front door. The tiles in the vestibule were cracked, the paint was peeling off the walls and the door looked in serious need of varnishing. We turned round, looking out onto the street.

"And the road's quite a busy one, isn't it?" I added, watching a minibus taxi shoot past and brake hard at the lights two houses up. "I'm not sure it would be so much fun to live on such a main thoroughfare. And look at the view," I went on. "It's a bit stark, isn't it?" On the horizon was a massive mine dump that might have looked like Table Mountain if it hadn't been a kind of monochrome dust colour.

"Hmm," Bill agreed. At least, I thought he did. But then he went on: "Although apart from that, the location's ideal. There's a Spar just down the road, plus a petrol station and other shops. It's a hop and a skip to the ice rink for the girls. They can bike there from here, and it's easy access to the Krugersdorp highway for you."

"You're right, yes, but what about the animals? I'd be constantly worried about them getting run over."

"True, but we could make sure the cats don't come out to the front and we can put a gate across the driveway to stop the dogs getting out."

"You sound quite keen," I frowned, looking at Bill.

"It's got loads of potential, don't you think?"

"Yes … I suppose it has, but we'll need to find out how much they want for it before you get too excited."

"Don't you know the price then?"

"No, this one was advertised in the local paper's small ads, but I don't remember the details."

"When can we find out?"

At that moment, I knew it was going to be the one. I'd rarely seen Bill so eager, although I thought I knew why. He was already mentally cleaning his paint brushes, fixing up the roof and increasing the height of the front wall. Even I became excited when I called the number on the ad that evening and found out how cheap the house was. At something under a hundred thousand Rand, it was eminently affordable, especially in those days of crazily high mortgage rates. In the past year, they'd risen to about 19%.

We arranged an official viewing to make sure the house had everything we needed, but we were already pretty certain we wanted it. Our imaginations had gone into overdrive, visualising what it could be and what our lives in Krugersdorp would be like. Much to my relief, the interior hooked us instantly. It was empty, which was just as well since someone else's furnishings might have obscured our vision. It was the floors that grabbed us first; they were the most beautiful Oregon pine everywhere except in the main bedroom. Although dirty, we knew they would polish up perfectly. Then there were the high ceilings, the wonderful old bath on legs, the scullery with an original stone sink and the pantry, or *spens* as it's known in Afrikaans. The only problem was that while it had a large lounge which led into a separate dining room and then into the kitchen, a typical layout in older houses, it only had two bedrooms, not the three we needed.

"The lounge is quite big enough to have the dining table in it as well, so we don't need this," Bill mused, pointing at the large empty dining room. "What we could do is put up a wall from the kitchen door to the lounge. That would close it off and give us an extra bedroom."

"We don't need a fancy kitchen either, do we?" I remarked, gazing round another empty space. The sink and the pantry were the only clues to its use. "I've always liked free standing cupboards. We only need a couple of dressers and a table."

"A stove might help too," Bill commented with a sideways look. "I know you don't like cooking, but I like eating."

"Oh well, if you must," I sighed. He swatted me and laughed.

By this time, it was clear we were intending to put in an offer for the house. Even the disinterested estate agent couldn't have overlooked these buying signals, so we all piled back in our cars, promising to be in touch. That evening, we emailed our offer through, and within a matter of days, it had been accepted, subject to arranging the finance.

The girls were pleased with our decision; delighted even. The prospect of being closer to the rink and all the friends they'd made there made them extremely happy. The only downside for them was the thought of changing schools again, but we all agreed they'd be better off going to Krugersdorp High. It was closer to home and easier for transport.

It would mean new uniforms yet again. Fortunately, I'd got to know about the school thrift shop system when the girls were at Buccleuch. It was standard practice that when pupils left, or grew out of their uniforms, they handed them in to the schools to be sold on as second-hand items for those who couldn't afford to keep buying new.

The collection point was usually just a room in the school building and was politely called the thrift shop. As far as I knew, no one was ashamed to make use of it. Uniforms were expensive and the children grew so fast some of the items were practically new. Even at Fourways, I'd initially bought both girls the essential clothing second-hand and replaced them with new items when necessary. I could do the same at Krugersdorp.

As for the house purchase, we knew we'd have to wait around three months for everything to go through, yet it would still mean we'd be in the new house by the end of the year. There was no question that we would pay occupational rent again and we waited for the transfer to go through before taking possession. We'd lost one home that way and didn't want to risk this one by making a similar mistake. All the same, Bill brightened visibly and the future looked much more optimistic.

Before the move, Bill and I went on a short holiday to the UK and France on our own, which we both enjoyed; a work colleague of mine stayed with the girls, which they didn't enjoy, but we weren't away for long and despite their complaints about my bossy friend, they'd clearly been well-fed during our absence.

Company travel with company

When I returned to work, though, I was called in to Christine's office about a different kind of travel.

"Val, you know Mr Dee's retiring soon?"

I smiled and nodded. He'd been suffering from ill health and decided it was time to rest up.

"Okay, good. Well, I know you enjoy doing the firm visits in Gauteng, but since Mr Dee can't do them anymore, I'd like you to start coming with me to do the Cape and Durban visits."

I didn't know what to say at first. We were probably about to move, the girls were most likely changing schools and Bill had work that would either take him away from home more often or require him to be on location for complete days. I couldn't afford to be away from home at short notice.

"Christine, I'd love to, but I'm not sure if I can."

I explained the problem to her, but for once, she didn't seem to be very sympathetic.

"Firm visits and presentations are part of your job, Val. You can't afford to pick and choose what you do."

Her reaction worried me. I'd never been asked if I'd be prepared to travel before. To me it felt as if this was changing the goalposts, and such pressure wasn't really fair.

"I'm sorry, Christine, but unless I can have a good month's notice to make arrangements, I just can't do it. You'll have to replace me, and I'll go back to the call centre."

That surprised her, I know; she was expecting me to capitulate.

"If that happens, you know you'll have to take a drop in salary, don't you?"

I swallowed hard and nodded. What could I say?

"Well, I'll talk to the other managers about it and see what they think. With Mr Dee coming up for retirement, it's not worth involving him and we don't know who'll be the next CEO yet."

This must have been the first time I'd hesitated to do anything Christine asked me to do. I had the feeling she wasn't impressed. However, the other managers agreed I shouldn't be required to go on trips without being given a chance to make plans for the girls, as it wasn't part of my original job description. I was relieved, immensely so, but sadly, it affected my relationship with my boss; the mutual trust and respect we'd enjoyed was disturbed. On the occasions when I accompanied her for these trips, things weren't always easy, not for me anyway, although on the surface we got on fine. That aside, they were a great way to see other parts of the country.

One of the places we went to was Mmbatho, the capital of what used to be the Bantustan (homeland) of Bophuthatswana. We travelled there in a very small sixteen-seater prop aircraft. I was terrified. I don't like flying at the best of times, and this plane was a serious teeth rattler. I was sitting next to one of the wings and the noise of the propellers was deafening. Not only that, the whole plane seemed to shudder as it ploughed its way through the clouds and I was sure all the rivets were about to pop out.

To make matters worse, there was so much buffeting at times it felt as if we were being chucked around between a pair of giant hands. At one moment, the aircraft suddenly fell into a stomach-lurching drop. "Just a bit of turbulence," the captain said by way of apology. "Keep your seatbelts fastened." It was a bit late for that. He might rather have told us to hang on to our lunch. I don't think I was the only one to feel like disposing of mine.

By the time we landed, I was sweating freely and gripping the arm rests so tightly I almost needed someone with a chisel to come and pry them off. To my joy, we hired a car for the drive back so we could see some member firms on route. Even Christine seemed pleased we didn't have to fly again; I don't think she liked it much either. Mmbatho itself wasn't particularly inspiring and the flight eclipsed any impressions I had of the city forever more.

As a rule, we drove to all our clients in the Free State and Northern Province. Nowhere was so far away we couldn't reach it in a few hours and we'd only flown to Mmbatho to save time. After our visits, we would generally stay in a local hotel, travel to the next town the following day and then return home after a couple of nights on the road. Other towns we visited were Bloemfontein, Kimberley and Mafikeng, none of which I'd spent time in before.

Bloemfontein has been both the provincial capital of the Free State and the judicial capital of South Africa since the early twentieth century, although prior to that, it was already the capital city of the independent Orange Free State Republic and many of its rather grand classical style public buildings gave it an air of importance suited to the home of South Africa's Supreme Court. Interestingly, when South Africa became a union in 1910, Bloemfontein was granted the status of national judicial capital in compensation for no longer being the administrative centre of an independent Boer state.

In keeping with its general air of gravitas, the main streets were wide with buildings set on large plots of land, each of them standing aloof and solitary much like the statues of dignitaries that graced the city's open spaces. The only problem I had with Bloemfontein was that it was slightly dull. There seemed to be little life or atmosphere in its centre. It was fine, noble even, but somewhat lethargic and soulless. Quite recently, I heard someone saying "Bloemfontein? It's got to be the most boring place I've ever been!" Slightly harsh perhaps, but it seems nothing much has changed. For all that it was pleasant there. It felt safe, a bit pompous maybe, but comfortable.

Kimberley, by contrast, was vibrant, noisy and colourful. It had its share of fine buildings too, but the streets were busier, the pavements scruffier and overall, it was livelier. To reach Kimberley from Bloemfontein, we drove west about 165 kilometres across flat prairie-like farm and grass land. On my first trip, we did our duty and visited a couple of firms in the town centre before heading to the place everyone goes: the Big Hole.

Kimberley's monument to the South African diamond rush of the 19th century is not a building, or a statue, it's a monster crater in the ground that is about a third full of incredibly blue water. Looking down into its massive depths, it was almost impossible to believe it was dug out by hand with picks, shovels and spades. It was so deep and so vast. Many people made and lost fortunes in the process; many more lost their lives.

Between 1871 when diamonds were first discovered here and 1914 when it was closed, 50,000 men slaved away to dig what is now a World Heritage site. There wasn't much I could say looking into its mystifying depths. Its past, its history of wasted lives, energy and passion spoke for itself, but for all that it was a huge testament to man's endeavour, and, let's face it, greed.

Of the three, Mafikeng (or Mahikeng as it is now known) was probably the one star rated town when we visited it. Formerly a seat of government of the Bechuanaland Protectorate (later Botswana), it had an impressive history that it didn't quite live up to. I'd read the stories of how the town was founded by the forward-thinking Molema Tawana, a man who believed in education as the path to progress. I'd also read about the siege of Mafikeng that brought Robert Baden-Powell, the founder of the scouts, into the limelight during the second Boer War. The importance, or rather usefulness, of his actions during the siege has been disputed in recent times, but there's no doubt he was a key player during this period of South African history.

After driving 365 kilometres north from Kimberley, it was a shame to find Mafikeng in such a run-down state. The buildings surrounding the town square where we had clients to visit were faded, peeling and sadly decrepit. The rich coloured paintwork had long lost its sheen and there was litter lying on the pavements and in the gutters; heaps of it.

What I didn't know was what had caused the decline, but the general dilapidation was a sorry sight for a town with such a wealth of history. Maybe it was because of its loss of government status, or maybe there was high unemployment in the area; it wasn't possible to find out in the space of a few hours. I could only hope that one day its inhabitants would be able to benefit from their heritage. The stories of the town's early years and its founder were worth commemorating. It seemed such a pity that most of Mafikeng's significance lay in its past; it had yet to find itself in its present.

All the roads we used were good and straight and driving was easy. There was never much traffic and although many people drove too fast, the comfortable conditions kept it relaxed. Accidents were fewer on the roads in the Free State too. This may have been because much of the land was given over to massive farms. The population density in these areas was low, so there were fewer buses and minibus taxis than there were on the routes to the major cities like Pretoria, Durban and Cape Town.

However, this wasn't the case when we travelled back to Johannesburg from Mafikeng. The route that made most sense to us was via Rustenburg. We had clients there too, so we could see them on the way. Being just short of 200 kilometres, it wasn't a long drive, but it was much more taxing than any of the other stretches.

At the town of Zeerust, the road became part of the main route to Botswana; it was also used for transport to the mines at Rustenburg, as well as being quite a tourist area with private game parks and lovely natural scenery; in other words, it was a relatively busy road. This was not helped by the hills and bends, as well as the racing taxis and the careering buses. The latter were made even more hazardous by having trailers attached to them that swung around the curves with terrifying abandon.

Like most of the main routes, it was only a two-track highway with emergency lanes on each side, meaning it was quite narrow for the amount of traffic it handled. I learnt to both love and hate this road: the scenery was beautiful, but the driving was not. My eyes were on permanent alert for the next lunatic to overtake us on the crest of a hill, on a blind bend or when another lunatic was racing equally fast towards us. Near misses became the norm; we played dodgem cars or dice of death for real.

As for the landscape, it was no longer grassland. We were back in *bushveld* country. Plains and hills studded with thick clumps of thorny shrubs and bushes gave way to more open areas dotted with trees, the Acacia being the most prominent and, for me, the only recognisable shape. In some places the trees were quite sparse, leaving space for grass to grow beneath them; in others the bush was dense and too thick for cattle, but it was perfect country for game lodges, the signs to which we saw occasionally along the road.

Now and then, I'd look out and see a small herd of buck grazing, a secretary bird walking alone through the grass, some vultures circling overhead, or a lone horseman cantering over the brow of a hill, his cloak a blanket and his hat wide-brimmed. "Where's he going?" I'd wonder, as there was nowhere in sight, not a house nor a *kraal*. That was the magic and mystery of Africa, even so close to a huge urban sprawl.

The *bushveld* scenery dominated our horizons all the way from Rustenburg back to the town of Magaliesburg with the almost constant backdrop of the Magaliesberg mountains to the north (and yes, the spelling is different). But as we came closer to the urban areas of the Reef, farmland took over again, a sign that we were nearly home.

The entire loop from our Randburg office to Bloemfontein, Kimberley, Mafikeng and back was around 1400 kilometres and we did it easily with the breaks for firm visits and overnight stops. That said, it was a long trip and the first time I did it was my first time in all these towns. Nonetheless, it was the country between them that left the most lasting impression on me.

Moving on again

The transfer on the Krugersdorp house went through before the end of the year. We packed up our possessions yet again and prepared to move to our new and, we hoped, more permanent home. Since arriving in Sunninghill in 1989, we'd had moved four times and this was to be our fifth: five times in six years sounded more than enough to me. I was determined we wouldn't have to move again any time soon.

Whatever happened to Bill's business, the cost of the mortgage was affordable on my salary alone even with the ridiculously high interest rates. If we could also manage to live on my salary, then we wouldn't be at risk of losing our home again. That was my theory anyway. Regrettably, theories and practice don't always match. Although Krugersdorp proved to be our longest stay in any house, it wasn't as permanent as I would have liked, but that is the next part of the story.

By December we'd said goodbye to Olivedale, bid farewell to all the gang at the 'Sniffy Bum Club', and shut the door on our rental life. In some ways it was sad. Olivedale had been kind to us, but we were all excited about the move to the West Rand, especially my daughters, who would be so much closer to their social circle.

Our new view would take some getting used to, and we'd have to accept that we'd be living on a busy thoroughfare, but the little tin-roofed house appealed to me greatly. In many respects, it had the feel and atmosphere of Melville or Norwood, Johannesburg's older suburbs, and I liked the idea of living in a real, small town where we could walk to the local shops and even into the centre. For once, this was a move that felt right and I welcomed it.

KRUGERSDORP

Painting it perfect

From the day we arrived in Krugersdorp North, activity stepped up several notches. Bill stopped pacing around and found his purpose in life again. Out came the paint, the rollers, and the tools. We painted the lounge, then sanded and polished its lovely floor to a magnificent gleam.

The next job was to erect a double-sided stud wall clad in plasterboard to form a passage between the old dining room and the lounge, and then to find a door for it that would fit in with the rest of the house. The smaller space the wall enclosed became Jodie's bedroom, which had its window onto the back garden. Mo's room was next to hers and also had a window at the back making both girls safer from possible intruders. All very neat.

They both chose their own wall colours: Mo's was a gorgeous marine blue and Jodie's a rich deep terracotta. With white ceilings, skirtings, door and window frames, they looked lovely, and the effect of the contrasting paintwork was still more stunning against the golden glow of the newly polished Oregon pine floors.

When I looked around at its perfect proportions, warm wood and great sense of space, I knew this was the house for me. I felt completely and totally at home, more than in Bryanston and definitely more than in Sunninghill or Noordwyk. I'd been quite happy in each of the others, especially Bryanston, but I felt this classic cottage with its corrugated iron roof suited us, or rather me, in every way, and the quirky neighbourhood of homespun Afrikaans folk mixed with arty types was right up my street.

The absence of a kitchen didn't present too much of a problem either. We bought a four-ring stove that had a spacious oven and connected it to a large bottle of gas that stood against the outside wall. A small hole in the brickwork fed the gas pipe through to the kitchen. We could buy bottled gas from the garage down the road, making replacements easy and we always kept a spare one.

The existing scullery, which led to the back door and garden, had hot and cold running water to its old-fashioned porcelain sink; the *spens* offered more than enough space and shelves for our groceries; and we bought a lovely old yellowwood dresser and a pine sideboard in keeping with the scrub-top table and chairs we already had. It was simple, cheerful and, I thought, quite charming.

It didn't matter to me that the sink was chipped and had rickety shelves underneath. I just put a fresh print curtain over the shelves and scraped the old, hardened paint splashes off the surfaces. It also didn't matter that the stove was on the small side; the smaller the better as far as I was concerned. It was Bill who liked cooking, Indian food being his speciality. If it was enough for him, I wasn't about to complain.

Within a month or so, the only unsightly areas other than the exterior walls and roof were our own bedroom, which faced the street, and the garden: a rather overstated word for what was just a bare piece of ground with some patchy grass on it. To some extent, it was like our squash court garden in Sunninghill, being small with high walls all the way round, but there the resemblance ended.

The ground was uneven and would need levelling; it had several depressions in it which soon became craters with Polly's new digging craze. She'd started this new obsession in the flower beds in Olivedale and her work continued in Krugersdorp, taking on Kimberley Hole proportions. In addition, the perimeter walls badly needed rendering; there were large patches where paint and plaster had fallen off long ago.

Initially, the only thing we used the garden for was to do the laundry. The house didn't come with appliances (or anything else for that matter), and since there'd been one in Olivedale, we'd sold our fully automatic, front-loading, ocean-sailing (well, nearly) washing machine with the Bryanston house.

Our short-term solution was to buy a twin-tub, something rarely seen these days except for mini-camping versions, but I soon became attached to mine and chose to keep it even when we could have had an automatic machine. It was light and mobile, so I put it outside the back door and fed the pump-out hose straight into the rainwater drain.

Washing became an outdoor event and fun to do in the sunshine. We couldn't leave it to itself, of course; the only automated feature it had was a timer. The clothes needed to be transferred from the tub to the spinner and rinsed several times, but I found it much more effective than an automatic. We then pegged the clothes onto the circulating windy dryer that Bill erected for the purpose. With Joburg's climate being so stable, it was a rare day that we couldn't leave our laundry out to be sun-dried

The garden thus remained purely functional until further notice although the cats and dogs clearly enjoyed it. They didn't care if there were no plants or neat borders, especially crater-crazy Polly. What they liked was the sun trap it proved to be, and Mitten, our elderly tortoiseshell cat and queen of her realm, could regularly be found basking on the warm flagstones at the bottom of the backdoor steps, a habit that didn't endear her to the dogs.

If Polly or Daisy wanted to go out when Mitten was sunbathing, they would stand on the steps, tails wagging, worry wrinkling their brows as they looked down in consternation at her feline ladyship. Needless to say, she wouldn't budge and they wouldn't risk jumping over her. She looked harmless lying there, purring up at them, but they both knew that if they took one step further her claws would snap open and she'd lash out at them in a flash. I didn't blame them for being nervous. They'd have needed high-jump practice over vaults to avoid her well-honed paw skills.

The situation required our intervention, which we usually provided once we heard the familiar and slightly panicked woofs one or other of the dogs would utter. Claude was the only one oblivious to Mitten's regal control. He was so old and blind he just stumbled over her regardless. The resulting scuffle involved much snarling, hissing and spitting but once they'd extracted their various legs from each other's mouths, he'd resume his bumbling progress, leaving Mitten looking cross, indignant and outplayed.

That being said, the cats settled in quickly, which was good. They took up residence on the sofas and discovered the fireplace, which was not good. Whether there was a residual smell left as a parting gift by a previous owner's cat we didn't know, but whatever the case, all three of ours seemed to believe the hearth was an indoor toilet.

Lighting a fire in it didn't help much either. They waited until it had burnt out and strolled right in, as was evident from the paw shaped ash prints weaving numerous pathways across the gleaming floor and glass-topped tables. They were probably all over the sofas too, but since these were a forgiving cat hair and biscuit crumb colour anyway,we didn't see them. Other than this, we didn't know what to do, so we gave up and screened the fireplace off until we needed it.

The girls also settled in well. From day one we barely saw them. They took themselves off to the ice rink at every opportunity. Adding to their entertainment, there was a pool room right next door to the rink which they made for after skating, and then Nando's Chicken, our favourite Portuguese fast food restaurant, was in the adjacent building.

For the first time, my daughters had a proper social life independent of us, and it was good for them. On the other hand, I had to start acting like a real mother and setting curfews, a new challenge for us all. I'd never had to do so before because we'd always collected them from wherever they were going. In Krugersdorp, they could make their own way home most of the time.

Once they started back at school in January 1996, timing became something of an issue. Jodie was fifteen and boyfriends were beginning to appear on the scene. My eldest, however, wasn't very good at playing the street-wise teenager. I set an eleven o'clock deadline for her to be home, which I thought was reasonable considering we were up so much earlier in the mornings, but I wasn't totally inflexible, not really.

"If you know you can't make it by eleven, Jo, phone me. Okay? As long as I know, then I won't worry."

"Okay, Mum, will do," she'd say, dashing out of the door to meet 'the one' waiting in his cranky old Opel Manta, known as the Green Mamba, on the grass outside. It was a car Bill had sold him and I was always anxious about its reliability. We'd driven it ourselves for a while and I had personal experience of its fickle ways.

Now of course, I, like all mothers, knew Jodie wouldn't make it home on time all the time, irrespective of the car's temperament. She wouldn't have been a normal teenager if she had, but I thought she'd be savvy enough to phone me before pushing out the boundaries.

Unluckily for her, she was too innocent by half and would forget to call, turning up in a mad flurry of apologies half an hour late and so getting herself grounded. I didn't like doing it but felt I had to. There was no point in laying down the law and then not enforcing it. Poor Jo.

It was the same when it came to smoking. I followed my nose one day and found a cigarette butt in her school blazer pocket.

"Oh sorry, Mum, Jenny must have dropped it in there."

I looked at her.

"Okay, if you say so, but if Jenny wants to do that again, tell her you'll be grounded … again."

She had the grace to go pink.

Mo, in contrast, was much cannier at playing the parent game. She phoned me religiously when she knew she'd be late, which was most of the time; I never caught her with any evidence of smoking, although I knew she did; and I didn't know if she had a boyfriend, other than the dozens who buzzed about her like bees round a honey pot at the rink. Apparently, she had more than one, but I was never introduced. Mo also used me to make excuses for her if she didn't want to go to a party or some other social event.

"Will you phone them and say I can't come, Mum?"

"Why? Of course you can go!"

"But I don't feel like it. If you tell them I can't, then I don't have to explain."

"All right. If that's what you want, but don't go making me out to be some kind of ogre. That's your father's job."

We both laughed, but I had the impression I was considered to be unjustifiably strict in some quarters. It depended on the friends, though. If she liked them, I was the coolest mum on the planet. If she didn't, I was unreasonably restrictive. It didn't matter to me, but I won't deny I preferred being cool.

Small town life

L ife in Krugersdorp was everything I hoped it would be. I revelled in the simple pleasures of walking to the Spar to buy groceries and fresh bread. The shop bakery was excellent, and they made the most divine *melk tert* (milk tart), which rapidly became an addiction. It was typically an Afrikaans confection, probably brought to South Africa from the Netherlands.

Made like a flan in a pastry case, it tasted like a cross between custard tart and cheesecake with cinnamon sprinkled on top. Heaven. Afrikaans confectionery was generally too sweet and sickly for me. The worst were *koeksisters*, deep-fried and syrup-soaked plaited donuts. They made my teeth hurt just thinking about them, but the milk tart made by the Spar baker was a taste sensation to dream about and something to be savoured – although not slowly. It was almost impossible not to eat the whole flan in one go.

The hardware store was another regular haunt, as were the second-hand shop, the pharmacy and the video store. We became known in our small neighbourhood and it felt good to greet the store owners every day when we went to fetch our fresh milk and bread. It was a novelty because we'd never been so close to the shops before; not having to use the car was a real blessing.

There were regular 'helpers' outside the shops too; these were unemployed men from the nearby township of Munsieville. They would offer to carry customers' shopping bags or push their trolleys to the car if need be. Since we walked the roughly half-kilometre from our house, we didn't need either service, but we normally slipped them a few coins. The resulting toothy smiles suggested that should we ever need them, we'd be sure of the help.

Across the road from the Spar was an Aladdin's cave the girls referred to as the 'crap *winkel*' (*winkel* being Afrikaans for 'shop'). Whether this was its real name or not remained a mystery to me, but it was one of those buy-anything-for-practically-nothing shops that proliferate in most large towns these days. In Krugersdorp, it was quite a find and we often went there just for fun. Jodie was going through a gypsy fashion phase and bought a couple of lovely floaty skirts for just a few Rands. And it was always good for last minute presents when, later on, living on shoestrings came to be the order of the day.

Historically, Krugersdorp was a *boer* area and in 1996, the culture was still largely Afrikaans, as was the language. It was an eye-opener for me as I hadn't lived among Afrikaners much previously. In demographic terms, they were considered to be a specific ethnic group, but this was not strictly true. The Afrikaner is a person of surprisingly mixed background and stems directly from the activities of the East India Company, the Dutch merchant navy giant that established Cape Town as a supply (re-victualling) station in 1652.

Although the first settlers were predominantly Dutch in origin, the Company saw the advantages of developing the Cape area and offered conditional immigration to a few groups of people, including its own German soldiers returning from Asia, French Huguenots and other Europeans among whom were the Portuguese who'd been trading along the coast since Vasco de Gama's first landing in the late 15th century.

In essence, the condition was that these approved immigrants had to agree to start farming and supply the Company with their produce. Despite their different origins, all the settlers came to use a common language, which (put very simply) was a mixture of colloquial Dutch from the southern Netherlands, vocabulary absorbed from the East India Company sailors and words adopted from Madagascan and Malay slaves as well as from local tribes.

The resulting blend was Afrikaans, which was mostly recognisable as a derivative of Dutch and Flemish but quite different in many respects, notably in its grammar and adapted vocabulary. Oddly, it only achieved status as its own distinctive language in the early twentieth century.

What I found so interesting was that many of the surnames most common to Afrikaners were still of Portuguese, German and French origin. In our local phone book, we had extensive lists of Ferreiras, Schneiders, Jouberts and Du Toits, maybe not quite as long as the Van de Merwe, Visser and Coetzee lists, but still significant. What was even more interesting was that they'd integrated elements of all these nationalities into the Afrikaans culture, although conformist Dutch still appeared to be the most dominant.

The community we lived amongst was typical in that it was fairly conservative and religious. We often watched the locals walking past the house on Sundays to go to the nearby Dutch Reformed Church. Dressed in their Sunday best, they carried their bibles openly, the outward symbol of their Christian faith. The custom of walking to worship was probably linked to the original Dutch church practices where any kind of labour on Sundays was frowned upon. Driving was work, so they walked.

During the week, we witnessed another Afrikaans custom when we saw the children going to school barefoot. I'd heard about it but not seen it until we lived in Krugersdorp and my surprise was even greater when I realised they not only went barefoot in summer but in winter too. These were hardy children. They didn't appear to feel the cold or hurt their feet on loose pebbles as they bounced happily across roads and broken paving stones. A testament to their former farming background, these youngsters must have been healthier, stronger and more immune to illness than their well coddled English counterparts. It cheered me to see them skipping along, unencumbered by ill-fitting shoes, and I hoped the custom would endure.

All told, it felt like a different world, especially when we heard Afrikaans spoken around us so much more than we did elsewhere. From the conversations we could hear over the garden wall, our immediate neighbours on one side were undoubtedly an Afrikaans family. There seemed to be dozens of them in the small house and their front yard was always full of cars in different states of assembly, but more often than not permanently disassembled.

On the other side, we had Wally. I was never sure of his cultural background; he mostly spoke English, but his language was peppered with Afrikaans and he had a strong accent. His origins were anyone's guess. Wally bought and sold bric-a-brac and his home was bursting with the fruits of his purchases. It didn't look as if he managed to sell much, so maybe his sales technique needed some polishing. Since he claimed to be an ex-policeman, this probably wasn't the best background for a life of trading. Whatever the case, he was kind and friendly and kept an eye on us when Bill was away.

Driving disasters

My journey to work from Krugersdorp was longer than it had been in any of our other homes, although it was a much nicer drive. Door to door, it was about forty kilometres, and a large section of the route was on the road we called the Krugersdorp highway, the R28, which I joined at the ice rink. I found it wonderfully exhilarating to descend the long, steep hill out of Krugersdorp with its breathtaking panorama of the valley spread out before me. To the north west were the Sterkfontein caves, a series of limestone caves rich in ancient fossils. A little further to the north was the Rhino park, a nature reserve dedicated to those massive herbivores. Krugersdorp also had its own small safari park. We were blessed to have these special, if not unique, places so close by.

Once I'd reached the foot of the hill, a four-way stop sorted all those heading east into Johannesburg with those like me going further north before turning off to Randburg. After this junction, the road opened up into the highway proper and I revelled in putting my foot down, flying up and down the hills until I took the Muldersdrift off-ramp.

The scenery was rural farmland, African style, with golden *veld* grass blanketing the slopes and red earth scoring the banks. There were few houses and for the brief time it took me to reach the exit to Randburg, I could almost imagine I was back in the rolling beauty of the Natal midlands. From the turn off, I wound my way through the pretty Muldersdrift village, sometimes stopping for petrol and a paper at the small garage. The village was also home to the gracious Drift Inn, where we occasionally indulged in a cup of coffee when we wanted to experience its atmosphere of timeless peace.

The rural environment lasted until I was quite close to Randburg, although the main through route became increasingly busy and by the time I reached the junction with the N1 concrete highway, the congestion had slowed the traffic down to a crawl.

At other times, I would keep off the main roads and drive through the small holdings on the dirt tracks before joining the next main arterial route into the city. On a good day, it took me forty minutes. If the traffic was bad, it could take up to three times longer, so I made it my habit to leave as early as possibly to avoid the worst of the delays, dropping the girls off at school first.

I enjoyed the 'me time' my journey to work gave me despite having a dreadful series of misfortunes with the cars I drove. Bill had replaced my Fiat Uno with a clean but elderly VW Jetta when we decided to prune down our monthly outgoings in Olivedale. It didn't last long after our move.

One misty, wet morning, I turned onto the R28 and started down the hill, taking extra care because the visibility was poor and the road was slippery in the wet. I could barely see a few metres in front of me. The rain was lashing down and the hill was shrouded in cloud, so I was surprised when I was overtaken by another car going at some speed. A few seconds later I rounded the bend and was confronted with the horrible sight of the recently speeding car crushed against the rear of a large lorry up ahead.

The next thing I knew I too was sliding straight towards them. The smash had damaged the crushed car's sump and oil must have poured out onto the road before the two vehicles came to a halt. There wasn't a thing I could do. I had little steering and no control, especially no brakes, so the unavoidable happened and I slid into the back of the now stationary car before I could steer myself into the verge.

What occurred next was a classic domino effect. One vehicle after another got caught in the pile-up and I later learnt that altogether twenty-two were written off that day including my Jetta. Thankfully no one was seriously hurt, not even the driver of the car that had set off the whole chain reaction. I could hardly believe he'd survived the impact.

Needless to say, I didn't get to work that day. I went home in the back of a police car and stayed put on the sofa in a state of dazed shock, watching replays of the aftermath on the national news. The towing companies must have made a fortune out of the wreckage; they were already circling the accident site like vultures looking for pickings before I'd even left.

Nevertheless, I continued to enjoy my trips to work, especially when it came to the Alfa Junior sports car Bill bought me as compensation for losing the Jetta. I'd mourned my Alfa Sprint, the car I'd had in Noordwyk, but the Junior was even more fun to drive and twice as pretty. It had a two-litre engine which took the hills with smooth ease while making a gorgeous throaty growl with its exhaust.

I revelled in it and the girls adored it. Mo made me promise to leave it to her in my will, optimistic child that she was. Unfortunately for me, someone in its past had enjoyed pushing it to its limits even more than I did and I quickly ascertained that it drank nearly as much oil as it did petrol, which usually meant filling up with both every time I went to the garage.

During the first winter after we bought it, there was an extremely cold snap when the night-time temperature dropped to well below zero. We had an unusually heavy frost in Krugersdorp North, which was close to being the highest point in the area and therefore prone to extremes. There was ice on both sides of the windscreen the following morning. If nothing else, this should have warned me, as I knew the car needed time to warm up on cold days, but I was in a hurry to get to work and didn't stop to think. After loading the girls and their bags into its small back seat, we managed to drive five hundred metres up the road before my lovely Alfa died. Apparently, the oil remaining in the sump had thickened to a sludge and the engine seized. I was devastated and I don't think Mo has ever forgiven me for destroying her inheritance.

My replacement was a rapidly acquired Renault 5 convertible, which I also became fond of, more because of its quirks than its reliability. It was much more economical than the Alfa and very nippy but without a high top-speed. As a result, I tended to take the more rural routes to work instead of belting along the highways.

On one occasion, I was scooting through the back way when I was appalled to see an African woman lying by the side of the road. I'm ashamed to say I didn't stop because by then, the use of decoys to trap innocent drivers and rob them was increasing, but I couldn't forget the sight and still hope she was simply sleeping and not dead. It wasn't unusual to see people taking a nap on the grassy verges of the city roads and the way they lay often made them appear corpse-like; I'd never seen anyone doing so in such a lonely spot, though. However, when I went home, she'd gone, which relieved me, if not my conscience.

Eventually, the Renault also fell victim to the rigours of nature. Its soft top was vulnerable, especially to the hail storms that hit us now and then. One weekend, we watched the approach of the standard afternoon storm without any suspicion of what it was about to dump on us. Because the garage was in use as Bill's motorbike workshop, his car was under the carport and the Renault was parked in the open driveway. It was a case of whoever was first home got the shady cover, protection from the sun being the more usual requirement in Johannesburg.

On that afternoon, the sky looked more threatening than usual. Even so, we didn't anticipate what was coming and before we could do anything to prevent disaster, hail stones the size of golf balls started crashing onto the roof of the house. The noise was beyond anything we'd ever experienced and the four of us stood helplessly, silenced by the row as we watched the hail rip through the roof of my car.

When it was over, we inspected the damage. The engine cover was pitted with dents but still whole; the vinyl roof, however, was completely destroyed and the interior looked as if someone had tipped a huge bucket of ice cubes into it.

"Oh my word, it looks like someone's attacked it with a knife," I gasped, gazing at the jagged tears in the fabric.

"You think this is bad," Bill said, arriving back from a brief recce along the road. "The Smits' red Jetta two doors up has holes in its roof too, and that's steel. They're not impressed."

"Oh no, poor things! Just as well we didn't try coming outside to save the Renault then."

"Yep, we'd have been a goner for sure. Stone dead. Literally."

I wanted to laugh at his quip, but it was too true to be funny.

It was sobering to think that even if we'd had anywhere to put the car under cover, it would have been madness to try. Luckily, our corrugated iron roof was undamaged and only lost a little more paint, which brought me to two conclusions: firstly, the corrugated shape was probably what made the roof strong, and secondly, the large bare patches may have been the consequence of previous hail damage.

Anyway, from that day on I had to drive everywhere without a roof over my head, which made winter even more interesting. But at least I got priority under the carport, a distinct bonus. Before setting off in the frosty early mornings, I would put my fluffy floral dressing gown on over my coat and the girls and I would wrap blankets around our legs. I shamelessly kept my furry slippers on too. I must have made an eccentric vision as I joined the commuter traffic into town every day, but I didn't care. Being warm was much more important. On one occasion, I needed to stop by the side of the road to fetch something from the boot. Before getting out of the car, I exchanged my slippers for shoes, but my dressing gown stayed on. If there were any bumper bashings on the road that morning, they were probably my fault.

Conquering the Argus

With the move to Krugersdorp, my cycling training also intensified as 1996 was going to be my Argus year and March the 10th was the date. I'd been keeping in touch with Annette, my neighbour from Bryanston, and she still wanted to do it too. We weren't able to get together for rides out much, although we managed the challenge of cycling up the Krugersdorp hill together one weekend morning. The sense of achievement it gave us both convinced us we should go for it and we kept up the mutual encouragement by phone and email.

We'd both sent in our applications and were equally terrified and excited when we found we'd got in. Because there was a limit to the number of participants the organisers would allow and a seeding system was in place, there'd been no guarantee of acceptance. The Argus attracted thousands of cyclists, and anyone who'd done it before was given priority over new entrants. After that, it was down to a first come, first served system until the cut off number, so I was elated to know we'd made it.

Krugersdorp's environs were ideal for cycling. There were long hills all around us. If I woke up early enough, I could do a round-trip of roughly eight kilometres by following the perimeter of the northern Krugersdorp suburbs. It was a good warm up before I went into work.

At the weekend, my trips took me further. Robert Broom Drive, effectively the northern ring road, crossed the Krugersdorp highway and followed a long, very hilly and scenic ridge, quite possibly part of the reef that was the source of Johannesburg's gold mines.

The road was usually quiet on a weekend morning, and depending on how far I wanted to go, I could cycle about ten kilometres of this stretch before cutting through to the more or less parallel Ontdekkers Road for the return trip; alternatively, if I felt really brave, I could continue until the road reached Roodepoort before circling back. This latter route made up a distance of nearly forty kilometres.

One Sunday I decided to push myself by doing the longer ride and kept going on Robert Broom Drive along the ridge. What I hadn't appreciated before was how steep the hills were and I hadn't thought to bring anything to eat or any kind of energy drink.

On one particularly long and steep climb near Kloofendal (Kloof means deep ravine in Afrikaans, hence the steep gradient), my legs simply gave up. My racing bike had twelve gears, somewhat meagre by today's standards although it was generally enough for our terrain. But not this time. Half way up the hill, my body went on strike: my calves turned to jelly, my ankles seized, my arms shook, and I promptly toppled over onto the grassy verge – not very gracefully and more than a little heavily.

My first feeling was acute embarrassment. I was mortified that my ride had come to such a humiliating demise. Untangling my legs from the frame, I crawled out on my hands and knees and looked around. There was nothing and no one about, thank goodness. The indignity of my situation was only relieved by knowing no one had seen me plunge into the grass; that would have been sad after all my months of work. But the fact remained that I was reduced to a lump of quaking mush and couldn't move for several minutes. There wasn't any doubt; I was having a major energy failure, a power cut of note.

That was when I discovered the wonders of Coke; not the white stuff, I should add, but the sickly sweet, sugar-loaded brown stuff that children seem to thrive on. Pulling my bike back onto its wheels, I staggered my way up the rest of the hill to a junction and to my great joy, saw there was a petrol station just a few metres down the road to my left. I hobbled into the forecourt, dumped my bike outside their shop and delved into my bum bag for some coins to buy a can of soft drink. All they had was Coke, but it more than did the trick. Several swigs and some not so discreet burps later, I felt my energy creep back. By the end of the can, I was completely revived.

I wasn't sure whether to be amazed or alarmed by this almost magical recovery. The ingredients of Coke are a mystery to me, but whatever it consists of, it was the sugar saturation that most likely put me back on my bike, probably not something my doctor would have recommended. But he wasn't watching and I managed to complete the rest of my ride back home without further collapse.

After that and regardless of its evils, I always made sure to have a can of cola with me in my small saddle bag and never had a problem again. With this comforting thought, I felt sure that nothing the Argus could throw at me could be worse than Robert Broom Drive. Well, I was wrong.

One of the other managers at work had also entered the Argus. Stephen was the IT manager and we'd always got on well, especially when it came to discussing cycling. He was much more experienced than I was and had done the race before. Consequently, I made sure to glean as many tips from him as possible. Take food, he said, dried fruit, nuts and muesli bars were good, and make sure to have plenty of water. Drinks would be provided on the route, but it was essential to have liquid to spare as it could get hot. And then there was my Coke. I had to have that too.

Stephen and his wife, Shirley, offered to take me to Cape Town with them as Annette was going under her own steam with Granville. I hoped we'd see each other on the course, but I knew that with twenty odd thousand other riders, the chances of meeting up were fairly remote. Without Stephen and Shirley, I would otherwise have been alone as Bill stayed at home with the girls and the animals. I was not only grateful for the lift down but also for the company before the race.

We travelled down to Cape Town by car on Friday, March the 8th, knowing we'd have Saturday to collect our race packs and acclimatise before the big day on Sunday. I think I slept most of the way down and to make up for it, spent all of Saturday feeling sick with nerves.

Our accommodation was in an apartment Stephen had rented for the weekend, so after collecting our entry numbers, we did some Argus sight-seeing around the city; in other words, we went to check out the starting point and to see how close to it we'd be able to park the following morning. In the evening, we consumed plates of pasta loaded with cheese and vegetables which Shirley prepared for us, although I was so keyed-up I didn't feel like eating at all.

"Come on, Val, you must finish your meal," Shirley urged me. "You'll need the energy tomorrow."

"I know, but I'm not so hungry now. I'm not a big eater at the best of times," I said, grimacing at the mound of food in front of me.

"Shut up, open up and shovel it in," she grinned without sympathy. So I did my best but didn't manage it all. Butterflies had taken up all the remaining space in my stomach.

On Sunday morning, we needed to be at the starting point in the city at a specific time depending on where we were placed in the open categories. We donned our cycling gear and pinned our race numbers on our shirts before leaving the apartment. I'd bought a special top in the colours and design of the South African flag which made me feel absurdly proud. It was also useful as it had handy pouches for my dried fruit and nuts, and other essential items. My bike's tyres were new, I had a pump and a water bottle fixed to the frame, and in my tiny saddle bag, I had a new inner tube, a puncture repair kit and a can of cola. I was set to go if I could get going at all.

The official start was at 6:15, but that was for the 'elite' professional and top riders. Following them came the seeded riders whose position was based on previous performance. Then a new batch of cyclists started off every four minutes to avoid too much of a bottleneck type crush. In spite of having done the race a few years before, Stephen was still in the open categories with Annette and me, but we were all in different groups. Our start times were somewhere between 9:00 and 10:00.

Stephen set off a few minutes ahead of me and I didn't see him again until he greeted me at the finish line. He'd come in with an impressive time of under four hours.

When it came to my turn to start, I found myself intimidated by the throng of other cyclists around me. I couldn't see Annette and it felt far too crowded. A moment of panic overwhelmed me; I was used to cycling alone, and the sudden press of bikes in my space was quite terrifying. I tried to mount my steed, wobbled madly and stumbled off it again. The mouse in me took over. I was too much of a wimp to stake my claim to the road, so I waited for all the others in my bunch to get going before I followed in their dust. Once I was stable and moving in a straight line I settled down and managed to find my place in the pack. At the back.

I'd barely got going before the next bunch had caught up and overtaken me, but at least I met up with Annette again and we urged each other on, the result being that for the first ten kilometres I had no real awareness of where I was; I was just intent on holding my place and keeping going. After a while, I started inching ahead of my friend. She was riding a mountain bike, which by design wasn't as fast as my racer.

"You go on, Val. I'll just hold you back," she said, generous as always.

"Okay, but I'm sure I'll see you again. I'll probably need a rest before long," I laughed, feeling a bit guilty for leaving her behind.

Given a free rein, I thought I'd see how fast I could go. I put my head down, crouched over my handle-bars and went for it, covering the remaining distance across the peninsular to Muizenberg in good time.

Then disaster struck. We'd been cycling on reasonably level ground up to this point but when we joined the coast road towards Simonstown, the wind was blowing hard and we began doing some serious climbing. With my *Highveld* lungs, I made good gains on some of the other cyclists who seemed to be struggling. Pleased with my pace, I was overtaking a small group when a gust of wind blew one of them off balance. He wobbled madly and fell into me, his wheel catching mine and then hitting another bike behind me. We all tumbled over.

It was a veritable pile up and a big tangled mess. Other riders got caught up in the mêlée as well and by the time we'd sorted ourselves out, there must have been about ten bikes involved. Luckily, no one was hurt, but we were all grazed, bruised and a bit dazed. Nonetheless, the festive atmosphere came to our rescue; this was the Cape Argus after all and it was supposed to be as much fun as pain. The locals helped us on our way, apologising for the wind, and we all laughed, or at least smiled, shook hands and climbed back on our saddles to set off again. This time it didn't take me long to pull away from the group and at last I felt I was benefiting from all those kilometres I'd burnt at high altitude along Robert Broom Drive and the Krugersdorp hill.

At various stages along the route, I grabbed drinks from the refreshment tables and munched on my dried fruit supplies. The scenery was spectacular. The Cape coast is one of the most beautiful in the world. There was no better way to see it, and the supporting crowds were an incredible inspiration. They did so much to cheer us on at all the most challenging spots.

My moment of huge personal triumph was when I topped the famous Chapman's Peak Drive and gazed down at Hout Bay far below. I still have the official photo taken at the check-point on Chapman's Peak showing me laughing with the exhilaration of having made it. The view over the sea and across to the steep cliffs beyond was stunning and I felt I was on top of the world in every sense.

During the early stages of the climb, I remember cruising past a young man, who was cursing everything he could think of and more besides as he struggled to pedal his way up the hill. I couldn't help grinning and feeling rather smug. He must have been in his early twenties; I was forty. It helped me to appreciate that the months of practice on the *Highveld* had paid off.

Conversely, there's another photo of me at Llandudno after I'd battled my way up the final test, the Suikerbossie hill. In this snapped moment I looked positively wasted. Having completed ninety kilometres of the race, Suikerbossie was a killer. It was only a two-kilometre climb, but with a 7% gradient, it was solid uphill cycling of the worst and most taxing kind.

From the foot of the rise, I looked up, and up, and up some more, and nearly died. Did we really have to do that? After everything we'd done? My memory of Robert Broom Drive was nothing by comparison, and it seemed like an exceptionally mean trick to play on us. Had it not been for my grim determination to finish and not to walk up any of the hills, I might have given up before hauling myself and my bike to the top. Suikerbossie had broken many an Argus contender in its time, but I did it, thankful that it hadn't beaten me and relieved yet again that I'd done so much high-altitude training.

On the plus side, the following descent was a joy: a long, long, glorious spin down to Llandudno. Still, the face in my photo tells the story of how tough that final ascent had been. I was exhausted and very glad that Stephen was there at Maiden's Cove, Camp's Bay to welcome me in. He helped me lever my aching limbs off my bike, and we both waited for Annette to arrive. As I recall, she made it not long after me, just as tired and just as elated.

We were so proud of ourselves. It felt like a huge achievement. I wasn't a natural cyclist having started so late in life, but I'd learnt enough to keep myself on my saddle for this ultimate endurance ride. My certificate tells me I finished my 105 kilometres in five hours and thirty-four minutes but for me, the time didn't matter; making it to the end was what counted. Crossing that finish line still rates as one of my most rewarding moments ever.

In the following two years of our Krugersdorp life, I carried on cycling, but no longer alone. Mo was bitten by the bug as well and we bought her a second-hand racing bike, a striking red and yellow model, which she used with great aplomb screaming down hills at three times my speed. Then our new Krugersdorp friend, Bobbity, started coming too.

Bobbity was a kind of colleague of Bill's in that she was the bookkeeper for one of the production companies he used when making his corporate videos. She and her husband, Garth, lived at the bottom of the Krugersdorp hill, but on the north side not far from the Sterkfontein caves.

They had a large plot with a hacienda style house that they kept adding to as their family grew. Garth had his own truck sales business which he operated from one corner of the plot. On any given day, there would be up to a dozen or so vehicles in stock, some being repaired and overhauled, others being offered for sale.

It was a thriving enterprise and he did very well – not surprising given his genial nature. I don't think I ever saw Garth without a smile on his face, even when he was cross or frustrated about something. He was a great story teller too, and often had us laughing at his truck buying escapades.

"You know what, guys," he'd say, leaning back in his chair and folding his arms, a bottle of beer tucked in the crook of his elbow. "It was crazy. There we were, Dev and myself, out in the sticks, trying to get this old truck out of the mud. It must have been there for twenty years, man. I'm not lying! It was buried up to its axles, but the engine still ran! Well, we had to have it, didn't we?"

And so the stories went. His excursions into the *bundu* in search of a bargain were the stuff of urban legends, but in Garth's case they were true.

The rest of the domain was under Bobbity's care and she employed two maids and at least two gardeners to maintain the spread. I always felt like calling it South Fork after the famous Texan TV series. With its rambling Spanish style home and its large acreage that nearly always seemed to be basking in the sunshine, it felt quite ranch-like.

As soon as we met, we clicked, and visiting Bobbity quickly became essential to my Krugersdorp life. I loved the vibrant, lively atmosphere that surrounded the family. They had dozens of dogs, several cats, and numerous children. Their employees were treated with direct but warm good humour and, in turn, the household staff clearly adored them. One of their maids, a smiling girl called Thembi, was my favourite. Always ready to laugh, she took Bobbity's no-nonsense teasing style in good heart and never seemed to be out of sorts. My daughters enjoyed going there too and Thembi loved them both.

Bobbity had a pool and frequently entertained large numbers of friends with *braais*, but my favourite was to head for her house straight from work or on a Saturday afternoon when we would break open a bottle of incredibly cheap, very bad wine and chat about anything and everything while downing glasses of severely awful, mildly fizzy, barely alcoholic plonk – if we managed to stop laughing, that is. She was bright, funny, practical and bossy and we became firm friends.

When Bobbity found out about Mo's and my cycling, she was determined to join us.

"Val, is it true you did the Argus? Really? And you and Mo go cycling around here? With all these hills? I want to come too," she rushed on, without drawing breath. "I need to get fit again. I've got an old bike in the garage. I'll get one of the guys to fix it up and I'll come with you. I want to do the Argus too."

It all burst out with typical Bobbity enthusiasm, and within a week or so, she'd got herself geared up and started coming with us.

In a group of three, we could explore further without too much risk of getting lost or running into trouble and we started taking different routes to the north and west of Krugersdorp. It was great fun and there were plenty of jokes along with the groans of despair when the hills became ever longer and steeper. I have to say I never found the uphill runs easy, no matter how much I cycled, but racing down the other side made it all seem worthwhile. For some reason I was always last to the bottom, although if I'm honest, I think Bobbity and Mo were much braver about just letting go and hurtling down the long straight descents than I was.

The West Rand was not so well known at that time and we rarely saw other sports cyclists on our morning rides, which meant we had the roads to ourselves and we used them to the full. What helped even more was that Krugersdorp was still its own place. The huge sprawl of metropolitan Johannesburg hadn't yet spread out like a giant puddle, spilling into all the rural spaces and filling the gaps between the two. The only other people we tended to see on two wheels were local Africans who used their bikes as transport and were undoubtedly fitter than we would ever be.

In the end, we didn't do the Argus as a trio; instead, we entered several other 'fun rides' as they were called and some of these were pretty challenging. Competitive cycling on the *Highveld* was much tougher than riding at sea level. A sixty-kilometre ride around Johannesburg was every bit as gruelling as the Argus had been; just not quite as beautiful and without the same level of kudos.

Introducing Solly

Much though we'd done at the little house, we still needed help with the more structural jobs. For one thing, the roof needed painting and while Bill was happy to get up a ladder, he didn't have time to do the preparation as well. Added to that, the garden walls needed attention with some re-plastering and re-building in places. We wanted to raise the height of the wall between us and our car-wrecking neighbours, mainly so we wouldn't need to see into their growing scrap yard. For all these jobs, we decided to employ some local labour.

Up on Robert Broom Drive, there was a stretch of grass verge next to the Munsieville township where unemployed painters, builders and plasterers would gather and wait for business to come their way. Anyone looking for a specific type of labourer could go there, select an individual with the appropriate skills and make an offer of work. It was something like an informal labour exchange and the hiring was done on a casual basis with mutually agreed rates. This was how we came by Solly: painter, builder, plasterer, plumber and general factotum, not to forget gardener, guardian and totally trusted helper.

Solly lived in Munsieville and worked for a number of people in Krugersdorp, but when we hired him, he was between jobs and had some free time. Bill found him wearing paint and plaster splashed overalls and carrying a bricklayer's trowel. He sported a pocketful of paintbrushes and had a large spanner in his other pocket. He was clearly a Jack of many trades and therefore the right person for our numerous jobs.

I took to Solly immediately. Brighter and wiser than poor Wilson, Solly was tall, thin and gentlemanly. I've no idea how old he was, but probably not as old as he looked, which was about forty. His face was heavily lined without being wrinkled as such and he was very dark, probably from spending so much time out in the sun. He spoke quietly, offering opinions about how jobs could best be done but in an unassuming way that Bill liked, which was a relief. Patience wasn't Bill's strong suit, but Solly didn't try anyone's and knew how to listen and take instructions; a major plus. The clincher was that the dogs, especially Polly, trusted him.

Solly proceeded to work methodically on scraping, sanding and painting the roof. When he'd finished, it looked magnificent; a brand-new hat for our old lady.

He then set his skills to building up the dividing wall in the back garden, which he managed without fuss and without incurring Bill's displeasure; another big plus. When that was done, he did the re-plastering needed and then painted the whole house. Meanwhile, Bill laid a brickwork drive, which Solly grouted and then built the piers to support the gates at the end of the drive. Not to labour the point, Solly was a gem. He should have come with a sign saying 'no job too big or too small'; he would do anything.

Of course, not all of these milestones were achieved at once. The work took place over more than a year, but when the jobs and the money for them came to an end, we didn't want to lose him, so I offered him some gardening work to keep him going. Sadly, this was where his skills fell short of perfect.

We had some large beds at the front of the house that needed digging over and weeding. I'd planted several succulent tropical plants in them, which were obviously meant to be there. However, there were also numerous small perennials that I'd put in to fill the gaps. These included Michaelmas and Shasta daisies, Phlox, Golden Rod and Bergenia, all flowers that would come back year on year. But there were also weeds among them. For once, I didn't give Solly enough instructions and after asking him to weed the beds, he went at it like a bulldozer and pulled out everything other than the large tropical plants.

"Solly, where are all my flowers?" I moaned, genuinely distressed.

"But madam, you tell me to take out the weeds. I think they are all weeds. I'm so sorry," he responded, equally genuinely distressed. I was now used to being called 'madam'; many of the Africans in Johannesburg did, but it made me feel ancient. I preferred 'mama' or 'auntie'.

"No, Solly, they weren't, but it's my fault. I should have shown you."

What else could I say? He'd been so eager to do the job thoroughly, and I'd assumed he knew about plants too. My mistake. After that, I confined him to watering the remains and cutting the grass in the back garden, which he did with his usual diligence. It couldn't quite be described as a lawn, but Solly treated it like a cricket pitch. We'd already filled in the Polly craters, smoothed it out and seeded it. Now, the grass was growing nicely even though it was still a bit lumpy. Nevertheless, before it had really taken root and settled, Bill invited hordes of people for a *potjie-kos* lunch.

For those not familiar with this typically South African fare, *potjie-kos* is a complete meal cooked in a huge witches' cauldron that stands on three legs just like the ones in the fairy stories. For Bill, a *potjie-kos* feast meant loading layers of meat, potatoes and vegetables into the cauldron with lashings of hot Indian curry sauce and cooking it all slowly over a charcoal fire. It was always delicious and our visitors made short shrift of it as well as the gallons of punch we made to alleviate the searing heat of the spices. None of this was good for our developing lawn.

When everyone had gone, Solly came and raked the grass over again, tending to it with the devotion of a green-keeper and removing all the cigarette butts that had been carelessly thrown down. His patience and acceptance of our visitors' slovenly habits were quite touching and I promised myself I would find a way of supporting him as long as it was feasible to do so.

Furry farewells

Our animal family were very happy in Krugersdorp, but two of our furry crew were very old by this time. Mitten, the cat we'd acquired as a kitten when we first lived on the farm in Natal, was fifteen in 1996, and Claude, our Shih Tsu, must have been close to that. It broke our hearts to lose them both in fairly quick succession.

Claude went first. He'd deteriorated to the extent he was rarely awake, had no control over his functions and lost all joy in life; he barely even acknowledged our presence. None of the family could bring themselves to agree about putting him to sleep, so I took the decision for them. I felt he'd given up and it wasn't fair to keep him going when he was most likely in pain. One afternoon, I picked him up and carried him round the corner to Anneke, the vet.

She was young, full of compassion and very caring; she also agreed that for Claude it was the kindest solution. I held him as she injected the drug that put him finally to sleep, and she held me when I cried. It felt like treachery somehow. I knew Jodie would be devastated, and she was. It took her a few days to forgive me for taking her little friend from her, but even she understood in the end that he was probably very ill. He'd had an unhealthy smell about him that suggested things were very wrong inside. Poor Claude.

Even worse for me was losing Mitten about six months later. She'd been losing weight and looked like the old lady she was, but she continued to be as feisty and bossy as ever. I'd always loved the way she managed the dogs. In fact, I think she believed she was a dog and that our other cats, Stanley and Spooky, were nothing to do with her.

When I arrived home from work, Polly, Daisy and Mitten met me at the gate and Mitten was always in front as befitted her senior position. By day, she rubbed round their legs, purring at them but also bullying them without mercy. At night, she curled up in their baskets with them. They were a gang of three and she was the boss.

What made me realise she was at the end of her days was an uncharacteristic change in this behaviour. Mitten started spending more time sitting alone on the wall in the garden or curled up on my lap. She stopped bossing the dogs around and became fragile both physically and in her demeanour. On the day she refused to eat, I took her round to Anneke fearing the worst.

"I'm afraid her kidneys are failing, Val," she concluded, after examining an unusually docile Mitten. "She's probably in pain. Do you see the way she's sitting all hunched up?"

I nodded, tears already threatening with the knowledge of what this all meant.

"She's been sitting like that a lot in the last few days," I told her.

"That's a sure sign of kidney damage. It must be hurting her badly. You know what I'm going to recommend, don't you?"

I nodded again, unable to speak.

"Will you stay with her?"

"Of course."

And so I went home without my beloved cat. She'd been with us since we first moved to the country, starting life on an African farm and then moving to Richmond before learning to be a city slicker moggy in Johannesburg. I'd adored her and missed her badly when we went to England. Losing her rocked me and I was a mess for several weeks, but I knew she'd had a good and long life; Claude had too. All the same, there were two big spaces in our lives without them.

And then we were three

Where our work was concerned, my job was still going well, and by 1997, I'd shifted from being Assistant Customer Services Manager to Corporate Communications Manager, a rather grand title for a department of one: me. My main function hadn't changed as far as external communications went, but I was now answerable to Stephen, my Argus companion, and not to Christine.

That said, I no longer took customer service calls, although I still gave presentations and went on firm visits. Now the girls were older, I could take on more of these and I started flying to Cape Town, Durban and Port Elizabeth on short overnight trips as well; that is, I did until the crunch came.

In the autumn of 1997, Bill announced he'd been offered a job in the Netherlands. He'd been working with a Dutch company on a documentary film they were making in South Africa and they liked his ideas and approach so much, they asked him if he'd consider moving to Amsterdam to work with them. He was flattered, of course. To be invited by an international company to move to a city with such a creative and artistic reputation was immensely gratifying, but what made it still more appealing for him was the changing situation in the South African film industry.

Since 1994, things had become progressively difficult in the arts and film world for production teams run by whites. As was inevitable, affirmative action was being implemented across the board and notably at the SABC, South Africa's broadcasting company. Bill didn't work for them, but he made films for people who did. He also made videos for corporations that were obliged to apply affirmative action policies.

The implications were serious for small, independent film-makers and one-man operations like Bill's. As time went on, only his reputation for producing good work kept him from going under, but it was becoming increasingly hard to find the work in the first place. Tenders submitted by companies with non-white employees were given preference by default. Since Bill had no employees, his quotes, however competitive, were declined.

Until the end of 1996, he was still managing to work quite regularly, although the film world tended to be a famine and feast business and he'd often had periods without a project. For several months, however, he'd been struggling to gain the commissions, even from his long-term clients, and it had an effect on us all.

Flattery aside, the offer from the Netherlands was a godsend, from Bill's perspective anyway. But I was knocked sideways. I hadn't seen it coming at all. My job was growing and I was happy with the new developments; I just hadn't taken it in that he was so dispirited about his.

"But what about us? And the house? And everything here?" I was close to panic.

"It'll just be a trial, Val. I need the work, you know that, but there's no guarantee it'll go well," Bill replied. "I have to go, though. I have to see if it's what I want."

"Well, yes, I understand that."

"You and the girls can stay here. The girls need to finish school anyway. We don't need to make any permanent decisions yet. Then if I'm not happy there, I can still come back."

"And carry on? How would that work if you're finding it difficult now?"

"Agh, I'll find something. I always have done, haven't I?"

I didn't answer because I knew he'd made up his mind and there wasn't anything I could say or do to change it. I didn't mention either that Jodie was planning to go to England once she'd left school. She was due to take her matric exams (the South African version of a high school diploma) in November, and then she'd decided to fly to England to take a gap year. That would leave Mo and me alone in Krugersdorp. And that's what happened.

By the end of spring 1997, Bill had packed a suitcase of clothes and flown from a beautiful September in Johannesburg to a cold, grey and damp autumn in Amsterdam. Fortunately for him, he was made welcome there and embraced the lively vibe of Europe's hippest city.

Following Bill's departure, I tried to cope with the new situation of once again having to earn a living and be responsible for two daughters, a house and all the bills. My countrywide travel was also curtailed. Luckily, I now had a boss who understood my situation and promised I would have plenty of time to make arrangements if need be.

"Here we go again," I sighed, but at least the girls were now more self-reliant. I was even teaching Jodie to drive, so she was well on the way to full independence and it wouldn't be long before she fled the nest too. Even so, it wasn't exactly plain sailing.

The first thing to happen was a break-in, but in truth I couldn't really call it that because we more or less invited the burglar in. Running a bit late one morning, I forgot to check that the house was properly locked up. We were so used to feeling safe in Krugersdorp I wasn't in intense security mode. In fact, we'd often joked about how the burglars drove past our house on their way to richer pickings in Sandton. In any event, on the morning in question I bundled the girls into the car without thinking further and off we went.

Early in the afternoon, I had a frantic call from Mo. She'd arrived home and surprised someone in the house. The next thing she saw was a person escaping over the front garden wall with a huge well-filled rubbish sack, followed shortly after by the vision of Wally haring down the road after the burglar waving his gun. I excused myself from work with Stephen's blessing and rushed home to find out what had happened.

It transpired that Jodie had left her bedroom window open and I'd left the garden gate unlocked, so between us we'd provided an ideal opportunity for a chancer to take advantage of our lax ways. Wally happened to be looking out of his back window when he spotted a furtive-looking individual testing the back gate. Finding it unlocked, the intruder sneaked through into the garden, saw the open window, and pulled himself up and disappeared inside. Realising this was not the conventional form of entry, even for Solly, Wally called the police and went to find his gun before running round to our house.

Meanwhile, Mo arrived home and surprised the intruder, who beat a hasty retreat the way he'd come in, but not without a bag full of our possessions, including my cell phone. As he vaulted over the front wall, he caught sight of Wally charging along the road with a gun pointing at him. In panic, and not knowing the gun wasn't loaded, the would-be thief dropped the bag of booty, vaulted over another wall and made his escape, thereby cheating Wally of the satisfaction of a citizen's arrest, which I'm sure he'd love to have made.

"I saw him climb in as calm as you please, the low-life *tsotsi!*" Wally spluttered (a *tsotsi* is South African slang for a 'no-good thief'). "And what's with those doff dogs of yours? They didn't do a thing!"

"Well, I'm actually quite glad they didn't, Wally. He might be dead by now if they were the sort to attack people."

"Not that one, *schat*," he said kindly. "He was a coward. He'd have run first. Did you see how he scarpered just now?" he asked Mo.

"Yes," she nodded. "But you can't blame him for not wanting you to shoot him, Wally. He didn't know your gun was empty. It's no wonder he took off so fast."

"*Ja*, well, that's one thing cowards do well...run fast!"

"Anyway, thank you so much, Wally. If it hadn't been for you, we'd have lost a heap of stuff," I soothed, not wanting to encourage a full-scale rant.

"*Moenie* worry *nie, schat,* no worries," Wally grinned, mixing his languages shamelessly. *Schat* (pronounced *skat)* was an Afrikaans term of endearment meaning 'dear'. I already liked Wally, but I could have hugged him then. He'd saved us a lot of money and heartache by coming to the rescue. He was the dear in this case.

The police came, but when they found we hadn't lost anything except my pre-pay cell phone, their interest waned, and they spent the rest of the time chatting to Wally and taking his statement.

Even so, the incident rattled me. I knew I'd have to pay more attention to the security details in future if we were to manage. Our thief had been an opportunist, I was sure; his actions fell under 'petty crime', but we couldn't rely on it to stay that way. We all needed to be more careful.

Another incident that made me more aware of the potential for danger was a personal attack on Jodie and her boyfriend. They'd been sitting in the 'Green Mamba' in the park, learning lines for a forthcoming performance of a play, when a couple of men stuck their heads through the car windows and threatened them at knifepoint. They wanted money, of course, and valuables, but being schoolkids neither Jodie nor Sam had anything other than books, let alone goods of any worth. Even the car wasn't worth stealing. For one thing, it was very old and for another, it was too distinctive.

Sam, however, had a remarkable gift of the gab and managed to talk the men into letting them go. They had to hand over the small amount of cash they had and a couple of cassette tapes, but they were otherwise unhurt and unfleeced. Nonetheless, I was horrified when Jodie told me.

"They could have killed you, Jo," I screeched, shock setting in.

"I don't think they would, Mum. Sam was amazing. He had them totally convinced that hurting us wasn't worth it and they'd only get into trouble."

"Yes, but if Sam hadn't been there … oh for goodness' sake, just promise me you'll never go and sit in the park again, not unless there are other people around, okay?"

"Okay, Mum, but it really wasn't so bad."

"Just promise me, that's all I ask."

And she did, but to this day I wonder if my child knew how lucky she was that her boyfriend was gifted with such charm. I still shudder to think what might have happened without his presence of mind and verbal skills. Krugersdorp was one of the least crime-ridden suburbs at the time, but these incidents proved we couldn't ever relax our guard.

Household humps

At the beginning of 1998, Jodie flew to England. She'd done well in her final exams and armed with her school certificates, she found herself a job in London. It was hard for me to see her go; she was only eighteen and South African teenagers lived a protected life compared with their northern cousins. To my great relief she initially lived with my sister, which helped me not to worry about her so much. Once she'd gone, Mo and I were left to hold the fort. We managed, but without Solly's help we couldn't have done as well as we did.

He moved into the old garage room with his wife and children when Jodie left. Originally designed as servant's quarters, it became Jodie's domain when she decided she wanted more teenage privacy. But when Solly mentioned he was having accommodation problems, it made sense for him to occupy it and in return he made sure to watch out for us. He worked for me two days a week, and for other people in Krugersdorp the rest of the time. The advantage of having him living on the premises was that he took over the handyman jobs Bill had always done, although his methods were not quite so conventional. I was also glad he was there for security reasons.

One morning, I was trying to flush the toilet when the handle fell off. On inspection, I found the mechanism it was attached to inside the cistern had broken.

"Oh dear," Mo sympathised. "Do you know how to fix it, Mum?"

"Erm … I'm not sure," I muttered, peering into the water and wondering what the bits of plastic floating around at the top were. "I'll go to the hardware and ask them."

It was a Saturday and when I went out to walk to the shops, I saw Solly coming up the road, carrying a loaf of bread.

"Hello, Solly, do you know anything about fixing toilets?" I asked, not imagining for one moment that he did, but it was worth a try.

"Why, madam, what is the problem?"

"I've broken the handle off. You know, the thing we use to flush the toilet?" I mimed the movements. He nodded.

"Ah yes, madam. Don't worry, I can do that for you."

"You can? Really?"

"Yes, madam, it's no problem."

"Well, I'm just going to the hardware to buy a new part for the inside. I'm afraid that's broken too," I said, making an apologetic face.

"Okay, madam, you bring the parts and I will fix it."

"Solly, you're a marvel," I laughed, practically bouncing.

At the hardware shop, I explained what I needed and the young storeman found a replacement mechanism for me. It came in a packet with all the parts together. I hoped Solly would know what to do with it as plumbing wasn't yet one of my skills.

I gave him Bill's box of tools complete with every possible wrench he might need, turned off the water and left him to it. A couple of hours later after much banging and clunking, some of which sounded alarming, Solly came to find me in the garden. He was smiling with triumph.

"It is ready, madam."

"Oh fantastic! Well done, Solly. I'm coming to look now."

"You must turn the water on, madam, to test it."

"Ah yes. I will."

I heard the water overflowing before I saw it.

"*How*, madam, turn it off, quick!"

"What happened, Solly?"

"I forget to take the tape off the piece inside," he said sheepishly. In the packaging, the floater that activated the filling valve was taped down to stop it waggling around and possibly breaking. Solly had forgotten to cut the tape. As might be expected, the valve didn't close and the water kept flowing. We had a minor flood in the bathroom to contend with, but in the end, that wasn't the biggest issue.

Once we'd mopped up, released the floater and filled up the cistern, I looked at Solly's work. Everything was neatly installed and it was faultless – except for one important thing. He'd put the handle on the wrong way round.

It sat on the side of the cistern, but now it faced the back wall instead of the front as it should have done. I opened my mouth and then closed it again. I didn't have the heart to tell him; he'd worked so hard and it didn't matter anyway. In future, we'd just have to get used to pushing it down at the back. The flush worked perfectly; it was just … well … different, and I have to admit visitors were sometimes confused by our eccentric front-to-back loo. At the very least it made a good talking point, and everyone agreed Solly was a man in a million.

As time went on, Solly endeared himself to us still more; he was such a kind man. I wished we could do more to help him and his family, but I was beginning to find the financial side of keeping things afloat quite a burden. Some kind of crisis point hit me the day I found the lawnmower wouldn't start. In the greater scheme of things, it was a minor detail, but there was something about keeping the house in good order that was important to me and cutting the grass was a part of that. Admittedly, it was probably Solly who'd damaged the machine as he was normally the one who did the mowing, but that wasn't the point; it was simply that things were getting on top of me and I had a minor melt down.

"I can't afford a new lawnmower," I wailed, "and I don't know how to fix this one."

"Don't worry, madam," Solly said. "I can help with it."

I was beginning to wonder what he thought of me. He was always telling me not to worry.

"What can you help, and how?" I sniffed. I was being pathetic, I knew.

"You will see, madam."

A few days later, I'd just arrived home from work and was closing the gates when I saw Solly walking down the hill from Robert Broom Drive pushing a lawnmower ahead of him. As he reached the crossing, he lifted its wheels over the curb like a baby buggy. I was transfixed, almost expecting him to lift a child out of the grass box when he reached me.

"Solly, where did you get that?"

"Another madam, madam," he said. I laughed, shaking my head. "I work for this madam every Monday. I tell her what happen because I know she have this extra mower. She say you can use this one as long as you need. But she say I must not use it, only you," he finished, shrugging. I smiled, understanding what he meant and amused by the instruction. But even so, I was struggling with my emotions.

"Solly, you really are an angel. I don't know what I'd do without you. You look after us so well."

"Madam, I am happy you say this, but it is easy. You look after me, so I look after you."

Seeing my eyes fill probably embarrassed him, and he turned and pushed the lawnmower towards the garage. Solly was pure gold.

Just the two of us

With Bill and Jodie absent, Mo and I spent more time exploring the more local attractions. We went to the Krugersdorp Game Reserve one weekend with Bobbity and her family. Small though it was, it had an impressive collection of animals including hippos, various types of antelope (buck) and even lions in a special enclosure.

With the country being quite open grassland, it was easy to spot the animals from the car and, as such, possibly more gratifying than going to the Kruger Park, which was the size of the Netherlands. In the 1500 hectares that made up the Krugersdorp reserve, there was a much better chance of seeing a variety of animals. We finished the day with lunch at their rather classy game lodge restaurant, looking out over the open *veld* as if we were right out in the bush rather than just a few kilometres from Johannesburg's expanding suburbs.

Even better than the game reserve was the Rhino Park. One Saturday morning, Mo and I joined a friend from work to make a guided walking tour around this large but lesser known reserve. At that time, it was located off the road to Rustenburg, just a few kilometres from Bobbity and Garth's plot.

We met my friend Shirley at the entrance and drove in together up a deeply rutted sand track until we reached the reception centre, a thatched building set in a shaded area under blue-gum trees. We'd booked to join a tour beginning at 11:00, so we arrived at the same time as other members of the group.

There were about ten of us altogether. We'd all dressed as instructed in neutral-coloured pants, T-shirts and hiking boots, careful not to wear bright colours that might disturb the wildlife we were going to be walking amongst. Our guide, Stefan, was a young and dedicated expert on herbivores who told us we would be following a path through the reserve along which we might or might not see any animals at all, but we would certainly see evidence of them.

It was a marvellous, almost magical morning. I felt closer to wildlife than I'd ever felt before, contrived though it was. This was Africa, albeit in a microcosmic state. Stefan showed us the traces or *spoor* of the animals and how to recognise the different species from their droppings. All the animals in the park were herbivores although the reserve was established principally for rhinos, even then an endangered species but not nearly as threatened as they are today.

We walked along the sandy paths through the bush that grew unchecked all around us. Stefan pointed out the weaver birds' nests and the *deurmekaarbos*, known as the puzzle bush in English. A densely packed and voluminous bush, it looked like a never-ending tangle of branches and twigs so it was well named. It also made a safe haven for a variety of small creatures in its thickly matted growth.

As it happened, we didn't see any rhinos that day, but we heard them crashing through the trees further on and had the feeling we were close, almost walking in their footsteps.

We also learnt that their droppings were completely neutral and harmless to humans. Since rhinos only eat vegetable matter, Stefan told us, their faeces contain no harmful bacteria. He demonstrated when we reached a clearing where they'd been feeding. The ground was covered with their droppings, which looked just like lumps of thick compost, full as they were with grass. Stefan picked up a handful of dung, and broke it apart. It looked quite dry and innocuous. He invited us to come and sniff it.

"It has a sweet, slightly aromatic smell, doesn't it?" someone said.

"*Ja*, it's really quite strong if you burn it, and actually, it's quite safe to eat it too," Stefan finished.

"Ugh, really?" Mo said, recoiling at the thought.

"Don't you want to try?" Stefan grinned at her.

"Only if you eat it first."

"*Nee*, I've had my breakfast this morning," he laughed, but I had no doubt he would have done so if pressed.

Rhinos lumbered around quietly in this peaceful territory and it seemed incredible we could walk through their habitat without risk. That's not to say they were completely harmless; they weren't. They could be vicious if threatened, but as long as we kept our distance, we had nothing to fear from them.

Another unique place we explored was on the Magaliesberg mountains. Said to be the oldest mountain range in the world, the Magaliesberg runs in an S-shape for about 120 kilometres from the north east of Pretoria near the town of Bronkhorstspruit to just south of Pilanesburg in the west.

In ancient times, the rocks from which the mountains were formed were part of an inland sea, and it was truly awe-inspiring to climb a steep path to the top of one of its ridges and see water ripples still evident in the surface of the great stone slabs we saw lying there.

The footpaths too were littered with ancient tools and evidence of early human life; it was a humbling experience to scrape the sand and find beautifully worked flints, axes and other well-hewn tools. Treading the tracks of these historic mountains was almost an experience in time travel and the view from the top was stunning. With their rolling wave formation, the mountains acted as a natural barrier between the northern *bushveld* and the southern grasslands. The landscape on both sides stretched away over bronze tinged *veld* to misty hills and endless horizons.

Before Bill left, we'd taken rides out to these mountains on his motorbike or in the car with the family. Now Mo and I could drive to one of these familiar spots close to the town of Magaliesburg, park the car, and walk up the mountain path with the dogs. They scampered ahead of us up the tracks, stopping only to look back and make sure we were coming. Bill's and then Jodie's departure had unsettled them both and they became more clinging, especially Daisy. On former excursions, they would have roared off ahead, but now they kept us in sight, bounding back now and then to nuzzle our hands before running off again, tails waving, noses pressed to the ground. It was such a special place and we could spend a couple of hours there enjoying the African wilderness at its loveliest before returning to the city and home.

That was the gift of living in Krugersdorp. Within minutes, we could be out in the country and feel far from the stresses of an overcrowded city.

For the next months, this was how Mo's and my life continued. We became close and sometimes I forgot she was my daughter and not my sister; she was mature beyond her sixteen years. One other incident brought us still closer together and that was the rescue of Namib.

The road we lived on was a busy one that led directly from Robert Broom Drive into the centre of Krugersdorp. Cars and minibuses roared up and down our section, always trying to beat the lights at the junction near our house. There was a four-way stop further down before the Spar and I was convinced the four-hundred metre stretch between the two crossings was used as a race track for time trials. At night, it wasn't quite as bad, but cars still tended to drive much too fast; it seemed that the speed limit was only there to be broken.

Late one night, a loud bang from the street made me jump just as I was locking up for bed. The bang was followed by a blood curdling howl that had Mo rushing to join me at the door. We opened it sure we were going to find a horrible and bloody sight on the pavement. But by the time I'd unlocked the gate, the howling had reduced to a pitiful whimpering, so it wasn't as easy to hear where it came from.

We ran out into the street together, unable to see at first where the injured animal was lying. When our eyes focused, all we saw was a pale lump in the gutter on the opposite side of the road, luckily out of further harm's way. Quickly crossing over, we reached the wounded creature, which turned out to be a beautiful young yellow Labrador. She (as later became clear) was panting with terror but unable to move. The injuries weren't visible; there was no blood gushing from an open wound, but from the angle of one of her legs, it was probably broken.

"What shall we do, Mum?" Mo asked. "Can we call the vet? Please?"

"I think we'll have to. I don't know how pleased she'll be to be called at this time of night, but we can't leave the poor thing here. She'll die."

"I'll stay here with her then."

"Good, keep talking to her. Your voice will hopefully calm her down."

"Go on, Mum. Please!"

I ran back to the house to phone Anneke, the vet. She listened to my story without interrupting until I'd finished.

"Don't move her, I'm coming right away," was all she said. I knew she would, and she did, arriving just a few minutes later.

What followed was a silent, but intense rescue operation as the three of us carefully moved the terrified dog onto a special stretcher and then off the road into her van. At the surgery, we got her out and carried her into the surgery hospital together. Anneke sedated her and once she was at rest, a quick examination suggested a leg broken in three places and a damaged hip at least.

"I can keep her here overnight and do some further examination in the morning … if she survives, that is," she said. "But we'll have to find the owner quickly. I'm afraid any treatment is going to be costly and if no one claims her, then..." She left the words unsaid.

Mo's face crumpled. I knew my daughter. Any suggestion the dog would have to be put to sleep was going to be met with floods of tears.

"Don't worry, Mo. We'll put a notice up in the Spar tomorrow and call around the police stations. Maybe someone will have reported her missing," I reassured her. "And, Anneke, if that doesn't work, we'll make sure she can have the treatment even if we have to pay for it ourselves," I finished, mentally crossing fingers and wondering what on earth I was saying. My mouth had clearly taken over my brain and locked up my reason.

"Are you sure? It'll be expensive. I can't leave it too long as she may have other injuries too that we can't see. I don't think there's any internal bleeding, at least I hope not, but I'll take pictures first thing and let you know."

We went home, tired and anxious, but the coming days were an education in how wonderful people could be. Firstly, Anneke called to tell us that the dog had survived the night and a scan showed no internal injuries. However, as we'd suspected, she had multiple breaks in one leg and the hip was also broken. She then said if we couldn't find the owner, she would perform the surgery at cost as long as we could come up with the funds to pay for it. The amount she quoted made me gulp, but I told her to do it. I had to. Mo would never cope if we didn't. We'd already given the dog the name of Namib because she was the colour of the desert sand we'd seen in Namibia. It was personal now.

I told Anneke she was a saint; she denied it.

"I'm just a vet," she said. "It's what any of us would do."

I doubted that somewhat.

The next uplifting response was from my work colleagues. When I told them the story, I was flooded with offers of donations to help with the surgery if the owner couldn't be found. The pledges came to more than half the amount we needed and I breathed a huge sigh of relief. After committing to it, I'd been plagued by apprehension as to how we would pay for the operation. With so much help offered, I knew we could do it.

I called Anneke and gave her the news. There'd been no word from the owners, but now it didn't matter and she went ahead with the surgery during the course of the day. That evening, Mo and I went along to check on Namib.

"How did it go, Anneke?" Mo asked.

"Well, I won't say it was an easy procedure, but the breaks were clean, so I've been able to pin them all and her hip as well."

She told us this as we walked through to the 'ward' where Namib was lying in her cage, this time with a large plaster cast on her back leg. She was still very dopey, but wagged her tail at seeing visitors. I just hoped we could find her owner.

Two days later, there was still no response to the notices we'd put up and the calls I'd made. Namib was making a good recovery, so I collected all the donations from work with much humility and heaps of gratitude. There was no reason for any of my friends to help; they hadn't even seen the dog, and it made me realise how unstintingly kind people could be. Their generosity saved Namib's life.

After paying the bill, I asked Anneke how long Namib needed to remain in her care.

"Well, I think she'd best stay a few more days. She has to keep quiet here; she needs to rest the leg, and there's still a chance the owners might appear. What are you going to do if they don't?"

"We'll take her, Anneke. There's no other option, is there? It won't be a hardship as she seems a sweetheart." I said this as I was stroking her lovely head. She wagged her tail as if to show her approval of the plan.

As it happened, we didn't get to keep Namib. Just as we'd become accustomed to the idea that she'd be coming home with us, her owner's son turned up at Anneke's. He'd seen the notice at the Spar and recognised the description of his father's dog, which had gone missing from a house up on Robert Broom Drive the day of the accident.

Anneke, bless her, wanted a bit more proof than the story he told, so later in the day, the son brought his father in. Namib's response at seeing her master was all the proof Anneke needed. She told them of the role Mo and I had played in her rescue and treatment and gave them our phone number assuming they would phone or come round to see us. They thanked her, took Namib with them, and nothing more was said. We never heard a word from them.

"I can't believe they didn't even call you," Anneke said next time I saw her.

"Such is life, Anneke. What's important is that Namib's on the mend and she's gone home. We didn't really need another dog, so it's probably just as well. I just wanted to thank *you* for all you did. You've been fantastic. I hope they offered to pay you your fees."

"No," she said, shaking her head. "And they didn't offer to reimburse you, either. But the best thing to come out of this for me is that you and your daughter and friends have restored my faith in human nature. In this job, we see some horrible callousness and lack of caring. It can be very depressing. You people have given me back my belief. Thank you."

If nothing else, hearing her say that was worth everything we'd done. For someone who loved animals enough to do what she did, the heartless cruelty she sometimes encountered must have been hard to bear and I was glad we'd inspired some optimism in her again.

I admit I was niggled that Namib's owner didn't make contact, but in the end, what mattered was that she was back home and was being well cared for. For us, the experience had been a good one and Mo and I never regretted it for a moment.

Facing the fax

Krugersdorp had become home in more senses than just a house and a town. We felt settled and as safe as it was possible to feel in big, bad Johannesburg. Except for the need to keep doors and windows locked when we went out, we didn't fear burglaries and never put bars on our windows. And of course we had Solly and his family as added security.

Home aside, I had my friends: Moira had left the company, but we still saw each other often and remained close. Bobbity was always down the hill and there for us if we needed help. Annette was a quick drive away in Bryanston and I managed to have coffee and chats with her now and then. My work was my safety net and my colleagues there were an important part of my life. I had a strong sense of family within the organisation.

Nevertheless, I missed Bill's presence and was finding it hard to cope with all the financial demands of a life that we'd started with a double income and was now down to just mine. So when later in the year he dropped the next bombshell, I had some major decisions to make.

The letter came by fax while I was at work. We'd taken to exchanging faxes rather than emails because when I had his letter in my hands, I knew no one else could read it. Our email system didn't feel quite so private.

His writing was usually bright and breezy with news of his latest activities in Holland and Germany. This time, though, it held a serious message: 'I've realised there's nothing left for me in South Africa,' it said. 'Would you be willing to come over here? There's no work for me in Joburg and I've made some great contacts in the Netherlands. I've even been offered my own premises in Rotterdam. I'm sure it would be better for us all.'

I was shocked and felt numb. I'd kept hoping he'd return home at the end of the year although I hadn't thought about what he'd do; I was just sure he'd want to come back.

I didn't answer straight away as I knew I'd have to talk it over with Mo. It would be a terrible wrench for her to leave. She had her friends and her ice-skating in Krugersdorp; she also had her schooling to complete. For me, it would mean leaving a job I loved and friends who were more than dear to me. The only upsides I could think of were having Jodie closer to us and being a family again.

The following weeks were spent mulling over the dilemma. I went round in ever wavering circles, but in the end, we agreed. The idea grew on Mo and she came to be excited by the thought of a new country and a new challenge. Despite my misgivings, I felt it was most likely the right thing to do for all of us, although the uncertainty remained.

Giving in my notice at work was awful. I hated doing it as it felt so final, but Stephen was kind and once the news was out, my colleagues' excitement for me made the move feel much more of an adventure.

There then followed the upheaval of putting the house on the market, planning flights for ourselves, two dogs and two cats and getting rid of all our household items ... again.

I had a garage sale, which felt very much like *déja vu*. We'd been in this situation before with all our surplus possessions spread out on the driveway in Richmond, Natal. Only this time, Solly looked on sadly as his fellow men and women competed with each other over the cutlery, crockery and clothing. They were laughing and joking, but he knew what it implied. As soon as the house was sold, he wouldn't have a home and he'd lose us as employers too. I felt his sorrow deeply.

"Solly, you can stay here as guard until someone buys the house," I told him. "I'm so sorry we're going and can't take you with us."

"Thank you, madam. Maybe the new boss can let me stay too."

"I hope so. I'll give you a really good reference, and you know you can take any of these things," I pointed to the household goods being squabbled over by the local maids and gardeners. Go on, tell your wife to take what she wants. You can have anything for free."

He smiled. His wife was one of those in the group sifting through the pile of clothes. He called to her and she came, her arms loaded with items. Her face split into a wide and sunny smile as soon as she heard his whispered news.

"Thank you, madam, thank you," she beamed and dumped the pile in Solly's arms so she could go back for more.

As for my job, I left the company on a high note. A dinner out, and a party in the office made sure I felt thoroughly spoilt and valued. I was given a Pierre Cardin watch (something light that wouldn't add to my baggage) and some lovely earrings, but best of all was the offer that 'if you ever want to come back, Val, you'll always have a place here.' That gave me a tremendous feeling of support in all the uncertainty of moving to the Netherlands.

In the weeks that followed my farewell from work, our furniture was sold piecemeal: the dining room suite to a colleague; the yellowwood dresser and sideboard to friends of Bobbity's; the beds and lounge suite to buyers from the local advertiser. Bit by bit it all went and once the house was empty, the final boxes were packed, addressed and sent off to arrive in the Netherlands whenever they got there.

The goodbyes were painful. I shut the door on our lovely home, locked it and gave one set of keys to the estate agent and a backdoor key to Solly. "You can use the kitchen and bathroom," I told his wife. There hadn't been an offer to purchase yet, but the agent would take care of matters regarding Solly's family when there was. I hoped he'd be kind.

The dogs, cats and Mo were already in the car as I looked at it all for the last time and turned away before Solly saw my distress. I just wished I could be sure someone in his future would value him as much as I did.

We spent the last few days of our life in Krugersdorp with Bobbity and Garth down on their plot. It was a good transition point. The lively bustle of their home buoyed our spirits, and it was from there the dogs and cats were collected to make their flight to the Netherlands. I'd bought the special boxes needed to contain them during the journey and the company that organised their transport was well-known and had a good reputation for animal care during the flights.

It was horrible seeing them leave without us, even though we knew we'd be travelling on the same flight. In my emotional state, I hated the thought of them being locked up in the hold of the plane, bewildered and unhappy. Predictably, I spent most of that last day with a lump in my throat, dangerously close to tears, but in the end, it all went smoothly. Bobbity and Garth took us to the airport, saw us off grandly and promised us a haven if we ever wanted to come back. It was a comforting thought to take with us.

Nevertheless, by January 1999 we were installed in a flat in Rotterdam, getting used to a new country, new culture and, most challenging of all, a new climate. To my joy Jodie came to stay too and settled quickly into Dutch life and society.

But the end of my South African story only came to its real conclusion at the end of 2000.

EPILOGUE

Prolonging the end

As things transpired, I went back to Johannesburg a few times during the course of 1999 to do special communications projects for my former employers and I continued working for them online as well. The CEO who replaced Mr Dee hadn't wanted me to leave and he knew I hadn't really wanted to either. Within a month of my being in the Netherlands, he'd been in touch and proposed the online work and periodic visits. It was an arrangement that worked well and gave me the Africa fixes I needed.

Then life's lemons started souring things again. Mo hated living in Rotterdam. She couldn't get used to the grey weather and having to start from scratch in a new education system. She begged to go home and we agreed, so she returned to South Africa later that year and moved to Grahamstown to live with her grandmother while she finished school. What resulted in even more of an upheaval was that I followed her in June, 2000.

The year's separation from Bill while I stayed in Krugersdorp had changed us both and we realised we weren't going to make things work. Just before Mo left the Netherlands, we bought an old barge that had been converted to a liveaboard houseboat in the 1970s. We moved onto it and into a harbour for historic boats in Rotterdam with the aim of doing a restoration job that would give the barge a more traditional appearance.

While life in the harbour went a long way to relieving my homesickness for South Africa, the stresses inherent in funding the work on the boat exposed the raw edges of the differences that had developed between us; a situation not designed for peaceful co-existence in the limited confines of a boat. The tension became tauter and threatened to snap.

When at the end of May 2000, my former boss offered me a six-month contract to go back to South Africa as the company's interim Marketing Manager, I jumped at the chance to create some distance from our personal issues. I knew it wouldn't resolve them; I just felt I needed some space.

But I didn't return to Krugersdorp. I couldn't.

The house we'd loved so much was sold a few months after our departure and it was too heart-wrenching to go and see it. Solly would have gone, and the pain of knowing I should have kept it after all would have been overwhelming.

Instead, I stayed with Moira in Olivedale and spent the second half of 2000 involved in exciting marketing projects, as well as travelling around South Africa.

It was a difficult time for me on a personal level, but to be in South Africa with no strings attached was another kind of heaven. I travelled on company business from Swaziland to the Cape with one of my team and saw even more of the country's glories than I had before.

We were on a kind of road trip campaign to show a new promotional video we'd made at our offices. Mel, my travelling companion, was my partner in both making the video and taking it on the road. We'd worked together throughout the intense process of producing it and she was no longer just my colleague. What's more we had the same birthday and although she was twenty years my junior, this added connection cemented our friendship. We became close on these trips, sharing confidences, hopes and dreams as well as plenty of laughter.

Driving through torrential rain down a mud-caked mountain road to Mbabane, Swaziland's capital, and staying in a stunning country lodge in the mountains near Tzaneen were two of the many memories I can recall with all the vividness of the impressions they made on me at the time. It felt as if we were on a great adventure and every stop brought new experiences that we savoured and stored.

On one visit to Cape Town to give presentations and visit member firms, we took the evening off and went on a champagne cruise around Table Bay. The boat was a traditional wooden sailing vessel, the wind was strong, the sailors were gorgeous and the champagne was, well, bubbly. Not being a good sailor, I just about managed to keep my stomach in place and enjoy the view. We not only had the human eye candy, we had an amazing sight of Table Mountain as the sun went down. Mel loved it; I nearly didn't, but I'll never forget it.

Another never-to-be-forgotten trip was one I took by train to Grahamstown to visit Mo. I hadn't travelled on a South African train since 1982 when we were first in the country. But in 2000, it was a different matter altogether.

It was an overnight journey, so when I booked a berth in a sleeper compartment, I remembered the luxury of our first and former trip on the Red Train to Durban. At that time, we'd had a family couchette with full service, and our bunks came with freshly laundered linen and soft blankets. We were brought tea and coffee on a tray and meals were served in a truly excellent restaurant car. It was the most wonderful welcome to South Africa. However, it was an expensive way to travel even then and we'd never done the trip again. So when one Friday lunchtime in September 2000 I boarded the train to Grahamstown at Park Station in Johannesburg, the contrast was only too stark, although in many ways the journey was much more colourful.

I was sharing the rather basic compartment of dingy green vinyl-covered seats with several rather large and full-bosomed ladies, all of whom knew each other. Their luggage consisted of massive carrier bags stuffed to overflowing with what seemed to be bedding for a house, clothing for a large family and grocery shopping for a whole community. We barely had room to move our feet, let alone spread out in any comfort.

Going to the loo involved taking on this major obstacle course, and since the train swayed constantly, the other test was in trying to negotiate our way out of the compartment without collapsing onto each other. Given the ladies' somewhat generous proportions, I was quite pleased I was in the corner by the window and out of harm's way when they undertook the challenge.

In the outer passage the problem of reaching the toilets was exacerbated by other bags and carriers, one of which held a couple of chickens. Their clucking accompanied us until darkness fell when they finally stopped trying to lay eggs and went to sleep. Unfortunately, my companions' clucking wasn't subdued by the dimming daylight.

The women talked non-stop in Xhosa or Zulu (I couldn't work out which) laughing and joking, their ample bodies heaving with mirth. With each uproarious chuckle, I was squashed still further into my corner. I had no idea what they were talking about, but it was all very jolly and I had to smile along with them.

In this lively close encounter with my African travelling companions, I passed the long hours and peered through the grubby windows for signs of our progress. By the time the sun was setting, we'd stopped at Vereeniging, Kroonstad and Bloemfontein, all places I'd been to by car.

As the evening wore on, the carriage became increasingly stuffy and the smells from six closely packed bodies began to take on a pretty pungent aroma, an odour intensified when I had to climb up to bed. Since I was the smallest, my fellow travellers appointed me to sleep on one of the two upper bunks.

"You sleep at the top, mama," they instructed. "We are too big to climb up there," they said, shaking with laughter at the mere idea.

They folded out the other top bunk for all their bags, which they hefted onto it. Then the bunk's intended occupant stretched out on the floor, making use of some of the bedding she'd brought with her. Both heat and smells rise, I soon discovered, and I didn't get much rest that night. What with the aroma wafting around from several unwashed bodies (mine included) the snoring and the warmth, I lay awake and restless in the darkness, vaguely aware we'd passed through Cradock, Cookhouse and Adelaide.

Nothing was visible through the grimy windows as the train made its laborious way through the lonely stretches of the Eastern Cape. Eventually, the regular rocking motion of the carriage and the rhythmic clatter of the wheels on the track lulled me into a fitful sleep.

The following morning about seven o'clock we finally stopped at Alicedale where I would be changing trains. By this time, the upper bunks had been folded back against the wall and we'd resumed our cramped seats on the lowest.

Alicedale was a railway halt seemingly in the middle of nowhere but one that was vital for the people in the area. Being an important education centre and university town, Grahamstown had its own branch line and a train went to Alicedale and back twice a day to connect with the main line to Johannesburg or Port Elizabeth. When I left the carriage with my single bag, my companions beamed with pleasure, wished me a nice day and shifted up to fill my space. It looked as if I'd never been there at all.

There was nothing of Alicedale to see from the ground, and it seemed almost surreal that this should be such an important 'station'.

In fact, there was no station as such, and other than a platform with a hut I could see no indication it was even a stop. Having said that, the number of tracks showed clearly it was where several lines converged.

Happily for me, the Grahamstown train was waiting, so I climbed aboard with a sigh of relief that I'd be able to move and breathe freely again. On the return journey after my weekend with Mo, there was only one other person in my compartment. While it was infinitely more comfortable, I have to say it wasn't nearly as interesting as my downward trip had been.

During those same six months, my friend Moira and I went pony trekking in Lesotho with her partner, Don. I hadn't ridden since we'd lived on the farm in Natal, but I suppose it's like cycling; you never really forget. However, Don had never ridden at all, nor was he the fittest of individuals. He bravely endured the steep mountain descents and bounced out of rhythm with every step his pony took, cursing volubly at the painful collisions between his buttocks and the pony's rump. The whole weekend was hilarious, magical and marvellous, even the moment when Moira used our drinking water for washing her face.

We were staying overnight in a tiny village in the Lesotho mountains and we had a bare and basic *rondavel* to sleep in. There were no services at all: we slept on camping stretchers with rough blankets over us; we had paraffin lights instead of electric; and we had a full bucket of water for drinking, making tea, cooking and washing dishes. Whatever was left, we could use for washing ourselves, but that came last.

Somehow or other Moira hadn't twigged that this was all there was and happily plunged her well-soaped hands in the bucket before we'd even had our first drink. The resulting roars from Don and me had the rest of the camp running to witness her shame. The roars were followed by howls of laughter. My dear friend never lived it down, especially when the tea and coffee we made tasted distinctly peculiar.

We went a second time a couple of months later and took Mo and Don's son, Ralph. Again, we had an exhilarating experience riding across the wild Lesotho hills although this time we just did day trips from the base camp, the gorgeous Malealea Lodge. It was the centre from which the pony trekking was organised, but it also offered hiking and cycling with hostel and hotel accommodation.

There, we slept in luxurious comfort in *rondavels*, ate in the communal dining room and enjoyed performances of local dancing in the evening. The kids loved it and mixed happily with the groups of young people staying in the hostel. As for the managers of the lodge, they were warm, generous people and I remember asking them if I could come back as a volunteer if all else failed when my current contract ended.

"Of course you can, Val, you'd be welcome. But you know there's nothing here at all, don't you? Other than helping guests, cleaning rooms and cooking, there wouldn't be anything to do."

"I don't think I'd mind that," I said, gazing at the incredible view across Lesotho's mountains. There wasn't a sound to be heard: no motorway, no cars, no planes, nothing. It was perfect.

"Well, you can always let us know. We're very laid back here."

Realistically, I knew it would be too difficult to make a living. I still had commitments: a child at school, another in the Netherlands, people who relied on me. But it was a very tempting thought.

At the end of the year, in December 2000, my six months were up and I had to make a decision about my future. During my absence, Bill and I had agreed to divorce. He would keep the barge and finish the restoration, a sensible decision in practical terms, but it left me without a home in either country. What this meant was that I had to choose between building a new life either in South Africa or in Europe.

After December, I would have no job in Johannesburg, nor would I have a place to stay, as I knew I couldn't keep lodging with Moira. I was sleeping in her son's room and he needed to be at home during the holidays in his own surroundings.

In the Netherlands, I still had teaching work I could pick up again and a good friend in the harbour offered to rent me one of his barges, a lifeline I couldn't ignore. Besides this, it was true to say I'd fallen quite heavily for life on the water. Not only that, I had the wandering bug after all my travels and some ideas were forming in my mind about the possibility of buying my own boat and then maybe moving to France, a dream I'd been nurturing for many years.

It wasn't an easy decision. I was happy and at home in South Africa and my youngest child was within a long drive's reach. I'd recently done it with Don's son as my partner-in-exhaustion. We'd driven the 1000 kilometres through the night after leaving work at five the previous afternoon, an adventure in itself but one that proved it could be done.

My problem was that while I loved everything about the country, I didn't know if there was a future for me in South Africa. I didn't even know if I could get another job. With affirmative action as policy, the only point in my favour was being female; my age, colour and background were against me.

It felt like my Krugersdorp dilemma all over again. I agonised over the decision during many sleepless nights. Eventually, the final balance fell in favour of trying my fortune again in Europe, if only because I was driving myself mad and knew I had to make a choice.

After all, I thought, if it doesn't work out, I can always come back; I'd done so more than once since saying goodbye to Krugersdorp.

As things turned out I didn't. As things stand now, so many years later, I know I made the right decision, but I miss South Africa and I always will.

Over the twenty years I lived there, the country claimed a piece of my soul, and it remains there still.

THE END

Many, many thanks for reading my tales of my life in South Africa. If you've enjoyed them, I would be truly grateful if you would leave a few words as a review.
https://www.amazon.com/Highveld-Ways-Recollections-Johannesburg-1990s-ebook/dp/B07QR3HB8Z/

If you are interested in seeing some old photos taken during this period, you can find them here:

https://www.flickr.com/photos/29479087@N04/albums/721576909 01038483

Every effort has been taken to proofread this document carefully and avoid errors. However, mistakes still slip through. If you find any, I would be really grateful to know about them. You can contact me via email on rivergirlsbooks@gmail.com.

I would also like to take this opportunity to thank all those who have read earlier drafts of this book. They are Jodie Beckford, Dee Tavener Paulien Wijnvoord, Teresa Bland and Koos Fernhout. I valued the feedback they gave me tremendously. In addition, I would like to thank all my readers, especially those who encouraged me to write this sequel to African Ways Again. Without you, I wouldn't have even started it, so in a sense, this is for you. Of special note are Margaret Hobbs, Caryl Williams, Patti St Marie Wilson, Sandra McKenna, Colin Pryce and Chris Moore.

Lastly, I would like to mention my wonderful contacts among the Twitter community: Terry Tyler, Peter Davey, Carol Hedges, Lynn M Dixon, Stephanie Parker McKean, Tonia Parronchi and all the authors and readers on the We Love Memoirs Facebook and Twitter pages. Your support and encouragement have inspired me to keep writing my African tales.

I have written several memoirs:

About South Africa:
African Ways
African Ways again

About my boating like in the Netherlands:
Watery Ways
Harbour Ways
Rotterdam Reflections (A collection of articles and blog posts)

About travelling in Belgium and France:
Walloon Ways
Faring to France on a Shoe

I have also written two novels:
The Skipper's Child
How to Breed Sheep, Geese and English Eccentrics
(this last is part memoir as it is heavily based on my years as a smallholder in England before moving to South Africa, even down to the names of the animals)

The link to my author page on Amazon.com is:
https://www.amazon.com/Valerie-Poore/e/B008LSV6CE/

Printed in Poland
by Amazon Fulfillment
Poland Sp. z o.o., Wrocław